Sex and the Single Parent

Sex and the Single Parent

How You Can Have Happy and Healthy Kids—and an Active Social Life

Mary Mattis, Ph.D.

Henry Holt and Company New York

Published by Henry Holt and Company,
521 Fifth Avenue, New York, New York 10175.
Published simultaneously in Canada.

Library of Congress Cataloging in Publication Data
Mattis, Mary.
Sex and the single parent.
Bibliography: p.
Includes index.
1. Single parents—United States—Sexual behavior.
2. Children of divorced parents—United States—
Psychology. 3. Children and sex—United States.
4. Parenting—United States. 5. Dating (Social customs)
—United States. I. Title.
HQ759.915.M37 1986 646.7′8 85-8692
ISBN 0-03-070488-X

First Edition

Designer: Kate Nichols
Printed in the United States of America
1 2 3 4 5 6 7 8 9 10

ISBN 0-03-070488-X

All case studies mentioned are composites.
Names and identities of individuals have been
changed to protect confidentiality.

Contents

Foreword

When Parents Without Partners was formed in 1957, single parents had few places to go for information on being single and a parent. It was a subject that the popular press did not address. After all, in the '50s, the "normal" family had two parents; one-parent families were considered "broken." And single-parent families numbered far fewer then than now.

Today, more than one out of every four families is headed by one parent, and one out of every two marriages ends in divorce. As the number of single-parent families continues to increase, so does the need to provide information and guidance that will help them with the difficult job of adjusting to a family life changed by death, divorce, or separation.

To be a single parent in this society is to be isolated to a degree. Communication developed by and for single parents is essential to understanding and dealing with the unique problems encountered in raising children alone. Both children and parent struggle for love, understanding, and security. Part of the parent's struggle includes the need to reestablish an active, fulfilling social and sexual life, a task which if handled improperly can severely strain the family relationship.

Mary Mattis's new book was written specifically for single parents. Mattis, a psychotherapist who counsels parents and children, approaches the subject from the position that single parents who feel good about themselves and are accepting of their own needs, including sexuality, make the best parents and are much more likely to turn out children with healthy attitudes.

Those searching for quick, simple solutions will not find them. There are no simple answers here or elsewhere. Being a single parent can and often does complicate one's social life, but it doesn't preclude having one. This book contains examples of single parents who have managed to balance their needs with those of their children.

Mattis does not merely inform readers: she also guides them through the difficult process of adjusting to their changing roles. Her book is informative and enlightening, and it will help its readers in making more rational decisions about this important aspect of their lives.

Paul Moss
International President
Parents Without Partners

Acknowledgments

My grateful thanks to Iris Bancroft, who helped with the writing of this book, and to Keith Bancroft, who also assisted me. A special thanks, as well, to Sandra Watt, a literary agent who is supportive, incisive, and effective. What treasures they all are.

I appreciate the cooperation of the many single parents who were willing to share their experiences with me, and of my many friends and colleagues who were generous in sharing their time, impressions, experiences, and recommendations. Their support was enormously helpful in developing this book.

For their contributions and support, I'm especially indebted to a group of professionals who have, for years, been my peer consultants. We are all very good friends, interacting with one another as the kind of "network" I recommend in this book. I wish to thank them specifically: Michelle Boffa, Cele Cooper, Arleen Kahn, Paula Machtinger, Naomi Malin, and, in particular, Marjorie Tasem, who has been my role model.

And last, my thanks, gratitude, and love to the most important single parent I have ever known—my mother.

Introduction

In the best of all worlds, this book would not have to be published. Children would be raised within warm, loving, and intact families that were not disrupted by discord and strife. These children would become adults who knew how to express and accept love, and they would in turn nurture future generations of men and women who were open and loving. Marriages would not be undertaken for any but the best of reasons. And divorce would no longer be needed.

But this, as we all know only too well, is far from a perfect world. Many couples enter into marriage because their friends are marrying, or because they want to escape less-than-happy family situations. They marry in the hope that they will never again feel alone. They marry for many wrong reasons. And when they finally recognize that marriage is not a solution but a problem in itself, they seek divorce.

Some of these couples have tried to save their marriages by having children. For others, children came early, when they weren't aware of the trouble they were in. Either way, some of the children now find themselves with parents who live in two separate households. Some are placed in the custody of one parent and see the other only occasionally. Some move far away and lose one parent altogether.

The loss of one parent also can come about through death. Suddenly, one parent is gone—never to return again. The comfort and love to which the children were accustomed are abruptly cut in half. For many it's wholly gone because the surviving parent is overcome by loss and is unable to carry even one-half of the burden of parenthood. Like the children of divorce, the children who have lost a parent through death may face the rest of their childhood in a broken family.

Today, because of our more relaxed sexual standards, many women opt to have children without marrying, often because they haven't found "Mr. Right," and they realize their biological clock is running out. They aren't willing to marry just anyone, so they go it alone. And once more a family is created that has but one parent. Other women who become pregnant accidentally, and who in past years would have given their child up for adoption, now choose to keep the baby. Again, a single-parent family comes into being.

In all of these situations, single parents must deal with childrearing, earn money, and at the same time attempt to maintain some form of adult relationships. And once more we're forced to accept the wide disparity between the ideal and reality.

In a perfect single-parent family, life still would be pleasant. The single parent would be well balanced, self-accepting, and self-confident; have a secure self-image with a career that is fulfilling and enjoyable; and be a competent or even superior parent, providing loving, consistent care in tune with the children's needs.

Single parents would not be burdened by multiple and often overwhelming responsibilities. There would be ample time for them to slow down and enjoy their children, savoring the time they had together. Parents would have adequate financial resources to pay not only for the necessities of life, but for extra comforts and recreation as well. They would never have to face an economic threat to their survival.

Support systems would be easily available if necessary. Ex-spouses would always be cooperative; the extended family would be ready to assist any time they were asked to care for the children. A housekeeper would be financially feasible, if that were the single parent's choice. And, in places where ex-spouses, extended families, and housekeepers were not available, the parent could easily afford good child care not only during working hours, but also in the evenings.

In this ideal world, single parents would have leisure in which to rebuild or create for the first time a personal life that included, besides time for their children, satisfying social and sexual experiences. These single parents would be at ease with their own sexuality and would easily convey healthy attitudes toward sex to their children.

Within a short time, they would meet "Mr." or "Ms. Right," thus eliminating the long and tiresome dilemmas that often surround dating. Their children would rapidly and warmly accept this newcomer into the family unit, and the newcomer in turn would embrace the children. A smooth integration would take place and everyone involved would live happily ever after.

But, again, these ideals are not yet attainable. Today's parents are the products of their imperfect pasts. They have doubts and guilts, worries and insecurities that interfere with their abilities to deal rationally with their children. Dating for them is difficult and filled with vicissitudes. Their children meet them with anger and opposition when they bring a lover home.

Money is not available for sitters and housekeepers. Ex-spouses are often antagonistic rather than helpful. Extended families live too far away or just don't want to take over the task of caring for children. What's more, the government is not prepared to lighten the child-care burden faced by single parents. Often, a single father or mother in need of adult social contacts must solve all of these problems alone.

Like all of us, today's single parents have inherited sexual hang-ups and inhibitions that limit their abilities to face their own needs and to instill in their children a healthy approach to their sexual natures. Often their own psychological burdens interfere with their attempts to be good parents. Overburdened by job pressures, financial problems, and their personal emotional needs, they can't give their children even the most minimal amount of love and support.

They need help. But again, our less-than-perfect world seems to interfere deliberately with their efforts to improve. Books that deal with single-parent issues often do no more than allude to the problems that confront the single parent who is striving to establish a new life while at the same time giving support to the children. One book advises single parents to "make liberal use of baby-sitters." But when most single parents are fighting to keep from drowning in the economic sea, such advice is useless.

Most other books now on the market seldom, if ever, address the question of how a single parent can maintain an adult social-sexual life without harming the children. They touch the issue lightly. Yet for many single parents, this is a major problem that worries them and blocks their attempts to establish fulfilling relationships with new partners.

Many single parents realize that to help their children adjust to their new lovers, they must themselves be happy and fulfilled individuals. But they have little or no help in reaching either goal.

During my many years as a psychotherapist, in private practice and in a psychiatric clinic for children, I have treated many single parents who could not handle the problems they faced. They have come to me alone and with their children. With them, I have explored the many facets of their most intimate relationships. We have devised methods for introducing a lover to their children that have helped them establish happy, balanced families both as they dealt with single life and when they decided to enter into new permanent adult relationships. The problems we have encountered and overcome have led me to write this book.

Within its pages I include advice and guidance for single parents who can't afford extended psychiatric help, yet who sincerely want to face squarely the problems they must deal with every day. Only one subject has been avoided. I have not discussed the many cultural and religious differences that affect the problems faced by single parents. This aspect of the issue is too involved to be included in this more general book. Nevertheless, many of the problems and solutions discussed in the following pages can be adapted to fit special cases. We are, after all, more alike than different, no matter what our color, religion, or language. Our children can give us the same joys, problems, and sorrows. And when we, as single parents, seek to build lives that bring satisfaction and happiness to our children as well as ourselves, we struggle with the same need for self-understanding and self-acceptance.

Read the following pages with an awareness of your own particular needs. You may find that solutions effective for one parent will present new ideas that speak directly to your own dilemma. When this happens, the insight you achieve may help you to see your own problems more clearly—and to reach, at last, a life that is closer to your ideal.

Sex and the Single Parent

1 *Our Little Mirrors*

Children Take Their Cues from Us

"*Y*our place or mine?"

The phrase is almost a joke—a parody on modern dating. But for the single parent, it can be both a reality and a dilemma. At one time or another, every single parent seeking a life of his or her own—yet concerned for the children—may be confronted with the uncertainty created by this simple query.

Why the uncertainty? The reasons are many. If you answer "Mine," your child may, at the very least, throw a temper tantrum that will put an abrupt end to your evening. Even more sobering is the very private, unspoken fear on your part that by bringing home someone to share your bed for the night you may be permanently damaging your child's psyche. Yet, if you answer "Yours," you worry about both the baby-sitter and your children, not to mention the discomfort and inconvenience of getting up from a warm bed and driving home late at night.

At the moment when you seek an answer to this simple question, it's easy to decide that your child is the one causing the problem. He/she is so possessive—so difficult to manage—so sensitive. He/she seems unnaturally dependent on you for a child of sixteen (or twelve, or even three). But children don't develop their attitudes full blown. They learn them bit by bit. They watch us, their parents, and are sensitive to the discrepancies between what we say and what we do. They pick up on our feelings and points of view, often magnifying them in an attempt to be in tune with the adults who are, after all, the only security they have.

It may be hard, at times, to accept the fact that you are the one primarily responsible for the way your children behave—but it's true. You call the shots. If you're having problems with them relating to your dating—or to a lover you feel more than casually interested in—look to yourself before you start a program designed to "straighten them out." After all, most often the children are simply reacting to you.

This isn't to deny that any child has other teachers. Peers, instructors in school, relatives, caretakers (such as baby-sitters), and other adults all contribute to a growing child's picture of life. But you, as a parent, play a particularly vital role. Your child looks to you for physical well-being and emotional nurturing. Security comes from trust in you. This is why a child is sensitive to parental attitudes and quick to respond even to those that are unvoiced—to those, in some cases, that are barely acknowledged by you.

The truth is that, whether children have one parent or two, they have the same needs. The difficulty with a relationship between a single parent and a child is that there's no one else nearby to act as a buffer if that one parent fails. If you, as a single parent, don't feel good about yourself, your child is in trouble. If you let yourself be a martyr, giving up what you want because of guilt or a feeling of obligation, both you and your child may be damaged. It's impossible for a person to be a martyr without becoming resentful—and no child who is resented can feel secure and loved.

Special Problems of Single Parents

Of course, a single parent does have special problems—many of which involve the other parent, the one who does not have daily custody of the children. Maybe your husband has called at the last minute with a feeble excuse for not taking the kids on his weekend. Or maybe the children have arrived unexpectedly on your doorstep after a quick call from their mother, who just had to have some time alone.

If you're like most people, you have difficulty coping with such sudden changes in your plans. Most of us aren't prepared to find—or to pay for—a baby-sitter on a moment's notice. We often end up canceling a date, which may work with a person we know well but may put an end to a new relationship.

In desperation, you may be tempted to leave your children alone for an evening. But such a choice isn't without its penalty. Guilt and worry often interfere with any pleasure that might have come from the evening out. One mother reported that she had once actually left her children alone all night, though she hadn't intended to do so. "I felt terrible about it for days afterward. I know the kids were frightened. My son said they woke up in the middle of the night and were scared and started to cry. They thought something had happened to me and that I'd never come home again."

Even if such an accidental trauma is avoided, the guilt is the same. A conscientious parent is aware that there's little enough time to spend with the children at best, and that only a portion of it can be spent in loving closeness. Your children have homework that must be done. They need time to play with friends. Or they misbehave—or simply get on your nerves—and get yelled at. The single parent, maybe even more than parents in a two-adult household, regrets any time with the children that isn't positive and pleasurable.

But these aren't the only problems that may distress you. There's the matter of closeness and dependency. Often, during and after a divorce, the parent who has custody of the children takes comfort in their presence, spending far more time with them than before. If this has been your situation, you know this new closeness may continue for years. Understandably, the children enjoy the increased attention and come to think of it as their due. Then, when they suddenly find your interest has expanded to include another adult, they feel threatened. They've had a number of years (maybe a large portion of their lives) during which they considered you as belonging exclusively to them.

A parent may fear that by bringing in a bed partner—or a live-in lover—the children's moral fiber may be damaged. No parent wants to set a bad example, but even in today's relatively enlightened society it may be difficult for a mother to entertain a lover without a feeling of guilt, knowing that if the children become aware of what's going on they may then consider such an arrangement acceptable behavior for them, as well, or veer as far in the other direction and condemn her.

Sometimes children will accept their father's lover without any apparent upset, but will be obviously resentful when their mother begins to show an interest in a man. In this way, the double standard that plagued past generations of women still affects life today. A mother faced with such a situation may wish she didn't have to deal with this frustrating, unfair attitude. But she loves her children and knows her love is important to them, so she tries to live with the problem. She does her best to keep her social-sexual life separate from her children. This is rarely a satisfactory solution.

A single father may have a similar problem. One man whose ex-wife had remarried and moved to a distant city found himself in a dilemma when faced with the request from his children that they be allowed to stay with him, since if they went with their mother they'd have to leave all their friends and the schools they knew. He had a number of women friends, most of whom had children of their own. He had no wish at that time to make a choice between them. When his children visited him occasionally, he could date the woman they already knew and liked or else take his lover to a motel. Even though his children seemed tolerant of one lover, he suspected they might be upset were they to find he had more. As a result, he was reluctant to accept his children full time.

Nevertheless, he did agree to let them live with him. It meant always going to a motel with his dates, and he didn't like that. But there was no alternative as far as he could see. "What could I say to my own kids? No, I don't want you? I had to take them. And most of the time it's fine. I love them and enjoy being with them. But it does put a crimp in my sex life."

He admitted he got a lot of gratification from his children. But he was aware they were entering adolescence, and he didn't want to give them any wrong ideas. "I hear kids get sexually involved at an early age now. I frankly don't know how to deal with that. I'm especially uneasy around my daughter. I just don't know how to relate to a maturing young female."

These parents have reason for their concern. Children are sensitive. If parents make inappropriate demands on their children, or if they allow other adults, such as lovers, to make their children feel inept or worthless, the damage may be lasting.

Often compounding the external problems single parents face are personal problems, perhaps rooted in their childhoods. It is not easy for anyone to be a good parent *all* the time, and many adults develop inappropriate parental behavior as a result of their own earlier mistreatment.

One woman, a patient who seemed both charming and capable, had actually internalized a very bad self-image that she'd developed early in life—a self-image that proved to be the result of conflicts between herself and her stepfather that were not recognized and not resolved by her mother. She had felt an insistent need to please this man so that he wouldn't leave as her real father had, but her stepfather seemed unaware of her dependence on his approval. He was critical of her and appeared to be unimpressed no matter what she did to try to please him. She became convinced that she was worthless.

With this attitude, she gravitated to men who treated her badly. The person she eventually married was such a man. Even though there were many clues that could have warned her away, she seemed unable to recognize them until it was too late. After she divorced him, the men she dated were much the same. She continually exposed her daughter to needless anxiety and to tears and self-recriminations following the breakup of each affair.

When she eventually managed to develop better feelings about herself, which resulted in her dating the kind of men who gave her respect and nurturing, her new attitude enabled her to deal more effectively with her daughter as well.

Single parents who want to have lives of their own, but who have a responsibility to their children, face many similar problems and dilemmas. They realize that an overemphasis on their own needs could harm their children, but they're confused as to how they should apportion their time, energy, and money. If they give up their own preferences in deference to their children, they feel resentment. If they take time for themselves, they feel guilty.

What they're seeking is a balance between all the factors involved. They want some freedom, but not at the expense of their children's welfare. They want their children to know that they are loved, but they have no desire to give up all adult relationships in order to achieve that end.

If you are able to adapt to and to cope with difficulties, you can serve as a good role model for your children, providing them with the strength they need to weather change. Your flexibility can be valuable to them and to yourself. Many communication problems will be easier to solve because your own security will color all of your relationships. The messages you give your children, both spoken and unspoken, will reflect your ease with yourself and with them.

Understanding the Messages You Give Your Children

It's important to understand that parents give their children messages on many levels. There are the things you communicate orally to your child and there are the various unspoken cues you give, many of which may escape your awareness. It's the unspoken cues that often carry the greatest weight. Your children are most apt to respond to them while ignoring what you verbalize. A few examples follow.

1. *Do you ask your child for permission to date?* I'm sure your initial response is a definite no. But many single parents

indirectly ask for approval from their children.

Sue often brings up the subject of her dating in this manner: "I'm going out tomorrow night, okay? You won't mind, will you? I thought I'd call Mrs. Getz. . . ." What she's saying to her son, Johnny, is that he's in control. If he objects, she won't go. Or, if she does go ahead with her date, she'll feel uneasy, aware of the conflict with her child. Sometimes, because of her son's obvious disapproval when she tells him about a date in advance, Sue calls the baby-sitter from work. Then, without going home first, she meets her date for dinner. She feels guilty about this subterfuge, but the pain of facing her angry son is put off until after the date.

If you feel comfortable about your dating and have made adequate arrangements for your children, you should face the issue directly and feel guilt-free enough simply to say, "I'm going out tomorrow night. Mrs. Burke will sit with you."

2. *Do you try to keep your dates a secret from your children?* If you do, you're reacting to a feeling of guilt about leaving them alone. What you're saying is that you know you're doing something very wrong. After all, if you felt that your activity was all right, you wouldn't be hiding it.

John knew his two boys became upset whenever he mentioned even the possibility of going on a date. Whenever he went out in the evening, they became very obstreperous, making it difficult for him to leave them with a sitter. So he began going out without telling them. He'd arrange for a baby-sitter to arrive after they were asleep, then slip out of the house, making sure he returned early enough and quietly enough to avoid waking them. He explained that his way of handling the problem avoided "hassles," but his secretiveness actually caused his children to think he was ashamed of what he was doing. Only when he was willing to face and deal with his young children's disapproval did he get control of this important aspect of his dating life.

3. *Do you call home often during an evening out?* If you don't anticipate special problems (that is, if your children are

well and you trust your baby-sitter), you shouldn't need to check in frequently during a one-evening absence. Repeated phoning when you've made adequate arrangements for your children shows that you're anxious, thereby creating a similar anxiety in them. What you're saying is you wish you hadn't left, that you *shouldn't* have left at all.

Sue would call home periodically throughout the evening on those times when she dated without giving her son advance notice because she felt guilty about her deception. Her anxiety was strong. Her son perceived this immediately, which added to his anger and feeling of being betrayed and left out of his mother's life.

4. *Do you feel you don't deserve happiness?* Many single parents don't date because of guilt and a poor self-image. In fact, they don't believe in doing *anything* good for themselves. Children sense this lack of self-respect and self-acceptance and react accordingly.

Eric's wife, Sally, left him shortly after it was clear that he was not going to get a promotion he had anticipated. He felt like a failure, in business as well as in life. Because he was depressed, he accepted the role of martyr. He didn't even try to date. A coworker suggested that he attend a singles group, but he never accepted the invitation. His children, reacting to his self-denigration, seemed to seal his isolation. They protested loudly whenever he was gone in the evening.

Then he was offered a better position. He came to therapy and was helped to recognize his own worth. When he began to regain his self-esteem, he could deal with his children in a more mature manner.

You may find that you've answered yes to more than one of these questions. You aren't alone if you have. A single parent will often give more than one signal to his or her children as far as dating is concerned. Such compounding of cues can only add to their confusion.

There are other questions you can mull over to help you determine what kinds of messages you're sending to your children. The next time you ask them to make a decision, think. Are you teaching them responsibility for themselves? Or are you expecting them to decide matters that you should deal with by yourself?

It's appropriate, for example, for your children to be allowed to decide which movie, from a number that are acceptable to you, they may see. In a moderate climate, it may be reasonable for them to choose between sweaters or jackets. But if you expect them to decide whether you have a right to date—or whether a certain partner you like is acceptable—you're backing down from your own responsibility. You should feel good about your adult relationships and not need your children's approval.

Often, a parent asks children for an opinion of a dating partner because of a conviction that they will be more secure if they're included in decision making. But the very question is a threat to that security, for it shows the children that their parent is uncertain about making decisions alone. Sue and Johnny, mentioned in regard to asking permission to date, serve as an example of this.

Sue is insecure about many things. She hasn't yet finished mourning her dead husband, nor has she permitted Johnny to show his sorrow. She feels guilty because of the anger that welled up within her when her husband, Jim, died, and because she knows more about sex now and is more relaxed with it than she was when he was alive.

Her inability to communicate limited her relationship with Jim, and now it's destructive to Johnny. With no guidance other than what he can glean from her subtle (and often not-too-subtle) changes in behavior, the boy is insecure. Until Sue manages to disengage herself from her past life with Jim, she won't be able to help Johnny—or herself.

Facing and Solving Your Conflicts

The compounding of the many problems that exist when you, a single parent, want to lead a normal adult life and still care for your children might convince you that there's no solution. Like Sue, you may be surrounded by difficulties.

1. You may be feeling guilty because you want to have some private adult life of your own—from which your children are excluded.

2. You may be anxious and frightened about "the big world out there."

3. You may be swinging from optimism about dating to feeling guilty or bored, so that you date sporadically. This ambivalent dating pattern confuses your children, since when you aren't dating you may be playing "superparent."

4. You may be denying your children the right to childhood, either by using them to substitute for adult companionship during those times when you have no dates or by reversing roles with them if you feel lost because your spouse (either through death or divorce) is no longer with you.

5. You may not be accepting of your own sexuality, or of sex in general.

6. You may feel uncomfortable with the choices you've made.

Though these problems might seem insurmountable, they *can* be overcome. You and your children can reach a level of communication and understanding that will allow you to enjoy an adult life and at the same time be a good parent. But first, you must face your own inner conflicts. When you've dealt with them, you'll be better equipped to work out the difficulties that exist between you and your children.

These six problems are dealt with in this book. Consider each one. Analyze those that apply to you. As you do, you'll be on the way to solving your dilemmas and building a happy and satisfying life for you and your children.

Irrational Guilt Messages

Irrational guilt has been defined as "the useless emotion that destroys pleasure." It can also interfere with making normal decisions. Guilt affects judgment and limits choices. There are many situations that appear to trigger guilt. You may feel you have no right to a life independent of your children, or you may feel responsible for your divorce. You may even be carrying guilt from your childhood that you've never faced and eliminated. There are as many causes of guilt as there are people who experience the feeling.

Guilt comes in many disguises, but identifying it doesn't always eliminate it. By its very nature, it has a way of holding on. It's not unusual for people to feel guilty about wanting to *eliminate* their feelings of guilt. They seem to feel that if they lose their guilt they'll have nothing left to "keep them in line." But guilt is not a healthy emotion. It handicaps its victims and makes them less able to deal with real problems.

Sue feels guilty because she was angry at her husband for dying and leaving her alone, and because she hasn't yet forgiven herself for the mistakes she made in that relationship. Sue also feels unworthy of life, since she wasn't as good to her husband as she now believes she should have been. She feels isolated and alone. Yet such feelings are common. Both widows and widowers have regrets, as do divorced persons who blame themselves for the failure of their marriages.

Already convinced of her unworthiness, Sue feels additional guilt because she takes time for herself, leaving Johnny with a sitter when she dates. She even feels guilty for needing sex. She's sure, internally, that she should be willing to give her son more attention, and she even believes that if she did she would, in some psychic way, make up for her failures with his father.

It would be foolish to assume that only single parents feel guilt—or even have *cause* for guilt. All parents feel the weight of guilt when they do less for the children than they feel is right. But the burden is twice as heavy when there's only one parent to bear it.

It might help you understand how guilt affects your life to list all those guilts of which you're aware. Don't bother to embellish them. You can do that later. What you need to see is just what your own burden is. When you face each guilt-laden situation squarely, you'll be better able to develop a feeling of self-acceptance and self-esteem. Only then will you find that you're equipped to deal with the problems and guilts your child is reflecting back to you.

Because people with poor self-esteem focus their energies on their perceived defects, it's important that you also make a list of all the nurturing things—emotional and material—you do for your children. Place the list where you can add to it whenever you notice some additional nurturing act you've done but taken for granted and not considered before. Keep this list in mind whenever you're feeling guilty or being critical of yourself. You're sure to be providing your children with good care on many levels. Don't let yourself begin to feel that you're *all* wrong just because you recognize areas where you need improvement.

Anxieties About the World Out There

Like most new single parents, you may experience some anxiety about reentering the dating world. You may wonder if you can "play the game." You may not be at all sure what "the game" is. Rumors are frightening to you, and you don't know who or what to believe. Is it true that all the good ones are married? Doesn't anyone want a committed relationship anymore? Are you really too fat? How old is too old? How plain do you have to be before you are unattractive?

The worries are sometimes overwhelming. Should you have sex on the first date? Will you be adequate sexually? Will you get herpes? Will you be impotent? These and other fears can't help but affect your behavior. They may even cause you to retreat from "the world out there," especially if you've never had to deal directly with it before.

Elizabeth had been protected as a child by her father. Her husband, Kenneth, took her father's place when they got married. When Ken left her for a younger woman who had no children, she was suddenly forced to face a life that was entirely new. She's lonely without Kenneth, and she's frightened at having to make her own living and manage her own life. But most of all, she doesn't know how to handle her need for male companionship. That was something she'd always taken for granted.

Her daughter, Lorena, had been an outgoing child, but now she's become timid and fearful and overly dependent, like her mother. She grasps voraciously at what little security she still has. Since Elizabeth has begun going out with men again, occasionally bringing a date home for the night, Lorena has grown even more dependent. She "adopts" each man in turn, calling him "Daddy" and mentally placing him in the vacancy left by her father. This reinforces the message Elizabeth gives by *her* actions and scares away any man who doesn't want involvements in his love life. Then, with her mother, Lorena feels the disappointment of rejection that follows.

The problem appears to be Lorena's. But most of the child's attitudes originate with her mother. Elizabeth is afraid to face life alone. She's searching for a partner who'll care for her and protect her from the outside world. She considers every man she dates to be a marriage prospect, even though most of them aren't at all domestic.

Elizabeth's dependence upon others is reflected in Lorena's actions. Unfortunately, Elizabeth's behavior is self-defeating. Her fear of "the world out there" makes her try too quickly to establish a permanent relationship. Thus, repeatedly, she scares her dates away before they get to know her.

Because Lorena's dependence is more obvious, Elizabeth thinks her daughter is responsible for the men never calling again. She can't see that her child is simply acting out the signals that she herself is sending.

There are other ways of retreating from the reality of the outside world. Some single parents become obese and use their weight as an excuse to avoid contact that could result in rejection. Others immerse themselves in their work, using their parental obligations as a rationale to avoid dating.

Whatever the excuse used, children pick up on it and apply it to their own lives as well as to the relationships their parent tries to establish. Thus children cooperate in and reinforce the fears their single parent has regarding the outside world.

It's not easy to face your own fears, but the more of them you recognize, the more quickly you can deal with them. I suggest you jot down any thoughts you have about things, situations, and people that frighten you. Free associate. Even if you feel that some of the fears you list are foolish or degrading, put them down. Honesty is important here.

Sporadic Dating Patterns

An individual often goes through changes of attitude, sometimes feeling very outgoing and at other times wanting to be alone. If this pattern is applied to single-parent dating, the message it sends to the children can be upsetting.

Children who have only one parent, whatever the reason, are very dependent upon that person. They try to adjust their lives to whatever routine their single parent establishes. If this pattern changes unpredictably and abruptly, the children are confused. And confused children react with anger and fear.

Jenny has four children. She threw out her husband, Frank, when she caught him cheating on her. But she's a sensual woman, and now, without an adult companion, she misses his affection.

When she becomes too desperate, she visits a singles bar and picks up a man for the night. But because she feels ashamed when she brings him home, she locks the doors to the children's rooms so they won't intrude or be shocked by seeing their mother with a stranger.

These intervals of great sexual need are followed by periods of anger. Jenny feels revulsion at her own behavior, disgust at herself for sleeping around. At the same time, she resents Frank's alcoholism and blames him for her trouble. During these periods of ambivalence, she avoids singles groups and refuses to date any of the men she met during her last fling. To occupy her time during these nondating periods, and to alleviate her feeling of guilt at neglecting her children during her weeks of overt sexuality, she becomes a supermom.

Her oldest boy, Fred, fifteen, has learned to dread both times. He has a rope and a key hidden in his room so if there's a fire while his mother has him locked in he'll still be able to get himself and his siblings out of the house. When she becomes the doting supermom, he's equally uncomfortable. He's confused and uneasy most of the time because his mother doesn't give him consistent cues as to how he should behave.

Jenny at least realizes that guilt causes her to abandon dating from time to time. Some single parents won't even face that fact, blaming their withdrawal from the dating game on boredom instead. This rationalization may prevent them from seeing the true cause of their frustrating ambivalence and taking steps to overcome it.

It's not easy to admit your own inconsistencies, but try anyway. At this point, you need to list any binges you go on. Are you grossly inconsistent in what you expect of your children and in your behavior toward them? Do you go through periods when you are too doting? Do you become very solicitous for weeks and then slip into paying little attention to what your children are doing? Do you hit periods when you just want to be pals with them and overdo the "we're all equal in this family" routine?

If you're inconsistent in any of these ways, you may be expressing your own uncertainties as to how you should behave toward your children.

Denying a Child the Right to Childhood

Childhood should be a period during which young people learn about themselves and equip themselves to deal with life. If, however, a parent is incapable of providing the security children need while they complete that growing task, a vital portion of their childhood will have been denied them.

When single parents use their children as substitutes for adult companionship during those periods when they have no lover, the children are given false signals. They assume that their parents prefer them to be grown up, and so they reject many aspects of childhood. But this rejection on the part of children denies them important experiences that are the right of all children. They become confused and insecure, and they may reach maturity without ever resolving issues that should have been dealt with in childhood.

Another way of depriving children of childhood occurs when a single parent has difficulty accepting the responsibilities of dealing with childrearing. This may cause the parent to display helplessness in a way that is obvious, even to the children. When this happens, the eldest child, aware that children are unable to survive alone, will exert every effort to hold the family together, even at the expense of the rest of his or her childhood.

In this extreme behavior, the child is reflecting the parent's fears as surely as the child who reacts by displaying excessive timidity. A child who assumes the role the custodial parent has abandoned appears to show great inner strength, it's true. But, in fact, such children are often torn apart by insecurity and doubt.

The pseudomaturity they show is their way of trying to hold their crumbling world together. They feel their parent's inability to cope, and they know they can't manage alone. To other people they display a "false self," that of a capable and confident child. They suppress their own neediness and fears, which they feel aren't acceptable, and thus live a fragmented life without an integrated sense of self. I'm sure most parents would prefer never to inflict this kind of pain on their children.

Since they have lost contact with their true selves, such children often feel hollow, empty, and unsure of their identities. Alice Miller, in *The Drama of the Gifted Child*, emphasizes that "the child has a primary need to be regarded and respected as the person he really is at any given time."* If children know that the identity receiving so much approval isn't "real," their opinion of themselves can be badly damaged.

* Alice Miller, *The Drama of the Gifted Child* (New York: Basic Books, 1983), p. 7. (Originally titled *Prisoners of Childhood*.)

Confusing Attitude Toward Sex

Many people, even in this enlightened age, are still taught attitudes toward sex that can interfere with normal, healthy sexuality. Parents who can't talk about sex to their children, or parents who feel there's a set of unwritten rules that define a *lady*, *gentleman*, *mother*, or *father*, can end up conveying rigid, apologetic, and unrealistic attitudes toward sexual behavior to their children.

Tony has his own private reason for avoiding his apartment when he spends the night with a female companion: He's always believed that children shouldn't be made aware of parental sex. When he and his wife were divorced, he let her have the house with the master bedroom upstairs—far from the children's rooms. But now, he has a real problem. His apartment allows for no such privacy.

Because Tony has a strong sex drive and is attractive and affectionate, many of his dates do end up in bed. He has an elderly housekeeper who comes in when he has the children. Out of deference to her, as well as to the children, Tony has followed the practice of taking his lover to a motel or to her place when they have sex.

He's always home before the children wake. But he thinks sneaking home makes his relationships seem surreptitious and dirty. To compound this, he feels guilty about indulging his need for sex at the "expense" of the children, especially since he has so little time with them.

His children react to his attitudes. He was embarrassed when his daughters first asked him about sex. Now in their teens, they don't come to him anymore with intimate questions. Without anything being said, Tony has managed to give his daughters the impression that there's something wrong with his personal life. On the rare occasions when they've seen him with a woman other than their mother, they've been upset. Tony's reaction is to become defensive and rigid. He's giving his daughters a false signal—keeping his private life hidden and never letting them see him as anything but a conservative, overprotective father.

Ambivalence regarding sex doesn't always result in overprotectiveness. Sometimes, parents who haven't clearly defined their attitudes toward sexuality make unwise decisions that cause sex to be an important issue to their growing children.

Heide had been normally protective of her daughter's sexual growth until after her husband, Len, deserted her. Then everything seemed to change. Glenda, who was physically mature for fifteen, seemed like a roommate. Heide enjoyed this new equality, and so did her child. But when Heide found herself wanting to bring a man home, she became confused. She reached the conclusion that it would be all right for her to bring male guests home only if she permitted her daughter the same freedom.

Children need rules that give them the parameters within which they can safely experiment and grow. Heide gave conflicting signals to Glenda when she opened the door to unlimited sex. She also provided a role model that was damaging to her daughter. Glenda saw her mother's action as a "washing of her hands," as a statement that Heide no longer really cared what she did. Feeling abandoned, Glenda reached out for acceptance where she could find it.

Heide's confusion regarding the generation boundaries between children and adults was at the root of Glenda's problem. Heide's relationships were sequential and important to her. She didn't indulge in casual relationships or one-night stands. Yet, she felt very uncomfortable. She was unconsciously trying to put her own behavior in a more acceptable light by making it impossible for her daughter to criticize her.

Heide had always answered "my place" when the question came up. But when she realized Glenda was running wild, she felt betrayed and angry. She'd given Glenda freedom—but she expected it to be used in moderation. Outraged, she rescinded her approval of sex for her daughter. But now she once more felt inhibited in her own behavior. She was faced with the need to define her own attitudes toward sex, this time without complicating the issue by including her daughter. She searched for reasons that would justify her controlling her daughter's sexuality while being free to enjoy her own. Until she worked that question out, she limited her own sex life. When the question came up as to whose place should be used, she now answered "yours."

Discomfort with Choices

At one time or another every adult has come to a realization that an earlier choice was not the best that could have been made. A large purchase turns out to be useless. A marriage made in good faith becomes a battleground. But regret can't alter what's been done. We have to live with our choices—or make new ones.

A change of heart can also occur in parent-child relationships. At some point in a child's development, parents may momentarily wish they'd never decided to have children. But this fleeting thought is usually replaced by a realization that the same children who are so bothersome now can also give pleasure. This mixed emotion regarding a decision to have a child can be experienced by a single parent as well.

If single parents feel ambivalent about the presence of their children, the children will react accordingly. Some children in this situation run away. Others become very difficult to handle. Both reactions are due to parental uncertainty with previous choices.

A divorced father who demands the children's custody may never have noticed the difficult times when his children didn't obey. He may never have realized how different the problems of teenaged girls and boys really are. When his children reach their teens, he may suddenly try to relocate his daughter with her mother.

A woman who fights for custody may regret it later when she's overcome by financial and emotional burdens. She may have a son who shows a need for a male role model. At that point, she may try to reach a better balance of custodial responsibilities with her ex-husband.

Even a woman who deliberately chooses to be a single mother may have moments when she regrets her choice. If she's older, she probably had her child because she felt she would miss the opportunity since she hadn't yet met the right man to marry. But the years have passed, and "Mr. Right" still hasn't come along. She may consider lowering her standards regarding the kind of man she's willing to accept just to give her son some kind of role model. However, bringing a second-rate stepfather into the family could be very damaging to both her and her son. She'll show her disappointment with the arrangement in many small ways, and her son will become aware of her feelings and be forced to share her frustration and unhappiness.

Rowena, a single mother who had her son, Tim, without marrying his father, became convinced, when the boy reached his teen years, that he needed a male role model. Suddenly, she altered her dating pattern. In the past, she had occasionally brought men home, but she'd never let them intrude on her family routine. Now, her male companions are frequently encouraged to spend part of the next day with her and Tim.

The boy resents their intrusion, even though he sees them often enough so they aren't strangers. He feels that his mother's and his independence is being threatened. He's rude to the men, frequently going out to play with his friends until they leave. When he's alone with his mother, he's critical of the way they live.

Rowena has the right to change her life-style—if the change is made because *she* wants a specific partner. But if she's making the change only for her son's sake, there are better solutions. She can enter her son in the Big Brother program, enlist the help of male relatives or friends, encourage him to join the Boy Scouts, or find a neighbor who will spend time with him. Until she clarifies her reasons for bringing in lovers who would not have been accepted before and works out a better solution, her son will continue to be confused and upset.

Sometimes the choice a single parent makes has to do with sexual preference. Today, many gay men and women who once were married are now divorced and establishing themselves in a gay community. Some of these parents still have the responsibility of raising their children. Other gay adults may have adopted children.

In most cases, these gay parents believe they have a responsibility to raise their children so they feel free to make their own sexual choices. This creates unique problems. Usually, parents *expect* their children to accept their own general approach to society and sex. So gay parents who seek to give their children the right to make their own decisions in these important areas need to be very accepting of themselves. Otherwise, they may feel that their children, in rejecting their life-style, may be rejecting them, too.

Jack is gay. He has custody of his fourteen-year-old son, Richard, because his ex-wife, whom he divorced when he "came out of the closet," is in ill health. He promised her that he'd do nothing to influence the child toward the acceptance of homosexuality. He's proud that he seems to have succeeded.

Now, however, Jack feels very insecure. To date, he's kept his son from finding out about his unconventional life-style, but Richard is now old enough to understand such matters, and Jack is certain his son will hate him if it becomes known that he's homosexual. How can he, Jack wonders at this late date, open the secret part of his life to his son without antagonizing him? To complicate things, he's met a man he'd like to live with, but he's afraid of what Richard would think.

Despite Jack's relatively relaxed attitude toward his own sexuality, he still harbors some uneasy feelings. He needs to face his own emotions even more directly than he did when he made the change from heterosexuality to homosexuality. Right now, his discomfort about his own sexual choice *is* affecting his son.

A child can sense when an adult feels ashamed, even if the parent is barely aware of it himself. If Jack can't overcome his uneasiness about society's reaction to his sexual choice, he's almost sure to have a problem with Richard. However, if he's finally willing to discuss the entire situation with the boy, chances are the air will clear.

When adults discuss life-styles and attitudes with their children, it's important that they maintain a consistency with their actual behavior. Single parents whose life-styles include sex but who try to convince their children that sex is ugly and bad won't get very far. Children can tolerate having a parent who is different from other adults, but they can't accept uncertainty, deceit, and out-and-out untruth.

Children Mirror "Significant Others," Too

Children are influenced not only by a parent's cues about dating and sexuality, but also by the attitudes of others who are important to them. If an ex-spouse, a child's other parent, is critical of the custodial parent's social and sexual life, a child's reactions will be affected. If your child is receiving disturbing messages from your ex-spouse, communicate directly with that person and attempt to work out the differences.

Very often these disturbing messages are rooted in the unresolved problems that caused the divorce. An ex-spouse, in order to avoid any admission of personal responsibility concerning the divorce, may attempt to make the custodial parent a scapegoat. Unable to endure his or her own feelings of guilt and inadequacy, one spouse "transfers" them onto the other. In this way, blame can be pushed onto the other person for all the errors and "sins" that give rise to feelings of guilt. When this occurs, a child is sure to be confused and upset.

For example, one man's playing around contributed to his divorce, but he was unable to face that fact. He transferred his guilt feelings onto his ex-wife and became very concerned about *her* morality, even though she was actually a very good mother and had been loyal to him throughout their marriage. Every time their son visits his father, he's subjected to tirades about his mother's failures as a parent and how much of a "slut" she is. The child is confused and emotionally disturbed because of his father's hostile attitude. Unfortunately, this situation will not be resolved until the father is able to accept responsibility for his own behavior.

You Decide About Your Own Social-Sexual Life

Mental health professionals and most single parents interviewed agree that it is inadvisable to subject children to a series of sleep-over partners who do not remain around long enough to become real to the child. Children seem to react negatively to such casual partners, who affect their lives but who are nonpersons. One man, discussing the series of "uncles" he'd known when he was a child, remarked that they made him very uneasy. He fantasized that he, like they, would vanish some morning, and he worried about where he'd go when he disappeared from his own home.

Within some reasonable parameters, you have the right to make decisions regarding your own social-sexual life. Your choice will be acceptable to your children if you're comfortable with it, and if you don't ask them to judge its merits. Young children, or even teenagers, shouldn't have such a burden placed on them.

If you've analyzed your needs and feelings regarding all the areas we've discussed, you now have a reasonably good idea of what you want out of life. But until you know your children's needs, you may not be able effectively to include them in your new relationships. The age and maturity of each child count. The more you know about what to expect at each stage of your children's growth, the more successful you will be in providing them with support when they need it.

2 *They Seem Upset by Everything*

Understanding Your Children's Concerns

A child who doesn't get enough reassurance is more apt to be threatened by a parent's dating and involvement with another adult than is a child who feels secure. But, often the very way in which an insecure child behaves contributes to a situation in which his or her security is further threatened.

A single parent—struggling with the problem of earning a living, with adjusting to being alone, and perhaps with a feeling of inadequacy because of having been abandoned—is not always prepared to deal with a disruptive child in an understanding manner. When your son screams and throws a tantrum the minute a baby-sitter arrives, you may find it hard to treat him with love and sympathy, especially if, to begin with, you're ambivalent about going out.

For this reason, it will help if you can understand your child's most basic needs—the ones that, when not met, leave him angry and insecure. Children have certain common worries that develop when their lives are in some way upset. Since they have suffered the loss of one parent through death or divorce, they may fear losing you, too. They may also fear that you won't have enough love to go around, and that they will then be pushed out if you establish a new life.

Children may feel anxious because they believe the security you alone can give them is being threatened. They may experience conflicting loyalties for you and your ex-spouse, if you're divorced, or a continuing loyalty to a dead parent that is outraged when you seek a new adult companion. They may find themselves suffering from embarrassment because your life-style (and theirs) is very different from that of their friends. And each of these concerns creates a need for reassurance.

If not sufficiently reassured, children may behave erratically, simply because they're frightened. If you're able to see behind their often unpleasant behavior, you can help them overcome their fears and settle down. We've already mentioned the first step in chapter 1—recognizing that your children reflect your feelings. But after you see how their worries often mirror your own, you have to differentiate between your children's expressed concerns and their real needs.

This is not always easy. Your children may believe you should change your behavior so that your family conforms with those of their friends. But they are really asking for some reassurance from you that you feel good about what you are doing and are not bothered because your neighbors consider you different—or even a maverick. This is where your skill as a parent is called into play. As you become acquainted with the various levels of child development found in chapter 3, you will be able to distinguish real childhood necessities from what may be expressed by your children as their concerns. These basic essentials can be as varied as your children, but some are common enough to deserve special mention.

Fear of Loss and Abandonment

Even a child who has had a pet die cannot fully comprehend the impact of human death. Suddenly, one parent vanishes—often without even saying good-bye. The dead parent may be idealized, and the feeling that no one is quite as good as Daddy (or Mommy) can have a strong effect on a child who sees the surviving parent with a new partner.

Kristine's father, Luther, died when she was eight. Her mother, having problems herself facing Luther's sudden death in a car accident, hedged when she talked to her daughter. She informed Kristine that "Daddy's gone to be with God." It didn't occur to her that Kristine might not understand.

Kristine, however, somehow equated "going to be with God" with going anywhere. She reasoned that her father must have gone of his own volition. It meant that even though he'd always said he loved her and they'd had a lot of good times together, he still had walked away from her.

Kristine grew very apprehensive. If her father, who loved her, could just leave her to be with God, her mother might decide to go, too. She knew how much they liked to be together. As a consequence of this misunderstanding, Kristine became a "little leech," clinging to her mother all the time.

This fear of further loss is often very strong in children who have had one parent die. It may also be accompanied by guilt, since children cannot help but be angry at the dead parent, who has seemingly deserted them, and feel guilty for their anger. Unless death is explained, children may suffer in silence, feeling more and more insecure, and, as a result, become a hindrance to their remaining parent's social-sexual happiness.

Fear of loss can be just as strong if divorce has taken place, or if one parent has just run away.

Eddie, a nine-year-old boy, looked a great deal like his father, Carl, with whom he strongly identified. When Theresa separated from Carl, Eddie became afraid that she might decide to separate from him, too.

An inarticulate child, Eddie was unable to verbalize his fear. Instead, he used every possible opportunity to provoke his mother. He needed to find out whether or not she would accept him—no matter what he did. He was determined to end his worry and insecurity. If she was going to leave him or send him away, he wanted it to happen soon. The delay—the suspense—was a torment he couldn't bear.

Of course, his behavior did nothing to endear him to his

mother. Theresa, when she scolded him, often threatened to send him to his dad, even believing at the time she said it that such a move would straighten him out. This threat, which was sometimes taken seriously by both Eddie and Theresa, only compounded his insecurity.

Maggie, ten, whose mother had left her father for another man, faced the same fear, but she handled it differently. Because she was so afraid her father, Louie, might leave her, she reacted by becoming overly compliant and ingratiating.

At first Louie was pleased. Maggie had never behaved as well before her mother left. But it soon became clear that Maggie had a real problem. Her fear kept her from standing up for her rights. She became timid. Her awareness of her dependency made her fearful of being left alone for even a short time.

This kind of difficult situation is often compounded because, when a death or divorce occurs, the former primary caretaker now has to assume the role of breadwinner as well. It isn't unusual for a mother who tended children and house before a divorce (or the death of her husband) to be forced to seek full-time employment. This confronts a child with two losses, though the mother may be aware of only one.

Grace, three, had to be put in a day-care center when her mother, Vivian, returned to work after her father died. When Grace began to cause problems that made it necessary for the supervisor of the center to call her mother almost every day, Vivian realized that her daughter was in trouble. But it wasn't until a teacher at the center remarked that Grace had really lost both mother and father that Vivian was able to help her.

The loss a child experiences may be symbolized by a small action that assumes unexpected importance. Alice, sixteen and a half, seemed well adjusted after Emma, her mother, was divorced. She fell easily into a comfortable relationship with her mother that was not disturbed when Emma began to date. Even when Emma began to live with Shelby, Alice was pleased. Then a problem developed.

One morning, shortly after Shelby moved in, Alice rapped on

her mother's door, interrupting Emma and Shelby in their love-making. When no one responded, she continued to pound on the door. This unreasonable behavior upset Emma. Was Alice becoming jealous and possessive at this late date?

Fortunately, the cause for this departure from her usual behavior surfaced before real difficulties developed. It seemed that Alice had always made coffee for herself and her mother in the morning. When Shelby moved in, Emma changed to drinking tea, which he preferred. Alice saw this as symbolic of her mother's change of loyalty. When Alice told Emma what was bothering her and Emma made it a point sometimes to have coffee and conversation with Alice in the morning as she had in the past, the problem behavior ceased.

A child may feel threatened by the possibility of being forced out by a new family. If the new adult has children, too, rivalries may develop, since they may feel a need to establish a hold on the new parent in their lives. And all existing children may fear the birth of more babies, since these new arrivals will belong to both parents, not to just one.

Donald was fifteen when his divorced father, Arthur, met a woman, Louise, whom he decided to marry. Because he loved his father, Donald was glad to see him happy once more. But at the same time, the wedding plans made him feel insecure. Louise had children of her own.

Donald could see that his father loved Louise, and he was old enough to realize that they might have more children. He grew increasingly fearful that there would be no place in this new household for him, and his fear caused him to behave erratically. Sometimes, when he was particularly aware of his need for a nurturing family, he'd be very obliging, helping the marriage plans of his father and Louise in every way he could. At other times, angry at what he perceived as the threat of being cast aside, he'd become unmanageable.

There are as many variations of this fear of being abandoned as there are children who watch a single parent go out and meet new people. Each child has his or her own individual picture of how life should be organized. But the one thing they all have in common is an inner awareness of their own helplessness and the knowledge that they need protection, food, clothing, a place to sleep—and love. If any of these things is jeopardized—especially if the love appears to be threatened—they can't fail to become afraid.

Guilt About Separation

Few, if any, divorces come about because of something a child has done. However, children don't know that. They believe in their omnipotent power. Rhymes such as "Step on a crack, break your mother's back" may seem foolish to an adult, but most children are still very careful to avoid cracks in sidewalks.

Combined with this belief in the power of thought, and confusion between thought and actual behavior, a child is aware that there have been many times when he or she was angry at the parent who is gone, whether through death or divorce. Drs. Judith Wallerstein and Joan B. Kelly, coauthors of *Surviving the Breakup: How Children and Parents Cope with Divorce*, found that not all children felt responsible for a family's rupture. They differentiated between a child's feeling of having *contributed* to the family tension and one of actually *causing* the breakup. They concluded that children who believed that through some sin of omission or commission they were responsible for the separation were more likely to be eight or younger.*

A child who accepts responsibility for a family breakup often becomes troubled, trying to correct the imagined errors that caused the separation. Such a child carries a fantasy about reuniting the parents that, though often unvoiced, is, nevertheless, very deep seated.

Feeling loyalty to a missing parent, a child may actually contribute to the destruction of a relationship between the remain-

*Judith Wallerstein and Joan B. Kelly, *Surviving the Breakup: How Children and Parents Cope with Divorce* (New York, Basic Books, 1980), p. 50.

ing parent and a lover. However, even when a child is very disruptive, the decision to separate is made by the adults—for adult reasons.

One such child, Len, fourteen, became depressed when his father began to make plans to remarry, but his upset was greatest two days before the wedding and immediately afterward. He broke down and sobbed, "Now it can never happen!" Even though he was old enough to recognize that his father and mother were happier apart, he hadn't given up the fantasy that he could, if he tried hard enough, make things right again.

Sometimes the cause of this feeling of responsibility is not so obvious. Jeremy, sixteen, seemed to be determined to get his parents back together after his father, Robert, divorced his mother, Greta. He set up all kinds of situations that required both of them to be with him. He even got into trouble with the law, and both parents had to come down to court to speak with the judge.

Before the separation, Jeremy had been very competitive with his father for his mother's attention, and he felt it was his father's jealousy of him that had triggered the divorce. It isn't uncommon for a boy in his teens, at which time there is a rearousal of the Oedipal conflict, to have a crush on his mother and to wish his father gone so he can have her all to himself.

Jeremy also tried his best to sabotage any socializing either parent did with anyone else. When Robert began to date a woman from his office, Jeremy became very disruptive. Once when Robert went to the theater with his new partner, Georgina, Jeremy ran away from home. Another time, he got into a fight with his father just before Robert was to leave to pick Georgina up.

The difficulty culminated when Georgina and Robert went to a very important office party that began early in the afternoon and lasted until quite late. Robert arranged for Jeremy to stay with a friend overnight and gave him careful instructions about leaving the house neat.

When Robert and Georgina arrived at Robert's place, well

after midnight, they found the house a mess. Lint had been sprinkled over the rugs, clothing was strewn everywhere, and both Robert's and Jeremy's beds were unmade.

Robert was furious with his son. He couldn't think about anything but cleaning up the mess. Georgina tried to tell him that she didn't care, but he was too upset. At last she helped him clean things up. But by the time they were done, they were both too tired for sex. They went to bed planning to enjoy that pleasure when they woke.

Jeremy had other plans. He arrived home at six-thirty in the morning, making noise as he pushed the door open, then went directly to the kitchen, where he prepared breakfast for himself, for his father, and for Georgina. He brought the breakfasts to their bedroom, where he sat on the foot of the bed eating his own food, successfully interfering with any show of affection between them.

It's easy to get angry with a grown child who behaves in such a manner. But the problem could have been avoided had more been done to help Jeremy understand why his parents had divorced so that he wouldn't feel responsible. Then he'd have been able to let them live their own lives without undue interference from him.

One child who often does feel the weight of blame for a family's breaking up is the victim of incest. If a divorce follows the exposure of the incest, the abused child may assume all responsibility and guilt for having informed on the offending parent—typically the father.

Compounding this guilt is the fact that if the parent who's left after the incest is exposed is the mother, she has to support her children without any assistance from their father, who might even be in prison. The daughter or son upon whose word the father was convicted can't help but feel responsible, not only for the broken family and the father's confinement, but also for the mother's added burden.

Eleanor was twelve when her mother, Kate, discovered that the girl was being used sexually by her father, Paul. Kate filed charges against her husband and sent him to prison. Then Kate took Eleanor and her younger brother, Jack, to a city in another state so the children wouldn't have to face friends who knew of Eleanor's "shame." Before she left, Kate told the few friends she was willing to speak to that she wanted the children to be able to forget.

Unless Kate does something more than just move, her daughter won't be helped. Obviously, nothing that happened was Eleanor's fault. But she's apt to believe it was and react with guilt unless she's given competent counseling.

Anxiety over Unorthodox Life-styles

The children of single parents tend to feel different from their peers who have both mother and father. If you're a divorced parent, a single mother by choice, or a parent left alone by death of your spouse, you need to understand and consider this difficulty your children may have. It is unlikely they'll dare to speak of it to you unless you show unusual openness, because they may feel you'll take the complaint as a rebuke.

Greg was the son of Marcia, a lesbian who had deliberately mated so that she and her lover, Karen, could have a child. When Greg was four, Karen fell ill and was confined to a nursing home. Marcia brought Greg with her almost every time she visited her lover.

When Greg began school, he realized that this situation was not "normal." His classmates didn't have two women for parents. When Karen died, Greg, eight, pushed aside his grief, refusing to confront it because he felt ashamed of the life-style of which Karen had been a part.

Greg was in fourth grade when Marcia met another woman for whom she felt a strong attraction. They decided to move in together. Marcia was most surprised by Greg's reaction. He did everything he could to disrupt this new relationship. Marcia tried to deal with what she thought was Greg's loyalty to Karen, who had loved him dearly, but nothing she said helped.

His upset had nothing to do with the realization that Karen was being replaced. Greg's problem lay in his need to be more like his peers. He was embarrassed because his mother was a lesbian. He hadn't felt that kind of discomfort before he began school. It was the comparison of his life-style with those of his friends that upset him.

Children appear to have what some adults feel to be an inordinate need for conformity. But this need can't be overemphasized. Most children must internalize what is accepted by their peers before they can comfortably decide just how far from that norm they dare safely move. We all have seen children follow strange fads in order to be accepted by their classmates, and have then seen those same children, a few years later, perfectly comfortable even when they're totally different from any of their companions. It's a matter of growth and maturity. However, while that need for conformity lasts, a child may have a serious problem if his life-style, or his perception of it, is not identical with everyone else's.

A single parent who recognizes that the children are bothered because their household is not like others around them must face the issue directly. Communication should be open and free so the child dares to voice any anger at being different and so the parent can respond by explaining the reason for this special feature of their living. How parents accept their differentness from others in society can greatly influence children, who mirror the adults' attitudes. If a parent is comfortable and at ease with an unconventional life-style, the children will generally find it easier to put up with the teasing that might be their lot when they associate with their peers.

Unfulfilled Need for Mourning

When a spouse dies, the adult remaining needs to go through the six stages of mourning—shock, denial, anger, sadness, resignation, and, finally, letting go. So do children. They're usually allowed time to mourn. Mourning in such a situation is expected.

If the loss is brought about by divorce, it's still very real to a child. Sometimes the problems children create in the months or years following the divorce of the parents (or, in some cases, the loss through death of one parent) actually arise because they haven't been given permission by the remaining parent to voice any sorrow. Especially if divorce has taken place and one parent is no longer available, the remaining parent's anger may deny children the right to talk about the missing adult, forcing them to pretend that one parent never existed.

Shawn's father, William, and his mother, Shirley, were divorced when Shawn was twelve. William moved to another state and stopped sending support money for his son. Shirley reacted by refusing to allow Shawn to speak of his father. She was angry much of the time, berating William whenever Shawn tried to talk about him. As a result, Shawn was never permitted to progress through the stages of mourning for the parent he had loved and lost. As months passed, Shawn grew more and more introverted.

When his mother finally found another man she wanted to marry, her attitude changed. She became lighthearted and bright. But her happiness and her interest in a new man only angered Shawn. He wasn't ready for a new relationship.

Shirley should have seen and acknowledged Shawn's need to say farewell to his lost father. She should have recognized that, even though she was angry at William, Shawn might still love him. Only when she began to understand that Shawn's ties to his father had never been properly considered was she able to let him speak to her of his feeling of loss. This new, better communication between mother and son, and her allowing him to complete his mourning, did finally open the way to a good relationship between Shawn and Shirley's new lover.

Helping Children with Their Problems and Worries

Children are as eager as you are to forget worries and sadness and go on with living, whether the worries arose from death, divorce, or any other difficulty children may face. But children aren't capable of dealing with their own worries, guilts, and fears without some help. You can give your child the help he or she needs if you take the time to discover where the primary worries are rooted.

Children need security. If anything happens to disrupt the confidence that everything will be all right, they'll become upset and unhappy. But what is the real basis of security? We all know that it doesn't lie in material things. It comes from inside. We've seen people who, because of an inner strength, weather difficulties that appear overpowering. They seem to have a conviction that they can survive anything.

Children get that inner confidence if they feel that those upon whom they depend truly care for them—love them no matter what happens or what they may do. If you love your children—show it! Don't assume they know you love them because you're working nine hours a day to provide them with the material things they had before their other parent left them and you. Don't *assume* anything. A child believes what he or she sees and hears. Children aren't subtle. You won't convince them that they're loved because you give them new clothes. In fact, too many presents may actually lead children to believe you *don't* love them and that you are trying to make up for it with gifts.

Angela was six when her mother had a second child. Both Edgar and Serena, her parents, were thrilled—especially when that child was a boy. Now they had one of each. But Angela was very cruel to her baby brother, and to all babies, after little Gerald was brought home. Neither Edgar nor Serena could understand why.

Before Serena went to the hospital, they'd talked a great deal in Angela's presence about their wish for a boy. They didn't realize that by doing so they were saying to her that she was less important to them because she wasn't a boy. Then, when the baby was born, Edgar went out and bought Angela practically every toy she'd ever expressed a wish to own. Understandably,

Angela interpreted this to mean that they'd done her a great wrong by bringing a second child—a boy—into the family, and they were trying to make that up to her, too.

How does this apply to a single parent who wants a child to accept an adult relationship that appears to be leading to marriage? Very directly. You can't make children feel wanted by giving them gifts in place of understanding and love, nor can you get them to recognize your needs unless you first show your concern for theirs.

To reach this understanding, you must be willing to talk. Talk about the loss you and the children feel. Discuss your changing emotional reactions to the events that have left you a single parent. Let your children respond by openly expressing their emotions, too.

Timing is important. Don't foist a discussion of this kind on children before they're ready for it. Wait for them to express, either by action or by words, their need for emotional support and love. There's a time for everything. Comforting children must be done in *their* time—not yours. Only one requirement exists here. Your children will need that comfort before they begin to feel abandoned and become difficult. Be sensitive to their reactions, and be ready to listen when you're needed.

You still may find that your children manifest their unhappiness by acting rebellious. But children who behave badly are often most in need of your love. It may not be easy for you to act loving just then, but think how much harder it is for your children. They're probably afraid you're going to leave, too. If children have experienced a period in which a parent has given them companionship and love that are no longer forthcoming because of a new adult companion, that fear is very real.

One other worry may upset your children when you begin to look with love on a new partner. They may fear that there won't be enough love left to go around. If they suddenly begin to act insecure, you need to *show* that you're unchanging in your affection for them. They need reassurance. After all, if you've gone through a divorce, your children have witnessed the cooling of your love for their other parent. What assurance do they have that you won't cool toward them, too?

If you begin to date another person very soon after your separation or divorce or loss through death, your children will have more trouble than if you give both them and yourself a chance to recover first. However, this consideration of timing must be accompanied by common sense. Don't give your children wrong cues by asking for permission to date, or by keeping your dates secret. Remember that overconcern when you leave your children with a reliable sitter can make them think that you are doing something wrong when you leave them for an evening.

Spend the time after your divorce or the death of your spouse helping your children build their inner strengths. And do the same thing for yourself. Children and single parents with inner security will not be threatened by changes that would destroy insecure, worried individuals. I recognize that it's often difficult to find the time and energy to help another in the first months after a family breakup, when there are so many pressures on you. However, you should consider the long-term benefits. Time spent helping your children to free themselves of worries that make them unhappy can release you as well.

Most children aren't easily put off. If you failed to notice that first cue your child gave you, don't feel you have failed. Just be alert for the next. Children are persistent. They'll keep trying to get through to you in one way or another until they become convinced you really don't care. The time to worry is when they *stop trying*. What's important to note is that, with each succeeding attempt, children are apt to become more intense.

Sid was annoyed when Vernon, his ten-year-old, began to hang around him all the time. He teased him, calling him "Rover," even offering him a bone, in order to emphasize that he did not like such clinging, especially since it interfered with his social life and the dates he occasionally had. But Vernon had simply taken a long time to recognize—and feel—the loss of his mother, who had died two years earlier. He was beginning to mourn, and he needed Sid's comfort and love.

Because Sid teased Vernon so, he stopped the clinging, but his next expression of need was more disturbing. He began to act up in school and fight with boys he had been friendly with in the past. Vernon's teacher finally called Sid in to have a talk, after which Sid lectured Vernon on his behavior, reminding him that his mother would be very disappointed if she knew that her son was not doing well in school.

Fortunately, Vernon's teacher did more than call Sid's attention to his son's antisocial behavior. She asked questions that started Sid thinking. In the next few weeks, he began to analyze his son's behavioral changes over the months since Vernon's mother's death. He conferred again with the teacher, who suggested some possible reasons for the boy's unhappiness. For the first time, Sid realized that Vernon might be afraid of losing him, too, especially since Sid openly expressed his sadness at his wife's death. When Sid realized that Vernon was trying to communicate his own need to mourn, he reacted differently from the way he had before.

The next time Vernon had trouble—he joined with two other boys and threw paint on the steps of the school—Sid was better prepared. This time he didn't scold Vernon, but asked, instead, what was bothering him. This more sympathetic approach helped the boy express his sadness. Through a number of conversations, and by a change in his attitude, Sid helped Vernon air and discuss his feelings of loss and abandonment. He responded by showing a definite improvement in his behavior.

If you find that your children have already gone through a number of stages in an attempt to get you to recognize their troubles, and if you fear that you've shut the door to communication, you may need extra help. Some of the difficulties children face when they feel abandoned or fearful that they may lose you are more than a parent alone can handle. However, outside assistance is available. Family counselors, therapists, and child therapists can all give you guidance. A little bit of assistance at the right time can mean as much to you as it will to your children.

Make use of this professional guidance. Sometimes all that's needed is for someone who can look at the problem objectively to point it out to you, as Vernon's teacher helped Sid to see that the boy was afraid that Sid, too, might leave him. Sometimes more assistance is needed. Don't be afraid to seek help. Your welfare and the welfare of your children are important enough to be worth the cost of therapy.

3 *But They're Too Young to Be Jealous!*

Age, Sex, and Developmental Stages Do Make a Difference

Sylvia and Marvin decided to live together in Sylvia's house, just when Aaron, almost eighteen, was getting ready to go to college. She was pleased with the serendipity of the situation. She had worried all along that Aaron would object to any man she decided to marry or live with because he had always been so loyal to his father.

She was concerned about Joseph, her eleven-year-old. He was so very young. He might resent any time she spent with someone else. He seemed to need her a lot.

When she introduced Marvin to her sons, she was startled. Aaron, who probably would never return home as more than a visitor again, was outraged. It was clear that he felt Marvin was going to occupy "his space." Even though he had his own room, and she'd promised to keep it for him, he demanded to know where he'd stay on holidays.

Joseph, on the contrary, took to Marvin immediately. He seemed to get special pleasure from having man-to-man talks. He even began to copy Marvin's distinctive walk.

Maybe you've experienced something like this. You thought you knew how your children would feel about your plans, but when you put them into effect everything seemed to fall apart. You wonder how you could have been so wrong in your expectations. You thought children became easier to manage as they grew older. You assumed your late-teen son was past trying to run your life.

What we often forget is that no two children develop at exactly the same pace. Your child may be ahead of the "normal" schedule, but there's nothing wrong if, instead, your son or daughter appears to be behind. It's the developmental stage your child is in that has the greatest effect on behavior.

Dr. Judith Wallerstein and her associates, in a five-year longitudinal study of the relationships between divorce and the developmental stages of children, concluded: "Despite significant individual differences, the children's age and developmental stage appeared to be the most important factors in governing their initial responses. The stage of development profoundly influenced the child's need of the parents and perception of the stress, as well as the child's understanding, coping, and defensive strategies."*

Although these developmental stages generally occur at specific ages, no two children are alike, either in how they react to the various stages or in the degree to which they overlap. It's easy for a parent to assume that every two-year-old child is at the "terrible-two" development stage, when the child is seeking to establish authority and often says "no" just to demonstrate independence. But some children pass through that stage before their second birthday and others don't reach it until they're almost three. Furthermore, what may be a traumatic period for one child is passed over easily by another.

Even more confusing is the fact that some children get stuck at one particular stage of development. In some cases, the "lock-in" to one stage may persist even after the individual has grown up. We've all met adults who, in some particular area, act like emotional teenagers or even petulant two-year-olds.

*Wallerstein and Kelly, *Surviving the Breakup*, p. 312.

During therapy, many such adults finally separate themselves emotionally from parents who may actually have been dead for years. Then, for the first time, those individuals are able to make decisions and choices based on personal needs rather than on a need for the approval of long-gone parents. During this growth process, some adults relive what appear to be delayed adolescent issues.

If such adults, burdened with some unresolved stage of emotional development, are also parents, the problems they face may be compounded. It isn't easy for immature adults to work through personal unresolved emotional development stages and at the same time handle those of dependent children. Feeling out of touch with inner reality and overwhelmed by problems, they may need professional help to gain self-respect and control of their lives.

The more self-knowledge parents have, the more capable they will be to deal with children's growing pains. Yet, no one is perfect. Often, a simple acknowledgment that problems exist and a willingness to face them honestly when they surface will put a struggling parent well on the road to finding solutions.

If you have more than one child, you'll be dealing with different reactions to the same event. What may upset a two-year-old may leave a five-year-old untouched and may strongly affect a teenager. If you have all three, your best is all you can do.

There's help to be gained, however, in understanding the major developmental stages through which children pass. If you augment this knowledge with some recognition of the parental support most needed during each stage, you'll be equipped to approach your children with more than just love. You'll be able to show them understanding and give them direction as well.

Infancy

Infants are helpless. They can't feed themselves or keep warm. They're totally dependent upon their parents for care and love. If, during this period, they experience support, affection, and attention—if they're cared for, fondled, caressed, and talked to—they'll develop a basic, lifelong trust.

As children grow more capable of independent action, they begin to explore the world away from their parents, returning often to reassure themselves that the environment in which they feel safe is still available. This testing of independence begins early, and to some degree it continues on into adulthood.

If children have two available parents, some of the burden of this period of emotional dependency can be shared. Growing children learn that the area of safety is large—encompassing two adults, both of whom love them. But if one of those adults leaves, either through death or divorce, some of that security leaves too, creating anxiety in the infants.

Frances found a job almost as soon as Len moved out. She was relieved to have him go. He hadn't been able to deal with her being a mother, nor could he accept his own child. Still, it wasn't easy for her to adjust. She'd anticipated staying home while Nancy was an infant—maybe even throughout the girl's childhood.

Her new boss was willing to let her solve her baby-sitter problem before she actually started work. Since she lived too far from her mother, she knew she had to find a sitter. But that wasn't easy. At last she met a woman who seemed appropriate. Other neighbors and the local minister assured her that her choice was good. Nevertheless, she noticed a definite change in her baby when she picked her up at the end of the day. Nancy seemed to cry and cling to her more than usual.

Matters got worse as the weeks progressed. At last Frances announced that she had to quit work. Her boss wouldn't accept her decision, since she'd already proven herself to be a valuable employee. He suggested that she ask the sitter if she'd spend at least some time in Nancy's own home. Frances did as her boss requested. Immediately, Nancy seemed to become less apprehensive.

Frances's employer had offered an excellent suggestion. Allowing Nancy to spend some time in her own home, even with her mother absent, reassured her. However, in this case, there were things Frances could have done to avoid the problem almost entirely.

1. If possible, bring a sitter into the home where the child feels safe. This may be feasible when the single parent goes on a date or is gone for a few hours of shopping, but it is usually too expensive a method of child care to be used during working hours.

2. If the separation is to be for an extended period of time and the infant can't be kept at home, then *give the child an opportunity to meet the person who'll baby-sit and to visit the baby-sitter's place in the presence of the parent.* Introducing an infant or small child to the baby-sitter is wise under all circumstances. The meeting should take place when the parent isn't going out, so that later the shock of being left with someone else for a period of time won't be so great.

What's important here is to minimize the stranger anxiety that many infants experience sometime around the eighth month. Infants can react with fear to a sudden disappearance of a needed parent. The goal is to minimize this fear by making the infant's new surroundings familiar and nonthreatening.

An ideal procedure is to start by leaving the infant for a short time. A quick return of the parent will reassure the child. If that experience is repeated more than once, an infant is far more apt to weather longer absences without trauma because the infant has learned to trust that life will return to normal in time.

Early Childhood

The anxiety associated with separation persists into early childhood, ages three through six, though it usually isn't as severe as it was in the beginning. Now, however, an additional complication arises. Children in this age group often compete with the same-sex parent for the affection of the parent of the opposite sex. This period is usually referred to as the *Oedipal stage*.

If both parents remain available and loving feelings for both are encouraged, this period passes without any trauma. Children, once more feeling a balance in their relationship to both parents, begin to model themselves after the same-sex parent, replacing rivalry with identification.

Erik Erikson, in *Childhood and Society*, refers to this period as a time for establishing initiative rather than guilt. If the passage through to the identification stage is made without creating guilt feelings for their earlier wish to take the same-sex parent's place, growing children are free to become outgoing and self-directed. But if something causes this development to be interrupted, guilt may block further emotional growth.

The most obvious interruption in this normal development occurs when one parent is lost either through death or divorce. If the parent who leaves is the one toward whom the growing children felt rivalry, guilt and subsequent fear can be enormous. Children often believe that parents can read their minds. In this situation, they may assume that the "rival" parent was put aside in order to fulfill their wish to possess the other, remaining parent.

Such a belief can make a child feel both triumphant and fearful. What if the remaining parent has a change of mind and goes back to the parent who's been excluded? It may be easier for a parent to understand this childish fear if a divorce has occurred. But it happens when death removes one parent, too.

Death isn't real to children. They have difficulty understanding its finality. Far too often an adult's attempt to explain death only confuses children further, especially if they're told that "Daddy's gone to be with God," as mentioned in chapter 2. Instead of being reassured, they become more frightened and insecure. Children may reason that if God called their father, Mother might be called as well.

Another danger also exists if the remaining parent is the opposite-sex parent, who is at the time the object of the child's

Oedipal desires—the child's reactions may not be recognized for what they are. The parent may take the child to bed for comfort, thus feeding the natural Oedipus complex. Carelessness about nudity may also affect the child, especially if the remaining parent has always been modest in the past.

If, on the contrary, the custodial parent is the one with whom the growing children felt rivalry, different problems may develop. Suddenly deprived of the parent they desired, children may assume that this deprivation is punishment for their "bad" wishes. Children with this fear may show undue resentment of the remaining parent as well as guilt and unhappiness at being abandoned by the parent they desire.

After their divorce, while the children were still living with Tina, Fred was so busy getting resettled that he had no time to take advantage of his joint-custody privileges. As a result, his four-year-old twins, Jack and Kristen, were deprived of their father. Kristen seemed most disturbed, objecting to everything Tina asked her to do. She fought with her brother. At the same time, Jack became proprietary toward his mother.

Fred finally got settled in a nearby condominium and, since both parents had custody, they completed arrangements for the children to spend every other week with their father. Kristen once more became manageable. Jack returned to showing a natural preference for his mother without the clinging that had been so upsetting to her.

Children between the ages of three and six who lose one parent, for whatever reason, need reassurance. They need to be told what happened, in language they can understand. The remaining parent must consider this of utmost importance to young children, whether or not the children show any overt upset.

Some special warnings:

1. Remember not to put down the parent who's no longer around. No matter how you feel, remember that your children love you both. It's enough to say that "Daddy and I just can't get along. You remember how we fought, don't you? It's

like you and Nick. You don't like to play with him, do you? Well, Daddy and I just decided we can't stay together. But we both still love you, and one of us will always be around any time you need us."

2. If your children don't verbalize their feelings, you should bring up the subject. Ask what they believe is the reason for your separation. Assure them that you won't be angry with whatever is said—and then stick to your promise. It's important that your children be relieved of any guilt feelings they may attach to your separation or divorce.

3. If, while your children are in this sensitive period, you find a new partner whom you try to integrate into your life, you may be met with resistance. No matter how jealous and irritable your children may be, remember that what's needed is reassurance from you that no one will replace them in your affection.

Dr. Wallerstein and her associates found that, following divorce, preschool children suffered more intensely than their older siblings. These children were more apt to regress, at least for a time, becoming more irritable, tearful, and aggressive in their need to hold on to what little security they felt they had.

These also are the children who generally feel most responsible for a breakup between their parents. Because they believe that their thoughts may control what their parents do, they're more fearful during daytime absences of the remaining parent and they fight to keep him or her from leaving them at night. Preschool children have little inner strength. They're more dependent upon their environment than are older children. Wallerstein and her colleagues found that "their fears are more easily allayed by concerned parents and their symptoms yield more quickly to appropriate reassurance and continued contact with both parents" than do fears and symptoms in older children. *

* Wallerstein and Kelly, p. 313.

Latency Phase

The ages between six and twelve have been labeled the latency phase, even though many authorities now consider that a misnomer. Specifically, it was once assumed that children of those ages were "latent" sexually, since boys and girls of that age group appear to avoid each other and show an obvious preference not only for playmates of the same sex, but also for the same-sex parent.

Recent research, however, has shown that even though children of these ages appear to be totally involved in physical activity, in getting acquainted with the world outside, in learning, and in exploring their own capabilities, they still are interested in sex and are developing as sexual beings. They can be hurt by a family breakup, for their sexual development demands that both parents be accessible to them.

Erik Erikson refers to the tasks of this stage as the development of "industry versus inferiority."* What he means is that children of from six to twelve will learn to apply themselves to outwardly expanding tasks if they aren't unduly worried about their relationships with their parents. If, however, separation, death, or divorce denies them access to one parent, they may feel inferior, and lose personal inner drive to achieve.

It's been found that early school-age children, particularly boys, tend to grieve more openly about divorce—especially in the absence of their fathers. Some of these children idealize their fathers and are inhibited in any expression of anger at their fathers no matter how or why they left the household.

These same children often freely express anger at their custodial mothers, younger siblings, and peers, however, even though they're afraid they might be sent to live with strangers. Any child who's threatened with being sent away for causing family problems will be upset, but a child of this age is especially vul-

*Erik H. Erikson, *Childhood and Society*, 2nd ed. (New York: W. W. Norton, 1964), p. 258.

nerable. These children are very fearful of further deprivation. If they're used as pawns in their parents' battle, their problems are multiplied.

Danny found himself in the middle of his parents' disputes even before the separation. After the divorce was final, both parents used him in their battle to get even.

His mother, Lena, often planned a special outing on the day when Paul was scheduled to pick Danny up. When his father arrived, Danny was asked to decide what he wanted to do—go with Daddy, or have fun with Mommy? After this happened a few times, Paul reciprocated. Now Danny had to make choices every time he went from one parent to the other. Whatever he decided was wrong. He was sure to displease one parent.

Danny was far too young at seven to understand what was going on. He felt deprived and guilty. His problem was caused by his parents' unreasonable behavior. Only when they were helped to understand what they were doing to their child did things improve.

Fortunately most children don't have to deal with such extreme parental behavior. Yet many children of divorce do feel they've lost their fathers. Concerned fathers with children of this age group maintain regular contact with them. Children need both their parents. They shouldn't be denied either because of the anger and hurt of divorce.

Both the custodial parent and the parent who isn't living with the children need to help six- to twelve-year-olds understand that it's normal for them to feel anger at both parents when a divorce takes place. Children are victims of their parents' decision to separate. If the parents refuse to accept their responsibility and aren't willing to allow their children to express their upset at the changes that have taken place, the children suffer. If they don't get help from their parents, they may displace their anger onto others—or themselves.

One more important issue involving the children's natural parents is that both should, at all costs, avoid insulting each other in their children's presence. They shouldn't ask their children to side with them in the marital battle. Especially in this age period, children need to be reassured that it's all right for them to continue to love both their mother and father.

Loyalty toward the missing parent may become an issue if the custodial parent begins to date. If the mother has custody, her children of this age may become fearful that the new man in her life expects to replace their real father. To avoid this fear, a mother who is dating needs to make it clear to her children that she wants them to continue to have a good relationship with their father. She needs to explain that her new friend doesn't intend to take their father's place, but that he's her good friend, and would like to be theirs, too.

If your boy of this age is unable to see his father regularly (due to death or distance), he may develop a premature attachment to your friend. Some of the boys in Wallerstein's study urged their mothers to bring in a daddy. There's some indication that this reaction is rooted in the earlier Oedipal conflict. Children up to the age of nine (and sometimes older) truly believe in the power of their wishes. If your boy is in the Oedipal stage, he might honestly believe that he's responsible for his father's leaving. Now, seeing you less happy and overworked, he wishes to make up for his past mischief.

According to Wallerstein's study, there appears to be a great difference between children of six to eight and those of nine to twelve, even though both are classified as being in the latency phase. The eighth to ninth year is a "time of rapid growth and strengthening in ego as evidenced by a newly available repertoire of coping skills, a time of greatly enhanced capacity to understand a complex reality and to withstand stress without regression. There appear, also, to be very significant changes in relationships with parents."*

Nine- to twelve-year-old children understand the realities of divorce more clearly than do younger siblings and they attempt to cope with—and master—their conflicting feelings and fears.

*Wallerstein and Kelly, p. 71.

Wallerstein found that these children often denied their pain and distress. Some felt ashamed and different if their parents were divorced. Where younger children became depressed and sometimes regressed, those between nine and twelve seemed to attack their problems by indulging in vigorous activity and creative play. Some of their activity was directed at reuniting their parents.

These children appear to have an additional burden. The consciences of preadolescent boys and girls were found by Wallerstein to be "harsh, unmodulated, immature."* Children of this age see things as either good or bad. This is why it is so important that parents not try to get such children to take sides. If asked to do so, they'll make value judgments regarding both parents. One will be all good, the other all bad. In some cases, this early judgment can affect the child even when he matures.

One such boy refused to see his "bad" father—or even talk to him—until he was almost thirty years old, even though his father had made many friendly overtures. In some cases this break lasts a lifetime.

Early Adolescence

The ages from eleven or twelve through thirteen or fourteen are considered the years of early adolescence, but the demarcation between them and both earlier and later periods isn't clear. These few crucial years actually contain so many phases that each year could easily be considered separately. Furthermore, since no two children develop at the same pace, there's a great deal of overlapping.

The most obvious change that takes place during these years is physical. Children begin to mature, and this change is accompanied by emotional upset. Most girls begin to menstruate at thirteen or fourteen, though some may start as early as nine.

* Wallerstein and Kelly, p. 80.

Some few don't start until they're seventeen. For boys, the onset of puberty varies just as much.

Growing children begin to seek independence, even though cautiously. Though the tendency to see parents as stupid and ineffectual is greater in the mid-teen period, there still are hints of it at this early age. These explorations into independence are still timid, however, and can be missed by a parent who's involved with other children or with personal problems.

Preadolescent children are often confused by their own new ability to find fault with their parents. They still need a great deal of parental care, and this limits their freedom to criticize. At this period in their lives, they need to "internalize" the guidelines they've been given by the very parents they're beginning to see as imperfect.

Now is when your children most need you to be consistent in your discipline. Time taken to explain your feelings and the reasons for your divorce, or to let your children grieve for their dead parent, will help them adjust. They need to feel continued respect for you and for their absent parent so they'll be free to solve the inner conflicts created by their alternating dependence and independence.

Combined with their need to accept their great body changes and to adjust to a new image of their parents is a parallel need to form some identity of their own. This building of self-concept is enhanced through close association with peers. Preteen friendships are deep and emotional. Fights can result in announcements that "I never want to see Johnny again." But such absolutes are soon forgotten. The need for peer association is too great.

Sometimes, during this physical development phase, the Oedipal conflict once more appears. Growing children now feel sexually attracted to their opposite-sex parent. This happens more often if the children haven't yet formed peer relationships. In a safe family environment children of this age may openly seek the attention of the opposite-sex parent and resent any interference by the same-sex parent.

If children of this age are involved in a divorce, this revival of the Oedipal conflict may further complicate their reactions. They may feel an increased anxiety and a slowing down of the normal separation process that should occur as children mature.

Sue was eleven when Kent and Louise divorced and Louise took custody of the children. Throughout the divorce proceedings, Sue remained aloof, gazing wistfully at Kent, who seemed barely to notice her. After the divorce, Sue stayed with her mother. Her father remarried almost immediately—a young woman of twenty-one.

Sue was devastated. She refused to go to her father's when she was supposed to visit him. She began to experiment with makeup, even though her mother disapproved. And when she did once more consent to visit Kent, she wore heavy makeup and a dress she'd picked up at a garage sale that was designed for a much older person. She insisted on wearing it, and her father, charmed by how "cute" this child-woman of his looked, encouraged her.

But when she and her father reached Kent's new home, Sue behaved in so obviously a seductive manner that he was embarrassed and scolded her in front of her stepmother. Chagrined, Sue walked all the way back to her mother's house, a distance of almost five miles.

Both parents were upset by her behavior but, fortunately, her mother recognized the symptoms. Sue and Louise had a long talk that helped the child understand what she was feeling. Louise also discussed the problem with her ex-husband and his new wife. The change of parental attitude that resulted eased Sue's distress. She once more returned to being the charming child she'd been before.

If you're a single parent dating with any regularity, you need to consider the additional problems that may upset your preadolescent children. You need to offer them increased reassurance and special tolerance for their periods of upset. This, combined with the clear understanding that you're not competing with them for the attention of your ex-spouse, will reassure them. You need also to make it clear to them that none of your dates is competing with them for *your* attention. If your children feel secure in your love and in the love of their absent parent, what may be a very difficult time for both them and you will become easier.

Midadolescence

Midadolescence lasts from around thirteen or fourteen to approximately sixteen or seventeen. By this time, most children have redirected their attention from parents to peers. However, the transfer isn't always complete, and so children of this age may still become jealous of anyone who appears to threaten the relationship they have with the opposite-sex parent. For example, the fourteen-year-old son of a dating divorcée may be very unfriendly, even rude, to any date she brings home.

A woman who maintains her youthful appearance and dates a younger man is very apt to hear from her midadolescent son. He may feel that if she accepts a younger man at all he should be the one. If she's aware that her son may have thoughts like this, she'll be better able to deal with him and to make him understand that there's a difference between his age and that of a man five or so years her junior. She'll also be able to reassure him of her love while she establishes her right to seek other companionship.

Children of this age who have younger siblings may try to take over some of the parenting. This should not be encouraged, but all children should be assigned appropriate household chores.

Adolescents in this age group typically alternate between increased independence and a regression to childish behavior. This fluctuation subjects them to considerable inner conflict. During a period of dependency their parents are idealized and admired. In the independent phase, children are convinced that both parents are stupid.

Midadolescent children are developing their own moral codes. They may be especially critical of what they believe to be parental failings. Adult sexual behavior will certainly be under scrutiny. A parent who's prepared will be able to discuss important issues so that understanding can be achieved. If children's attitudes were respected during preadolescence, they'll have an easier time learning to respect others as they mature.

Your children of this age are capable of discussing their problems and their disagreements with you. If you're bringing in an occasional partner, or if you're living with someone, your mid-teenagers may object. They're asking that you clarify your reasons for denying them the freedom to experiment sexually while you demand it for yourself. You don't need to be controlled by the standards you've given your children (and which they've internalized), but explaining your decision will help, and you may do some compromising that will relieve their worries.

Parents who don't want their children to have sex too soon emphasize the responsibility of sex, not only if children result, but also to the partner involved—and to oneself. One father put it this way to his daughter: "When I have sex with a date, it's because I enjoy what I'm doing. I try to make sure she realizes she doesn't have to have sex with me just because I ask her. That's a problem when you're too young. Boys often want sex partly because they think it will prove they're grown-up. And girls let it happen because they're afraid of losing a boyfriend if they say no, and because they think everyone else is doing it. Those aren't good reasons for sex. Sex is too special a way of relating to do it just because you think it's expected of you. When you get older, you'll be able to accept the responsibility that comes with intimacy and you'll have sex because you want it. If you wait to start until then, you'll feel good about yourself. If you do it because someone else wants you to, you might begin to feel you've been taken advantage of and cheated. And then it may be difficult for you to enjoy sex the way you could if you felt good about yourself."

This is a time when consistent discipline is important. In an intact family this is often provided by the father. The discipline, combined with clear guidelines as to appropriate behavior, can help the growing children control their overwhelming sexual and aggressive feelings.

But if their father isn't present, will your children of this age be seriously affected? Not necessarily. If communication channels have remained open, and if you're willing to allow your children to express their feelings of hostility, you can help in the process of maturing that's taking place. However, there will still be upsets. Nothing in this life is perfect.

If your divorce occurred because your partner was playing the field, and you are now trying to establish a new relationship, you may encounter a problem with your teenagers. Your children may expect you to admit that you had no right to get a divorce, since you aren't any different from their father now that you're dating and having sex with some of your dates. You may find that your adolescents are disillusioned with you and feel that you have abandoned the moral position you taught them. Talking can help, especially if you've had good communication in the past, but you must be sure of your own beliefs and not feel guilty if you are to help them understand the difference between your present behavior as a single parent and your ex-husband's infidelity.

Many of the adolescent's maturing processes mentioned in this chapter are affected when there is a divorce. For example, children typically alternate between increased independence and a regression to more childish behavior. It is normally a gradual process. However, when there's a divorce, the process is accelerated. This may be due to the fact that children with a single parent usually have more responsibilities. Single parents have less time to cater to the dependency periods through which their adolescent children are passing.

Most adolescents prefer to deny that their parents are sexual human beings. But adolescents living with only one parent seem to be able to recognize that even their dependable, loving custodial parent does have sexual needs. They see their parent dating. They may even be included in discussions about those dates. A single parent and his or her adolescent children may become confidants at this time. Because of this it is important for the parent to retain the position of adult in this new relationship. If the children are expected to make decisions that should be the parent's, they may be overwhelmed by the emotional load and their normal development may be interrupted.

Beth felt very much alone and rejected after her husband, Mike, left her. It was easy for her to turn to Greg for emotional support. He was so mature for a boy of fourteen. And he seemed to grow strong under the new responsibility.

Then Beth began to date Don. The first time she brought him home, she was astounded at Greg's reaction. But Don, a father himself, recognized the symptoms. He questioned Beth about Greg and finally convinced her that she and the boy should go into therapy.

When Beth was able to accept responsibility for her own life, Greg was free once more to develop his own personality. As a result, there were times when he was as difficult with her as he'd always been with his father. Don helped Beth understand and cope with these problems when they arose.

Wallerstein and her colleagues found that many young people between the ages of thirteen and eighteen considered a parent's leaving them through divorce as a substitute for their "own adolescent leave-taking of their parents and of the parental home."* Some children, however, react quite well to these changes. They take pride in their ability to assume greater responsibility for their own lives since they were moving in that direction already.

Other midadolescents, however, become very emotionally upset when their parents divorce. They act out their anger sexually, frequently with older adolescents. Yet others react by slowing down the maturing process, returning to a dependency that they had abandoned earlier. Such children may show no interest in their peers of the opposite sex, even though they are physically mature. Children in these two extremes need professional help.

In most cases, however, the dependency periods diminish in length and intensity and the periods of independence increase. As this change takes place, children are able to look more real-

*Wallerstein and Kelly, p. 81.

istically at their parents, seeing both their strengths and their weaknesses and recognizing them as human beings, capable of both good and bad, triumphs and failures. Difficult as it may be to believe when you're mired in adolescent problems, even teenagers grow up. And when they do, your trials are close to being over.

Late Adolescence

Late adolescence is generally considered the ages from seventeen to twenty. Although there are wide variations, children of this age are beginning to make a more definitive separation from their parents, both emotionally and physically. They're involved in a satisfactory way with their peers. Many even have their own sex partners. At this point in their lives they tend to see their parents more realistically as individuals with needs of their own. They're no longer as judgmental. Parents and children can, at last, begin to be friends.

If your late-teen children are still preoccupied with the issues discussed in an earlier section of this chapter, they might need professional help. By the time children are nineteen or twenty they should have developed a life and identity of their own.

Children over Twenty

There are some adult children who continue to have conflicts over their parents' dating and sexual involvements. Most such child-adults have not resolved the adolescent conflicts that developed as they began to internalize the standards they learned from their parents. Some may be having trouble forming their own sexual relationships and may be jealous of their parents who've achieved satisfactory intimate sexual relationships with others.

A divorced parent with such children may feel uneasy about dating if these children come home for a visit or if they still live at home. Some parents feel responsible for their children even after they are fully grown. But there must come a time when children assume responsibility for their own lives. When that happens, parents and children should be able to communicate as equals. If communication remains poor even after the children are mature, there most probably are unresolved conflicts from the past, when the child was a dependent, that need to be faced and resolved.

Ellen was twenty-three, her mother, Katy, forty-eight. Though they no longer shared the same home, Ellen spent a great deal of energy monitoring her mother's dating, which she felt was excessive.

Katy dated every weekend. She generally went out with three different men, and she had sex with all of them. She'd been very careful to conceal this until Ellen took an apartment of her own across town. Then Katy, assuming that they could be friends, confided in her daughter. She thought Ellen had moved because she wanted a more active sex life of her own.

However, this wasn't the truth. Ellen had moved out because she'd always been subliminally aware that her mother was intimate with her dates, and she'd condemned the practice. In her own apartment, Ellen led a celibate life.

Since Ellen's choice was not inspired by religious beliefs, Katy recognized that her daughter might need help. But Ellen refused to go alone. She was certain that, if her mother accepted treatment, she'd abandon her "loose" life.

It was, however, Ellen who changed during therapy. She was able to resolve the Oedipal problems that had been compounded when her mother divorced her father. With this resolution came a more relaxed understanding of her mother's right to live as she pleased.

If you face a problem with an adult child, remember that now, more than ever before, you can talk to each other on a mature level. You can resolve disagreements you couldn't face before. However, because of past unresolved difficulties, you may need assistance. I've found that therapy sessions in which both parents and their adult child are present can be very productive. Sometimes, the presence of an objective person such as a therapist can help open channels of communication that have been blocked for years.

Sexual Differences in Adjustment

Studies have revealed that though the age and sex of the child may influence greatly the initial reactions to divorce, these are not as critical as some believe. Dr. Judith Wallerstein and associates noted that "our findings suggest that in the long run, neither age nor sex are central factors in determining outcome. At the onset, young children tend to show more acute and more global responses to the divorce than their older brothers and sisters, and girls . . . tended to recover significantly faster than boys from the initial unhappy reactions to the parental separation. But, by five years, the factors that contributed to good outcome and to poor outcome were related to the configuration of factors . . . which reflect primarily the quality of the relationship with both parents, the quality of life within the divorced family, and the extent to which the divorce itself provided the remedy which the adults sought. Neither the age nor the sex of the child were as relevant at this time."*

There is some evidence to indicate that boys from single parent homes achieve less academically than do boys from intact families. However, it also appears that girls surpass boys, even if the girls are from single-parent family units and the boys come from intact nuclear families. Generally, girls appear to be greater achievers in school than boys, no matter what their home conditions might be.

Why are boys so often seen as being much more vulnerable? It's been suggested that the expectations we have for our male children play a critical part in creating this problem. Boys are expected to be more physically aggressive—to bury their emotions in action. Many boys are still taught that men don't cry. Girls, on the contrary, are permitted to cry and in other ways express despair and sorrow.

Another factor that may influence sexual differences in behavior is far more subtle. Studies of how parents handle their

*Wallerstein and Kelly, p. 313.

babies have shown that boy babies aren't treated as gently as girls. This may be a most critical discovery. An infant that doesn't feel total acceptance in the arms of its parents may be more vulnerable to rejection than one who's gone through the critical early formative years with total confidence learned through loving touch.

We still haven't solved this puzzle. Some researchers speculate that there's a congenital weakness in boy babies that's reflected in their emotional states as they mature. We know that premature male babies are far more apt to die than are females. Boys are more apt to have reading disabilities than are girls.

Custody of children still goes to the mother in 90 percent of divorce settlements. As a result, most research has been with children living with their custodial mothers. This raises the possibility that the absence of the father is the cause of at least some of the problems discovered. Possibly, since the father is most often the authority figure in the family, his absence results in an authority vacuum. The mother, suddenly alone, may not be able to establish her authority as quickly as is necessary.

Particularly vulnerable are boys between the ages of three and five who are actively into the Oedipal phase, and who may feel guilty because of their feelings of rivalry with their fathers. Even in families that remain intact, this period in boys causes difficulties.

When the father is removed and the boy is left with his mother, the move "resolves" the Oedipal conflict in the child's favor—an entirely unnatural conclusion to the affair. This makes it more difficult for the male child to accept his mother's interest in another man, give up his possession of her, and move on to the stage of positive identification with his father.

Another sexual-emotional conflict may develop. A male child may decide that it was his father's very maleness that caused him to be excluded from the family. Believing this, the child will fear and reject any signs of his own masculinity. Some male children in this position overreact in an attempt to end their dilemma. They seem to feel that if their mothers are going to throw them out, too, they want it to happen soon so they can go on with their lives.

A number of researchers insist that a good part of this conflict may be caused by the mother herself. They claim that a woman angered by divorce may transfer her resentment from her ex-husband to her son, especially if he resembles his father. The Wallerstein study reported that "there is evidence in our findings that many mothers were more responsive to their daughters than to their sons, and that there was a significant preference for their daughters in their parenting at this time. Similarly, fathers sometimes visited their sons and ignored their daughters."*

More studies are needed before we can be certain of the reasons for these important patterns. Possibly the new tendency to award custody to the father or to both parents will make some changes here. It has been found that boys showed definite improvement if their fathers remained involved in their lives. It also has been found that if parental conflicts are controlled, or minimized where they once existed, both boys and girls have fewer problems.

Certainly the attitude parents exhibit toward each other has an effect on the children. If divorced parents are too much involved in their own problems and ignore the needs of their children, both boys and girls will suffer greater stress.

Therein lies the basis of improving the situation for all children of divorce. Divorce is painful. It often occurs amid fighting and accusations by two adults who can't see beyond their own hurt and anger. Yet this is the very time when children most need consideration and attention. If parents can be helped through counseling to face their children's needs and consider them of prime importance in the divorce arrangements, their children will benefit.

Sue and Rick were at each other's necks all the time. When they filed for divorce, they seemed unable to think of anything but their anger. The judge insisted they get help in dealing with

*Wallerstein and Kelly, p. 101.

their problems, for they were unable to agree on custody, visiting rights, or child support.

It became clear that they had to express their anger and overcome it before they could deal rationally with each other, yet they insisted that there was no time for such a delay. Only when their children's plight was impressed upon them did they agree to cooperate. It was difficult, but when they returned to the judge they had a reasonable custody arrangement worked out.

During the years that followed, they continued therapy separately when they encountered problems. It helped both of them, but their children benefited the most from their willingness to continue to seek help.

The Use of Growth Charts to Plan

If you're approaching a divorce, and while you're still talking, you and your spouse need to discuss how the oncoming changes will affect your children. If you use the information regarding growth patterns that appears in this chapter to guide your actions, you can prevent many of the upsets that often seem inevitable.

Planning is necessary no matter how well your children seem to adjust. Problems can and do exist that children manage to keep concealed. If you spend some time in this form of preparation, you will be rewarded by having children who, later when you're alone with them, are far more able to recognize your human, personal needs. Many of the problems we have discussed already and others we will be discussing in the following chapters will then never disrupt your life.

4 *You're Important, Too*

Helping Children Understand a Parent's Needs

We've examined the many needs children have, especially in a single-parent family. It's not easy for your children to share you, the most important person in their world, with another adult—perhaps a complete stranger. If you are divorced or your spouse has died, your children may consider this newcomer a rival for the spot the missing parent used to fill. But if you give them a feeling of security, and a sure knowledge that you love them, many of these difficulties will be overcome.

Advice comes so easily. "Let your children know you love them." "Be consistent in your treatment of them." "Don't ask your children to fill your own emotional needs." But each of these directives requires control on your part. Each admonition expects you to be comfortable with yourself so that you can comfort your children.

But are such ease and comfort possible? Maybe you've lost your partner through divorce, in which case you can't help but feel rejected. Or maybe your partner has died, leaving you feeling lonely and uncertain of your future. Maybe you're fighting prejudice and discrimination because of your unconventional lifestyle, and the resistance you encounter leaves you feeling irritable and angry. Can you deal rationally with your children when you're so upset and insecure yourself?

Of course you can't. You cannot ignore your own needs for any length of time without becoming upset and distraught. Your welfare must be considered, too. You probably can't ever give your children everything they want, but for your sake as well as theirs you should make yourself as happy and as well adjusted a parent as you can. That will benefit everyone in the long run.

If you're nervous and upset because you miss the sex you shared with your absent spouse, how can you expect to deal calmly with your children? If you're longing for adult conversation and companionship, how can you listen effectively to your children's complaints, battles, and sorrows without getting impatient? The single parent has needs, too—needs that, if not satisfied, can undermine the happiness of the entire family structure.

Whatever the cause of your being alone, your actions and decisions cannot help but be, to a large extent, inspired by your adult needs. You cannot ignore those needs. If you do, you'll find yourself growing increasingly upset and irrational. It will be more and more difficult for you to deal with your day-to-day problems, and with your children.

Laura was a single parent whose every thought and action seemed to be devoted to her two children, a twelve-year-old boy and a ten-year-old girl. Her divorce from Frank had occurred over two years ago, but since then, despite her sometimes insistent desire for male company and intimacy, she hadn't allowed herself to date. She didn't dare take the time to develop another relationship. She felt she might possibly lose the children to her ex-husband some day if she didn't prove to everyone—Frank, the in-laws, the neighbors—that she was the best and most dedicated mother around.

She missed Frank a lot. She missed the companionship, the cuddling, the sex. It was tempting to substitute the children in some ways—to have Marilyn share that big, empty bed with her and to get deeply involved with Ricky's out-of-school activities. But she resisted, knowing it wouldn't be good for them. However, she was determined to be there, always, whenever they needed her. She promised herself she'd not add any more unhappiness to their already upset lives.

Nevertheless, as time passed, she found herself increasingly frustrated by the lack of a male partner. Along with the frustration came irritability and impatience. She snapped at the children for minor infractions. The daily routine of caring for them became a drudgery. She often cried herself to sleep at night. The children had not only lost a father, they had also lost the kind, gentle mother they had once known.

Laura was desperate. She knew something had to be done. A woman friend who had been urging her for months to get out of the house and meet some new men made the suggestion again. This time Laura acted. Despite some grumbling from Marilyn and Ricky, she joined a singles club.

It wasn't always easy for her to make the meetings, but she went. In time, she met Walter. He shared her desire to stay single but didn't hide the fact that he was very attracted to her. She felt sexy again—in a good way. Even before they became lovers, she began to feel better. She didn't snap at the children so much.

When Laura and Walter did become lovers, some problems arose. Ricky was jealous of this new man in his mother's life, and Marilyn, who had dreamed of getting her parents back together, did not hide her disappointment.

But still, things were easier for Laura. She was able to deal with each problem as it came along. She didn't feel upset and nervous all the time. And, because she didn't get angry at the children so often, she was able to talk with them and help them through their problems. Getting her own life back to normal brought normalcy into every phase of her relationship with her children.

Let Your Children Know What's Happening

As soon as you, as a single parent, realize there's something important missing in your life, the stage is set for the next step—

informing your children. Youngsters need to feel you aren't rejecting them if you bring new people into the family circle. They need to understand what you want—and why.

Maybe they've been your major interest for some years. You may have worked hard to make up to them the loss of their other parent or to make sure they never felt deprived because you've always been all they had. Unless you keep them informed of what you are doing, they may easily feel that you're leaving them—or at least threatening to leave them. A little time spent in preparation can avoid hours of upset and may help you sidestep some of the problems that confront many single parents today.

First, you need to clarify in your own mind what action you can take to round out your life. Is there a singles group near you that you can join? Maybe you've always wanted to act, and there's a class in acting at a local college. Maybe you already know someone you'd like to date. The choice must be your own.

Once it's made, you need to bring your children into your confidence. If you think back to when you were a child, you will remember how difficult it was for you to accept your parents as real people with normal, real human needs. Other adults could be sexy, adventurous, even daredevilish. But not your parents. They were different. Most children cannot easily accept their parents' sexuality, even after they learn the facts of life.

Yet, when we become parents we sometimes assume that children will naturally understand what adult needs are. And they do—to a degree. If the relationships between children and parent have been good and open, and they have been taught to be empathic, to comprehend the parent's feelings and points of view, children may feel that they understand.

Yet even then, the view a child has of a situation may not be the same as the parent's. A child cannot possibly realize the extent to which a single parent, or any mature person, needs another adult for companionship and sexual fulfillment. Such desires are beyond a child's experience and, therefore, beyond a child's ability to comprehend fully.

When you begin to talk to your child about your intent to

change your life-style, remember to keep your explanation simple and to give examples that have meaning to a child. Every so often, ask your child to explain what you just said. You may be surprised at how changed your ideas have become when they're expressed by your son or daughter.

Don't assume that your children agree with your decisions just because they say they understand. Give them a chance to express their disapproval. Don't quiet them if they tell you they can't see why you need anyone else—you have them, don't you? Don't let them make you feel guilty if they ask why you got a divorce if you want an adult partner around the house. Remember that, even though they need to consider both their parents as good, it doesn't mean you have to feel guilty because you and your ex-spouse were not able to get along. That matter has meaning only to you, an adult—not to your children.

One more point. The preparation of your children for your dating doesn't have to include a long discussion of your reasons for being single. It's better if those two subjects are dealt with separately.

John was an architect in his midthirties whose wife had gone off with another man, leaving him with the custody of their two young sons, ages eight and five. John worked hard, putting in long hours at his office. But feeling the added responsibility of being a single parent, and loving his boys very much, he spent every minute of his free time with them.

After a few months, however, the lack of a female companion began to inhibit the enjoyment of his work, his hobbies, and even his children. Fortunately, he realized what the problem was and decided to change his habits. He began dating again and at the same time talking to the two boys about his being lonely and missing having a "mommy" around the house. Although they complained a bit about his frequent absences from home in the evening and their increased time with a baby-sitter, the children could understand his wanting a woman around the house. They missed their mother, too.

However, they had already been made to realize that their own mother would not be returning to live with them, so they were somewhat prepared for a substitute when John decided to bring Angela home. They had also spent time with her before, so she was not a stranger to them.

He sat the boys down several weeks before she was scheduled to move in, and they had a man-to-boys talk. He kept his voice light. "We had lots of fun together at the zoo last Sunday, didn't we?"

Both boys nodded. Angela had been with them all that day.

"It feels good to have Angela around, doesn't it?" He let them talk about how much fun they had had on their last outing. Then he continued. "Well, Angela has said she'd come and stay with us. How do you feel about that?"

Now he let the boys express themselves without interruption. They began by expanding on the fun they had had with Angela the week before. Only gradually did some of their fears come out. Would she make them do things they didn't want to do? Would she boss them around? The older boy, Freddy, asked if they would still get to see their mother if she came back.

John made certain the discussion ended on a high note—a plan for more "family" fun the following Sunday. He didn't ask permission of the boys. They were too young to understand their father's desire for female companionship and sex, but his method of relating the situation to their own needs paved the way for a smooth transition into a new arrangement that benefited everyone.

Set the Stage

John prepared his children in advance for the inclusion of another adult in their lives. He allowed them to adjust to the *idea* before he confronted them with the *reality*. If you can plan ahead as to how you want to live in the future in terms of dating or seeing someone regularly before you actually start to do so, friction, misunderstanding, and open hostility can be minimized, and sometimes avoided altogether. Even if you aren't anticipating a sexual involvement, it's a wise idea to prepare your children any time you begin to be more social. A new person may come into your life quite unexpectedly. So, once you've decided to expand your life to include another adult, or adults, on an intimate basis, you can begin to restructure your time and living pattern with your children—preparing them for the introduction of another special person into the family group.

Ask yourself questions such as: "How much time should I spend with my children?" "What are my basic obligations to them that cannot be compromised?" "Are there hours during the week when they have meaningful activities that need not include me?" "How much time do I need for myself?" "What unimportant things can I eliminate that are now taking too much of my day?" "What are the times when my children will need me and miss me the least—times when I can enjoy adult friends without having to be constantly available as a parent?" After all, you can't do everything. If you're going to add a new facet to your life, something else has to go.

When you've thought over these and similar questions and answered them to your satisfaction, you can make an intelligent change in the pattern of your family life with the least impact on the children. You will have taken the first important step toward preparing them for your new role as an adult satisfying your own adult needs. By asking yourself important questions, establishing priorities, and making a sincere attempt to consider everyone's needs and wants, you will begin to structure your life with purpose rather than just letting it occur haphazardly.

But you still need to move slowly enough so that you retain your children's cooperation. This is why you will succeed best if you begin this readjustment before you have a specific partner you wish to see often and with whom you want to share your nights.

You Need an Adult Social Life

Start by spending more time with friends. If you have a few close acquaintances, go with them to places and activities you enjoy.

Leave your children with a sitter. These aren't family outings. In this way you will meet new people and begin to establish a network of friends who can be helpful to you in a variety of ways. You'll also be showing your children that you have a right *and a need* for a social life of your own. Then, when you start to become even more active socially—and include a new sex partner in your activities—it will be less of a shock to the children. You will not be suddenly disrupting your overall life pattern and the amount of time you spend with them. Because the change is gradual, you will avoid giving your children the feeling that you are withdrawing from them or making a choice between them and someone else.

Privacy Must Be Respected

Respect for privacy doesn't just happen. It occurs only after a deliberate acknowledgment is made that the rights of others are important. You teach your children respect for your privacy by making certain you show the same consideration for theirs.

In some families there is little respect for boundaries between family members. People listen in on one another's telephone conversations, read each other's mail, sneak looks at private diaries, interrupt one another's talking, or walk into a bedroom or bathroom without knocking. Clearly, this shows a lack of respect for privacy.

Perhaps you have been doing many of these things. And maybe a situation of this sort does not bother you now. It's just you and the kids, so what difference does it make? Besides, that's how it was in your family when you were growing up. You never had privacy until you were well into your teens and insisted upon it.

Maybe, when you married, you felt less need to have time for yourself. You enjoyed being with your spouse and it just seemed natural to do everything together. And that open relationship continued after the children were born. You expected privacy when you and your spouse were in bed, but you didn't think your children needed it. Like your parents, you forgot that privacy can be essential to a child's growth.

Now you've reached the point where you have a relationship that cannot always include your children. You don't feel the same about having someone you're not married to in your bed when your children rush in for a few minutes' loving before they get dressed for school. Abruptly, privacy has become an important issue between you and your children, because *you* want and need it. Yet, if you now suddenly insist on privacy you'll confuse your children. It will seem to them like rejection. They'll feel that you're pushing them away, out of your life.

You can avoid this confrontation if you prepare for it before it occurs. If you develop an atmosphere of respect for one another's privacy now, before the presence of another adult complicates the situation, you will not have to deal with hurt feelings and misunderstandings later.

Barbara had lost Bob in a car accident. Their only child, Penny, age seven, had been badly hurt at the same time. With the combination of her grief over the death of her husband, her concern for Penny, and her struggles to work harder to make up for the lost income, Barbara completely abandoned her former social life and most of her friends. All of her energies were focused on Penny. The child's recovery took several months, during which time Barbara spent every available free moment with her. They were inseparable. They played together, read together, bathed together, and slept together. Even after Penny's complete recovery, the pattern of closeness remained intact.

Eventually, the time came when Barbara realized how narrow her life had become. A fellow employee, Tom, had been indicating an interest in her for some time and had recently been asking her for a date. She decided to accept his offer. The evening was very pleasant. After three more dates, Barbara and Tom became involved sexually, going to his apartment for a brief time together at the end of each evening. Then Barbara would hurry home to her daughter.

However, this arrangement left both Tom and Barbara feeling dissatisfied. They each wanted the luxury of spending entire nights together. Barbara wouldn't even consider being away from Penny overnight, so Tom suggested they go to her place. At first, she resisted. Penny would have to be moved. She always went to sleep in Barbara's bed, even when Barbara went out. Finally, however, Barbara decided to make the necessary adjustment. She was beginning to hope that she and Tom might eventually marry.

It wasn't easy for Barbara to get Penny back into her own bed. Still, she insisted and, finally, the girl seemed to accept the change. But that was only the first step. Before Tom came to stay overnight for the first time, Barbara had several conversations with Penny, trying to explain her needs and wishes to the child, who was now ten. Penny listened with a scowl, obviously not in sympathy with her mother at all. However, she seemed to agree to give her mother and Tom the privacy they needed.

In practice, the arrangement proved to be a disaster. Whether by deliberate intent or ingrained habits, Penny always seemed to be intruding on the two adults whenever Tom came to the house. She would walk into the bedroom through the unlocked door late at night, when Tom and Barbara were engaged in sex, excuse herself hurriedly, and slam the door after her. And although she had a private bath of her own, she would, on some flimsy pretext, unexpectedly enter the bathroom Tom was using and then leave in a huff when he protested. Even in the living room or kitchen, Penny always seemed to be demanding attention—forever asking questions or carrying on a monologue that was difficult to interrupt.

Barbara had more talks with Penny, attempting to explain the reasons why she and Tom needed uninterrupted privacy. The child's response was sullen withdrawal. Barbara considered putting locks on the bedroom and bathroom doors but was afraid Penny would take the action as further evidence of her being rejected.

Finally, in an emotional exchange, Penny accused Barbara of being mean and unfair. Barbara could walk into her room at any time without permission or warning but she wasn't supposed to do the same thing in return. Barbara was shocked. She hadn't realized the mistake she'd made in failing, long ago, to establish personal privacy for them both. She determined to remedy the situation.

She began by agreeing with Penny that she had been wrong. Then, together, they began to work out a more equitable arrangement. Gradually, Penny began to accept her mother's right to privacy, especially since she felt more grown up knowing that she, too, had some independence. But all this came too late to save Barbara's relationship with Tom. He was thoroughly disgusted with the entire affair and broke off contact with her, even getting himself transferred to another department in the company.

Adults, by their own behavior, communicate to children their regard or disregard for privacy. In this, as in any other area of child-parent relationships, the child learns by copying the mother or father. A parent who consistently respects a child's privacy will receive the same respect in return.

Fortunately, it's never too late to develop this important facet of your family life. Knock on bedroom and bathroom doors and wait for an invitation before entering. Observe the privacy of your children's diaries and phone calls and conversations with other children. And don't pry into their relationships with your ex-spouse, even though it's tempting.

This doesn't mean that you should ignore your children or not be aware of what's going on with them. It does mean that you should treat each child with respect. Give them their private space and time when they *know* you won't intrude. Then let them know they are to do the same for you. They are to knock on your bedroom and bathroom doors, too, and wait for your affirmative response before entering. They are to allow you time alone when you need it and ask for it.

If they aren't already so equipped, put locks on the bathroom and bedroom doors before they're really needed. Then, when you have someone stay over and it's essential that you maintain your privacy, the locks can be used as a precaution. Even if your children come to your room and find the door locked, they won't be too upset. They'll understand that the lock just means you need to be left alone for a while.

If, on the contrary, you install the locks only after you have established a new adult relationship, your children may easily get the impression that you are locking them out of your new life. Then all sorts of problems may develop. Clearly, a little early preparation can make your life simpler and save your children from unnecessary distress.

If you are now in an intimate relationship, and the lack of privacy has already become an issue, sit down with your children for a talk. Be sure to choose a time when you're not angry. Make it clear that you, as an adult, need your private time and that you do not expect to be disturbed when you're in your bedroom or bathroom and the door is closed. Tell them that you realize they may also need such privacy, and so if they have their doors shut you will never enter without first knocking and getting permission.

This may be the time to install locks on your bedroom and bathroom doors and to explain that their use makes you feel more comfortable. Tell your children that when the doors are locked they are to go back and play for a while. Explain that you'll lock your doors only when it's important that you and your new friend be alone, and that they should never just keep on knocking at a time like that, because it upsets you.

Some parents are appalled at the notion of having a lock on their bedroom door. They feel guilty for excluding their children even to a small degree by its use. They assume that, if a child is told to stay out, that should be sufficient.

Ideally, that's true. But children forget. If you tell them they should come into your room only if there's an emergency, they will interpret the word *emergency* in their own way. It's far better to lock a door than to scold or to get into a power struggle over the issue when a child invades your privacy.

A child who continually has trouble respecting your privacy

may be demonstrating some emotional concern that needs to be understood and addressed. This will call for a very intimate discussion in which you make it clear that you are not angry but that you want to know why your child is troubled. Ask why it's difficult to respect your wishes in this matter. Then *listen*. Often what a child says is not as important as *how* it's said. Also, children have difficulty voicing things that they fear may offend. Be understanding. No matter what answers you get, don't scold.

If your child has difficulty telling you what's bothering him or her, ask some pointed questions. "Are you afraid I'll stop loving you just because I have Don?" "Do you wonder what we're doing when we won't let you come into the bedroom?" These can be questions that lead to new understandings and open the door to more questions that may be troubling your child. Help them come out. And when they do, answer them honestly.

Remember, however, to give answers that are appropriate to the age of your child. A three-year-old needs only to be told that "Don and I are loving and holding each other." A teenager will need a more thorough explanation, in keeping with past discussions you have had about sex. If you are fair and honest with your children, you'll be rewarded by having a peaceful house and children who understand your needs.

Some parents, after a separation or the death of a spouse, get into the habit of allowing their child to sleep with them. They rationalize that they are comforting the child. Or they frankly acknowledge that this arrangement makes them feel less lonely for the lost spouse.

This is an unwise practice for several reasons. For one, it establishes a pattern that will be difficult to break when you want to sleep with a new lover. A child will feel resentful and jealous and will be angry with both of you when displaced in this way. For another, it can be overstimulating for the child, especially a child of the opposite sex. And for a child dealing with Oedipal issues, it can create guilt as well.

If your child needs comforting at night, it is far better, although perhaps harder for you, to go to the child's room and offer reassurance. If you feel cold and lonely in bed by yourself, surround yourself with pillows. They will make the bed seem warmer and cozier and give you something to hold on to. Your child should not serve this purpose. However, both you and your child might find that a pet or a stuffed toy can sometimes be comforting in or on the bed when you go to sleep.

Help Your Child See You as an Individual

In a typical family arrangement, both father and mother tend to lose their individuality and become just "parents." But the fact that an adult is a single parent often helps a child's perception of that parent as a separate entity. Try, in every way you can, in both actions and words, to implant in your child's mind the concept of you as an autonomous person, deserving of all the rights, privileges, and privacy this implies. Take your children to your working place so they can see you as someone other than a parent. You should not allow yourself to be taken for granted by a child. You're important, too. Help your child to understand your needs as an individual and to allow you to be one.

Don't be afraid to engage in activities that exclude your children. You'll be giving them tacit approval to begin establishing their own friends and individuality. This is important both for you and for them. And don't let yourself feel guilty when you satisfy your own needs as well as theirs. In the long run, they'll benefit.

If You're Not Conventional

If you have an unconventional life-style, you may find yourself facing additional problems. Today, many women are electing to have children even though they aren't married and are not certain they ever will marry. They're free of problems dealing with in-laws, but they may have increased interference from their own parents or siblings, who don't approve of such a decision. Because of their choices, these independent women often don't receive much support from society and so they need to be more self-accepting than single parents with more conventional life-styles.

But if they decide to marry, or even if they choose only to have a live-in lover, they are going to need more privacy—and demand it. Far better that they establish privacy and respect for individuality beforehand.

If you have an unconventional life-style, consider it when you begin to approach the problems your socializing may present to your children. A gay parent may want to explain—at least minimally—something about being gay. One thing to remember is that a child cannot be kept in ignorance of these social-sexual differences. Children are thinking creatures. They notice if their household differs from those of their friends. It is usually far better for you, the parent, to talk over and explain any variation in your life-style that is important to you rather than have your child form an opinion about it based on the attitudes of others.

And there is the crux of the problem for any single parent, no matter what his or her life-style. If you want your children to understand you, you must communicate openly. Dare to bring up sensitive subjects—even if your child seems to shy away from them. They have to be faced and talked about.

Dare to make changes, too. Just remember that any change should be gradual. If you've been through a divorce, your children have already had to cope with one abrupt change in their lives. Don't force them suddenly to deal with more. Take things slowly. Think ahead. Be prepared *before* you meet that wonderful person who will brighten your nights and maybe your entire life. If you are, your children will share in your joy.

5 *Do My Children Hate Me?*

Coping with Children Who Sabotage Your Social Life

*I*n chapter 4 we discussed the problem of Penny, who seemed determined to destroy the relationship between Tom and her mother, Barbara, and who succeeded in her efforts. Unfortunately, this sort of behavior isn't rare. Far too many single parents begin to feel that their children are enemies whose sole aim in life is to make them unhappy.

Therapists recognize this reaction as an indication that the parent has lost control. If sabotage is an ongoing problem, the child has been given too much power in the parent-child relationship. Obviously, it's the rare adult who will deliberately give up parental authority. Most who find themselves in this dilemma aren't aware of how it came about. The shift in power is usually so subtle that it's unnoticed until accomplished.

In its extreme form, a child's unruly behavior can totally disrupt a parent's social life by destroying ongoing adult relationships. At the very least, it can cause embarrassing episodes that upset the family. After the disruptive behavior becomes habitual, the parent often has trouble recognizing the real problem. It's the behavior that receives the attention; the motivation for it is ignored. The parent feels helpless and frustrated. It appears to be too late to remedy the situation.

Where has the parent gone wrong? What positive aspects of childrearing have been neglected? If you are having behavior problems with your children now, especially problems relating to a lover, look back to their earlier training. Ask yourself these questions (many of these areas will be discussed later in this chapter): "Have I learned to listen to what they say—really listen?" "Have I looked for cues to what they're thinking in their actions and responses?" "Have I tried to anticipate their reactions so as to prepare them for new people and new situations?" "Have I rewarded positive behavior and punished unruliness—and been consistent?" "Have I provided them with rules and limits to guide their behavior?" "Have I reached an understanding with them by helping them to talk about and resolve their feelings?" "Have I given each child a special time to be with me and feel loved and secure?" Above all—"Have they been reassured that my love will always be there for them no matter who else I may bring into the family?"

Too many negative answers to the above questions could indicate that your children may be feeling confused and insecure. The fact is that unruly children are usually that way because they're reacting to unrecognized insecurity. They seldom know why they do the unkind things that so upset their parents.

Sometimes, the behavior even seems to have a physical basis. Donna, one patient of mine, was a typical example of the disruptive child whose sabotage appeared to be an ongoing illness. Because the parent was unable to deal with it, Donna took control of the family.

Janice, recently divorced from Gerald, was at her wits' end. At thirteen, Donna was a constant problem. Every time a man arrived to pick Janice up for a date, Donna became acutely ill. She was asthmatic, and the least upset would send her into painful spasms. Often, her behavior actually drove the date away, especially if he was concerned about children. But as soon as the date was definitely aborted, Donna would miraculously recover.

She was frequently remorseful and apologetic after an emotional binge, but Janice couldn't depend upon that reaction. If she accused her daughter of faking an asthmatic attack, Donna became very angry—which could lead to a second attack that appeared even more dangerous than the first. As a result, Janice eventually ceased dating entirely, and became convinced that Donna blamed her for the divorce, hated her, and wanted her to be unhappy. A friend suggested that she bring the child to therapy.

When they started therapy, Janice was disturbed to find that I did not immediately deal with her child's disruptive behavior. Focus was instead centered on how Donna felt about her father's departure from the home and on helping her express her feelings about the recent divorce. Only as the sessions continued did the reason for this procedure become clear.

It was difficult for Janice to accept the fact that Donna was truly sorry when her behavior caused her mother to cancel a date. But she was. Donna didn't consciously want her mother to be unhappy. She was actually a very frightened girl, convinced that her father had rejected her. She feared that if her mother found another partner, she'd have no home at all.

There was some reason for the girl's concern. Neither parent had seemed eager to take her. Her asthma had always caused difficulties, often interfering with plans Janice and Gerald made when they were together. Donna was aware of this and was convinced that, because of her problem, she didn't deserve to be loved. Because she felt so unworthy, she fell apart at the least threat to her security.

This information came as a surprise to Janice. She knew that in determining who should have Donna's custody the critical issue was the girl's welfare. Both she and Gerald had been concerned that Donna be near a doctor who knew her condition and who got along well with her. They also wanted her to remain in the private school that was equipped to care for her in an emergency. Because of these overriding priorities, both parents had set aside any personal desire to have custody of the child in favor of what they felt was best for her.

But neither parent had bothered to explain this—or even the

reason for their divorce—to Donna. She knew only that no one seemed in a rush to keep her. She concluded that her illness was the cause of her parents' breakup. Each time her mother was upset when a date was sabotaged, Donna became more convinced that she was right. Everybody wanted to get rid of her.

Her reasoning was totally illogical and not at all based on reality. However, the conflicting cues she got from her mother didn't help to allay her fears. When Janice wasn't dating, she was very attentive to Donna. In exchange, she expected Donna to be considerate of her when she had a date. But had she been more aware of Donna's real concerns, Janice would have realized that what she was hoping for was impossible. Donna needed to have her fears put to rest. Her own awareness of her illness made her exceptionally sensitive and created a special need for communication and understanding. Only when Janice recognized her child's need for security did things begin to change. Then it became clear that what had appeared to be deliberate sabotage was actually the cry of an insecure child for help and reassurance.

It is not uncommon for parents not to tell their sons and daughters the real reasons for their divorce. And custodial parents may appear to be giving contradictory indications to the children regarding their importance in the new, one-parent family. Like Janice, they are surprised when their children don't see a connection between excessive attention when no dating is occurring and the parent's expectation that the child will accept a smaller share of the limelight when a lover enters the picture.

Such conflicting cues, coupled with the lack of communication regarding the divorce, may lead children to assume that they are the cause of the separation, and of all the problems their parents have. This is especially true if, like Donna, they have some troublesome illness or affliction. The insecurity that results then triggers the disruptive behavior. The custodial parent becomes afraid to do anything that might be upsetting to such a child, and so control is lost. It's a logical sequence. But until it is recognized, no improvement can occur.

When Your Ex-spouse Is the Saboteur

After a divorce, the separated adults need to express their anger and grief, just as a surviving spouse needs to work these things out after a partner dies. Only when the process is complete can each individual move on to new relationships and a new life. But one of the two persons involved in a divorce will frequently hold on to the anger and hurt and repeatedly try to get even for what has happened. An embittered ex-spouse may use the children to keep the antagonism alive, placing them in the middle and making them tools for revenge.

Children are sometimes willing to cooperate with the antagonistic parent and sabotage the other's social life, usually because they cling to the hope that what has been destroyed can be repaired. Professionals who deal with children of divorce find that most of them harbor the dream of reconciling and reuniting their estranged parents. Many abandon the hope only when one parent remarries.

But few divorced couples are reunited. Divorce is an extreme solution to marital disharmony. When parents are ready to sever family bonds in that manner, they've usually tried reconciliation already—and failed. At least one of the parents is ready to go on with life either alone or with another partner. But if the abandoned parent wants a second chance, and enlists the children to help, trouble can develop.

Help Your Children Talk About It

It isn't enough for a parent to realize that an ex-spouse is at the root of the children's disruptive behavior. The unpleasant situation will continue until the parent is able to communicate with the children on their own level, helping them to recognize how their own desire for a reunited family makes them susceptible to being manipulated.

However, children frequently have difficulty talking about how they feel. When asked if they're happy or sad, they're apt to give monosyllabic replies. If they're sympathetic to an absent parent, they may be afraid to say so. Yet, until this sympathy is acknowledged by children, they are easily exploited.

To overcome children's reluctance to talk about their feelings, psychotherapists often ask their child patients to draw pictures, to write poems, or even to make up games in which they identify the roles played by the people in their lives. Sometimes the use of "family dolls" to depict the relationships with other family members is helpful. With the aid of such dolls, a child can act out, and therefore demonstrate, feelings that would be almost impossible to relate in any other way. If a lover has been brought into the family circle, the manner in which that doll is allowed to interact with the others can be very significant. All these devices are very effective in getting to the root of problems, especially with children who are too young to analyze what is happening around them. It is frequently beneficial for all family members to participate in such activities. Avenues of communication open as they draw and talk about pictures together.

Any of these approaches may be used by thoughtful parents without the assistance of a psychotherapist, although professional knowledge and experience usually get results faster and with more certainty. And for the parent who wants to allay a child's fears in certain areas, there are books on divorce or the death of a parent that can be read aloud and then discussed. They're written specifically to help children, and the language is on a level that's easily understood by younger family members.

When discussing serious matters with your children, it's always important to keep language and examples simple so they can better understand these complex ideas. With the proper approach, children may be able to see that perhaps neither parent really wanted the turmoil of a divorce but that it was necessary for the good of all. They might even understand how people who love each other may not always be able to stay together.

If your ex-spouse is directing sabotage that is disrupting your life, begin by considering your children's ages. If necessary, deal with each child separately. It's important that they be comfortable with you so they dare to be honest about their feelings. If you've had poor communication with your children in the past, you may need professional assistance. But if you already have some rapport established, you may be able to eliminate a disruptive situation by yourself or with minimal help.

Following her divorce from Sam, Rachel had a lot of problems with her son, John. After returning from an extended visit with his father, John somehow managed to upset every dating plan she had. After several discussions with him in which she attempted to discover the reason for his behavior, she managed to calm him down a bit and reduce the amount of sabotage. But the peaceful times didn't last. Whenever he visited his father, the boy immediately resumed his disruptive behavior. She became convinced that her ex-husband was responsible for John's attempts to destroy her social life.

The divorce had been very messy, with Sam contesting it every step of the way. He was an alcoholic who staunchly refused to accept treatment—the main reason Rachel had sought the separation. He had promised many times to change but had never succeeded. Now she began to realize that he still hoped for a reconciliation. In the meantime, he was using John to keep her from making any other commitment.

Fortunately, Rachel had available an additional line of communication to her son. Both she and John loved to draw. When he was younger, she had used art as a way to help him express his feelings. When we began working together, I suggested she use this method of reaching an understanding with John.

She started by reminiscing with him about the divorce. She drew a few sketches showing what had happened, then asked him to do the same. After they'd drawn a series of pictures, his wish that his parents would reunite surfaced. Now Rachel suggested they both try to imagine how Sam felt. But further drawing wasn't necessary. By this time, John was able to tell her how much his father wanted her to come back to him.

Children are very vulnerable to being hurt. Many need active support before they dare express ideas that might conflict with those of their parents. They're afraid of disapproval. Even if they've given up the idea that their mother and father might be reunited, they may still feel insecure if their custodial parent shows an interest in another adult. Because they resist any alteration in their lives, they quickly accept whatever situation they are in as being "normal." Any suggestion of *new* change, especially after they have just gone through a difficult change, is upsetting.

If you, like Rachel, are fortunate enough to have an effective channel of communication open between you and your children, you'll be able to help them understand the reality of your divorce and your need for adult companionship. If you can't talk with your children, then get help. Until they're allowed to verbalize their concerns, no solution to the problem of sabotage can be reached.

One further point. You don't have to change your behavior just because you get your children to express themselves. However, you may be able to help your children understand you better once you know what's upsetting them. They'll need reassurance and support, too. Children can adjust to a new life-style if they feel loved and secure.

It wasn't easy for Rachel to explain her reasons for divorcing Sam and for not trusting him to change. However, she spoke simply, using language that was understandable to John. But she also paid attention to what John said. Because she let him share his feelings with her, she managed to help him see that she couldn't go back, even though she, too, wished the divorce hadn't been necessary. The result of her listening was greater understanding for both of them—and eventually an end to John's sabotage.

Learn to Listen

Adults far too often find themselves talking *to*, not *with*, a child. Talking with means listening as well. When you're trying to understand and change a child's pattern of sabotaging your social life, you need to hear and pay attention to what's being said. It's easy to assume that children's sabotaging behavior is rooted in their desire to repair your broken marriage—and it often is. But in many cases, this may not be the reason at all.

When children are disruptive, don't make assumptions about the reasons without first talking over the situation with them. You may find that the motive for the unpleasant behavior is superficial, not deep-seated. Laurie found to her relief that such was the situation involving her daughter's resentment of her lover, Mel.

Phyllis was rude to Mel every time Laurie brought him home. Laurie was certain her teenager just wanted to reverse the recent divorce that had left her without her father. For a long time Laurie tried to ignore the behavior. Instead of Mel calling on her at home, she met him at the office after work and phoned Phyllis to tell her to stay overnight at their neighbor's house. But Phyllis became very difficult and eventually blurted out that she knew her mother was "running around."

When she finally sat down to talk with her daughter, Laurie expected a real argument. Fortunately, she listened before she started accusing. She began by asking Phyllis why she didn't like Mel.

Phyllis burst into a long explanation. Mel was patronizing. He actually patted her on the head once, as if she were a baby. Surprised, Laurie promised to see if she could straighten him out. She made it clear that she wouldn't like to be treated that way, so she understood how Phyllis felt.

When Laurie talked this over with Mel, he admitted that he didn't know how to deal with a teenage girl. But he was willing to work on it.

In time, Phyllis and Mel became good friends. The objections Phyllis had to her mother's dating Mel vanished. This would never have happened if Laurie hadn't been willing to listen before she condemned.

Listening becomes even more important if you start a new relationship after some years as your children's only parent.

They have become comfortable with their present life, so they feel threatened by the thought of another change. Many misunderstandings that develop between children and stepparents (or partners who move in with custodial parents) can be avoided if the parent shows a willingness to listen to any complaints without making judgments. Often, the problems are much smaller than they seem to be.

Again, an important point to keep in mind is that children who feel secure are able to accept changes in their parents' lives. They know they're loved and won't be abandoned. If you begin to develop a close attachment to a new date, take the time to let your children know what's happening. Let them tell you how they feel about it. In the long run, you'll save hours of worry and upset. Another thing—don't give up a relationship just because your children object to it. Instead, lovingly let them know you have your own needs and that this partner is important to you. Be sure, at the same time, to repeat that you love them, too, and want their happiness as well.

Anticipate Reactions

A single parent frequently has problems because of a failure to look ahead and recognize that children are both fascinated and repelled by any evidence of a parent's sexuality. Yet this curiosity should be expected. Children often feel an unacknowledged sexual attraction to one of their parents, which arouses envy and jealousy if that parent exhibits sexual behavior with someone else. Sometimes, as in the following account, the very person causing the jealousy and rivalry can, if perceptive and understanding, help work out the problem with comparative ease.

After he'd been divorced for six years, Edgar met Madeline. Before that, he'd always taken his dates to a motel. Now he wanted his seven-year-old daughter, Janet, to meet Madeline and love her as he did.

He brought Madeline home one afternoon, expecting that she could stay the night. But Janet reacted badly from the start. She threw a tantrum, barely spoke to Madeline, and when she was alone with her father for a short time she asked him if she'd been a bad girl. He didn't pick up on the cue. All he did was assure her that she'd been good and that was why he wanted her to meet his new friend.

Janet wasn't prepared for such a major change in her father's life. She had come to think of him as *her* partner. Later, when she saw Edgar kiss Madeline, she burst into tears and ran to her room. Even then Edgar didn't recognize the extent of the problem. He was too involved with Madeline.

In the following weeks Janet's behavior worsened. She did everything she could to sabotage her father's new relationship. Fortunately, Madeline was perceptive enough to see the real reasons for Janet's unhappiness and unruly behavior. She talked the matter over with Edgar, and suggested that he try to see this new situation from the child's point of view. It was the first time Edgar had recognized his daughter's childish crush on him. He realized that her behavior, quite normal for a child her age, could not be treated lightly. At Madeline's suggestion, he sat down with Janet and faced the subject squarely.

"I wonder if you know just how dear you are to me," he began.

Janet smiled smugly. Clearly, she expected him to tell her he was giving up on his interest in Madeline.

"You're the most wonderful daughter any man could wish for. I hope that someday, when you grow up and get married, you'll have children who are as much of a pleasure as you are."

Janet frowned. This wasn't exactly what she expected.

"You've never really had a mother who lived with you and helped you."

Now Janet gave a reluctant nod of assent.

"Well," Edgar continued, "Madeline is a nice person. I really think that when you get to know her you'll want to be friends."

"I just want to be with you."

"I know, dear. You're afraid that if Madeline comes to live with us, you and I won't have any special time together. But we will. I love the time I spend with you and nothing is going to make me give it up. It's just that I love Madeline, too, and I want her with me."

Janet was quiet for a time. But she seemed a bit less perturbed.

"Is that why you're going to marry Madeline, because you're lonesome?"

"No, I want to marry Madeline because I love her. She's a wonderful person, and she means a lot to me. I would never marry just anyone. I love Madeline very much."

"More than me?"

"Differently. You're my daughter. You have a very special place in my heart. But there's room in it for a wife, too. I want Madeline to be my wife and that means she'll be living with us someday. I want both you and her to be happy when you're together. So it's important that you understand how I feel."

Janet seemed to relax a bit more. "You're not mad at me because I was naughty?"

"Of course not. I know you were worried and scared. I was wrong not to talk to you before. Do you feel better now?"

Janet nodded.

"Good. Just remember, if you get scared again, tell me right away. I don't want you to be unhappy, and when we have special times like this, we both feel better, don't we?"

That ended the discussion, but there were many more. Whenever Janet was upset, she needed reassurance. In time, with a great deal of attention and care devoted to soothing Janet's feelings, she quieted down. She even came to love Madeline and to anticipate having her as a mother.

Much of Edgar's problem could have been avoided had he prepared Janet for the change well before he brought Madeline home for the first time. He should have been aware of Janet's attachment to him and her assumption that she was all the companionship he needed. Children usually give positive clues showing how attached they are to a parent. They *can* be recognized if the parent is alert. Edgar wasn't.

Read Your Children's Cues

You can be aware enough of your children's behavior patterns to anticipate—and avoid—trouble. Pay attention to how they act toward you. Are they proprietary? Does your teenager sometimes act like the other head of the house? Does your little one embrace you at every opportunity? These are some of the cues children give that indicate trouble may arise if you bring an adult companion into your life.

If you do bring a new partner into this environment, you may find your children acting in inexplicable ways, some of which may be very upsetting to your routine. Your small child may revert to a two-year-old's mannerisms and cling to you when dropped off at the day-care center. Your six-year-old may begin wetting his bed again. At any time, your children may exhibit annoying, irritating behavior designed to make you wish they were living with your ex-spouse. Yet, no matter how odd it seems, the root of all these actions is insecurity. They're pleading for reassurance.

It seems illogical; why would your insecure children do the very things that push you away? Wouldn't it be far more sensible to be extra pleasant, so you'd be reminded of how much you love them?

Yes, it would. And sometimes a child who fears losing a parent to another adult is just that. But an overly compliant manner is just as loud a cry for reassurance as the more objectionable kind. What's more, both patterns are very common, appearing in adults as often as in children. The point to remember is that either extreme of behavior—very good or very bad—is likely to be an indication that a child is insecure.

It's possible that you, yourself, have experienced an inability to control your emotional outbursts when you've felt unsure and vulnerable. If you have, you can better understand the plight of your child. Children haven't learned emotional control. When two youngsters play together, they often get into tiffs that end with one or both storming home announcing, "I'll never play with him again! Never!" Yet, half an hour later the two fighters may be back together. Their own mutual need and love for each other have repaired the rift.

The problem in parent-child relationships is that children don't know if their need for their parents is reciprocated. If there has been a divorce, or even if one parent has died, children realize the remaining parent is quite capable of going on alone. So if they then see their parent showing interest in a new person, they feel insecure. However, more often than not, when children feel unsure of their position in a new adult relationship, the cues they give are subtle and require a large amount of sensitivity from an adult. Sometimes, only a trained professional can determine the real causes for children's perplexing behavior.

When you anticipate any major change in your life, give your children increased attention and love. That will cushion the bumps and help quell the insecurity. Keep in mind your children's dependency. Give them reassurance that you'll continue to love them even though you might find a new adult companion. If you do this, you'll save yourself from hours of worry, and your children from unhappiness and despair.

Each Child Is Different

If you have more than one child, don't expect each to have similar reactions to the same situation. Every child is an individual, with a unique personality. Not only will each of your children respond differently, but none of them may respond exactly as described in the chapter on developmental stages in child growth.

You need to be prepared for a variety of reactions to any step you take to improve your social life. Keep an open mind. If your children are giving you problems relating to your dating, listen to their fears before you decide they just don't like your new partner.

Here'a a typical example of ways in which siblings may react to the same situation—and ways in which they may suddenly, and unexpectedly, alter their previous attitudes.

Jane, her twelve-year-old son, Frank, and her eight-year-old daughter, Kristie, had been without Tom, Jane's ex-husband, for a year when Jane met Richard. Frank, who had enjoyed giving his mother emotional support during the period immediately following her divorce, resented the newcomer. He viewed Richard as a threat to his position as man of the house. Kristie, on the contrary, seemed delighted at the presence of this new man.

In the weeks that followed Richard's moving in, Jane realized that Kristie's attitude was changing. The eight-year-old was now competing with him for her mother's attention. The child seemed uneasy any time Richard even sat close to Jane. At night, she had trouble going to sleep unless her mother sat beside her bed.

Frank, to her surprise, developed a definite liking for Richard, even though he had at first seemed antagonistic. Richard worked in the computer field, and Frank wanted to learn all he could about computers. The knowledge he got gave him status among his peers. It made the two of them solid friends. In fact, there were times when Jane felt that Frank barely cared if she was around.

The problems Jane anticipated when she brought Richard in to live with her were not the problems that actually developed. This often happens. One child may compete with the lover for a parent's attention. Another may fight to remain in the center of activities. Yet another, who first protested the loudest, may adjust quickly. And these patterns may change at any time. Much depends on how secure and loved the children feel and how well they get along with the new adult. When the initial period of settling in was over and Jane began to give more normal attention to Kristie, the child settled down and returned to her usual, happy self.

Reward Positive Behavior

Studies have shown that people tend to react quickly to things that displease them while failing to recognize or honor things that give them pleasure. We are all guilty of that. Our children may be good for days and receive no recognition. But let them do one thing wrong and we pounce on them immediately.

Further studies show that the learning process is improved if success is rewarded. Children whose only recognition is punishment when they do things wrong don't learn correct procedure as quickly as those who are complimented when they do things right.

In dealing with children and your need for more adult social life, you'll do well to consider these tendencies in human learning. Notice when your children do nice things and behave well. Let them know you appreciate them. You may find that the periods of less acceptable conduct diminish.

Clara came to me complaining that Jason, her four-year-old son, hit, bit, and pinched her, especially if she had adult company. When they were together in my office, he played for a time as she talked, but then he came and stood in front of her. This, in itself, is quite normal. He, like any child, wanted her attention and reassurance. But she ignored him. He tugged on her skirt. She paid no attention, behaving as though he were not in the room.

Uneasy, he stepped closer and pinched her arm. She looked startled. "Don't do that," she said, automatically putting her arm around the boy. But she continued with her monologue about her troubles. She seemed totally unaware of her child's need for some sign that she knew he was there—and that she loved him.

Clearly disturbed now, he resorted to more drastic measures. He bit her arm. "Don't do that," she repeated and lifted him up on her lap. Even then, however, she didn't give him any real attention.

When I reviewed for her what had happened, she was surprised. She hadn't realized how completely she'd failed to notice his age-appropriate attempt to get her attention. She had, instead, been rewarding his inappropriate pinching and biting by touching him and picking him up. She admitted she also did this whenever an adult friend visited her.

Clara's problem lay in her lack of understanding of children's behavior patterns. She hadn't recognized her son's abandonment of his play as a sign that he needed acknowledgment from her. She ignored his behavior, which was typical for his age, and responded only when he became troublesome.

It may take extra thought and attention at first to respond to a child's age-appropriate positive behavior, but you'll be rewarded if you do. Children want to please their parents, even though it often appears they don't. If you let them know what you want, and reward them with attention when they obey, both you and they will be happier.

Next time you plan a social evening, think specifically about your expectations. How do you want your children to behave when your date arrives? At dinner? When you and your date take them to a movie? Be clear in your own mind exactly what you'd like to have happen.

Now visualize the event. "Walk it through" in your mind. Consider any behavior on the part of your children that you'd appreciate. Then, when it takes place, show your approval. It won't take much. A smile, a touch, a hug, or just one complimentary word may be all that's needed.

Any positive action on your part says a lot to your children. It tells them that you're aware of them, even with your guest nearby. It reassures them that they're important in your life. And it reinforces their good behavior.

Reach an Understanding with Your Children

You've determined how you want your children to behave on various occasions, and you've remembered to reward good conduct. But you're still having problems. Are they just determined to cause trouble?

Probably not. Teachers learn that they often have to repeat instructions many times and in different ways before everyone in the class understands them. If you tell your children what you want them to do, hoping that one mention will be enough, you may be expecting too much. Maybe they don't understand you.

For example, words that make sense to you may carry your message to your sixth-grader but may have little meaning for your five-year-old.

Use an old teaching technique. Ask your children to repeat what you've just said. If it comes out substantially the same, you can expect them to behave as you want them to. But if you can't get a sensible response, tell them again. Use different words. Take another point of view. Teachers sometimes have to try ten or twenty different approaches before they get through to everyone.

Take this opportunity to discover your children's feelings regarding your new friend. Let them air these feelings. If they have to suppress their reactions, they'll have trouble being nice, no matter how much they want to please you. But if they can voice their anger and be met with understanding, they're far more apt to respond positively to your request for cooperation.

Give Them Rules and Limits

Children need to know what you expect of them. They must also learn that much of what happens to them is affected by their own actions. You can teach them this invaluable lesson not only by rewarding good behavior but by punishing their bad behavior in an appropriate manner.

Even if you do this consistently, you may still find that your children don't always live up to your rules. They may choose to take the consequences rather than obey—which is exactly what adults do much of the time. But the choice is theirs. Discovering the correct balance between compliance and independence for themselves helps them build their own inner set of rules, creating a standard by which they will live. And while this learning is taking place, your children have a feeling of security. Their world is ordered. *Cause* brings about *effect*.

Some parents have trouble setting limits. If you have this problem, examine the possible reasons closely. Are you still reacting to unreasonable rules your own parents set for you? If you are, try not to overcompensate. Maybe you avoid setting limits because your spouse has died, and you don't want to add too many restrictions that might upset your children. But children need *some* rules. Too much freedom is as bad as too little. Sometimes, it's even worse. Gloria certainly found this to be true. Before she sought professional help, her well-intentioned handling of her daughter almost ruined both their lives.

Gloria didn't believe in disciplining children. Helen was only five when her father died, so Gloria let the child have her own way most of the time. There were a few guidelines laid down, but infractions were usually overlooked. Only when the girl's unruly behavior became impossible to ignore did her mother scold or punish her.

Helen demanded her mother's attention exclusively when they were together, even if others were present. She felt very insecure, since she never knew why she was occasionally punished for what she was ordinarily allowed to do. As a result, she did not develop a clear understanding of the relationship between actions and consequences.

Gloria related *setting limits* to *punishment*. She thought that she was being kind to the child—far kinder than her father had been to her. After all, she punished Helen only occasionally, whereas her father had been very strict all the time. But her erratic reactions to Helen's behavior just confused the child.

What was worse, a different set of rules seemed to apply when Gloria's lover visited. On these occasions, any punishment was more frequent and more severe. The child now had two reasons to be insecure: her mother's inconsistent punishment pattern and the fact that someone outside the family seemed to be more important. Helen responded by misbehaving more and more, testing the limits, testing her mother's love for her, trying to determine just what the rules were that she could live by—and probably searching for some uniform enforcement pattern that she could understand.

Children *need* limits. Limits provide structure and a sense of safety, just as walls do in a room. If children can see the relationship between a violation of rules and the effect it has on their lives, the rules become meaningful. But if there are no guidelines, and children are scolded only when a parent gets fed up, they are then confused and bewildered. Such a form of reprimand is truly a punishment.

Teach, Don't Punish

Probably the most important lesson children need to learn as they grow is that *their own actions affect what happens to them.* For this reason, parents need to think through the ultimate results of their children's misbehavior. A wise parent recognizes that all adults are surrounded by rules and limits: They must work effectively if they expect to keep their jobs; they must behave decently to their friends or they'll lose them; they must obey the laws, or they'll be in trouble.

Children don't learn this lesson by osmosis. They need to be taught. And as their understanding increases, their behavior becomes more acceptable. This is what makes erratic discipline like Gloria's so disastrous. It teaches children that the world around them is unpredictable.

When you encounter undesirable behavior in your children, don't just lash out in anger. Try to help them see what the consequences of their actions are. Then every problem will turn into a learning situation. Lonnie handled the misbehavior of her two children in a way that not only corrected it but taught them a valuable lesson regarding responsibility for their own actions.

Lonnie told four-year-old Dan and seven-year-old Kari that Paul would be picking her up at 7:30 to take her to the theater. She told them she expected them to be nice and to go to bed without a fuss. She had engaged their usual baby-sitter, so she felt they had no reason to be upset. But when Paul arrived, Kari hung onto her mother's dress and begged her to stay home. Little Dan took his cue from his sister and began to cry.

Lonnie firmly disengaged Kari's grip from her dress and led her over to the baby-sitter. She picked up Dan and put him on the girl's lap. Then she crouched before them. "We'll talk about this tomorrow, Kari. This isn't the way you said you'd act, remember?" Then she quietly left.

The next morning, after she'd fed them, she sat down with one child under each arm. This was a time for reassuring them of her love. Only after she'd kissed them both did she bring up the tantrum of the night before. Her children were too young to respond to a long discussion, but Kari was capable of understanding that her actions had not changed the evening. Together with her daughter, Lonnie explored what might be an appropriate reaction to such a tantrum.

Because she felt safe, Kari's first response was to suggest that her mother not go on the date. But Lonnie made it clear that such a suggestion wasn't acceptable. Next, Kari proposed that she be spanked. Lonnie explained that she didn't like to spank if some other more suitable form of discipline could be found.

They finally decided that if Kari acted that way again, and as a result got Dan all upset, she'd have to give up one of her toys for a week. And if Dan was the one who started the ruckus, he'd be the one to give up the toy. Kari could see the cause and effect of that rule, even though she didn't like the idea of giving up a toy she valued. But she did get the connection. She had taken a large step in learning to recognize that her actions could affect her own happiness.

Be Consistent

Of all the principles you may apply to the training of your children, being consistent is the most difficult. Yet this rule is not as impossible as it may first appear to be. A very wise woman once remarked that one should never applaud a one-year-old for an act that will be punished when the child is three. That's a good beginning. We humans can base our concept of correct behavior only on our past experiences.

But children have very limited experiences on which to draw. They need guidance so that what they learn one year applies to what is expected of them in the years that follow. Nevertheless, that doesn't mean you're supposed to be superhuman. Children can understand that when you're upset you may not act the way you do when you're calm. So, if you generally behave reasonably and consistently, an occasional variation from this routine won't disrupt things very much.

You'll be helped as much as will your children if you've established a pattern for reacting to their misbehavior. If they're unruly when you bring a date over, and you all know what the consequences will be, you don't have to explode. Your prearranged discipline should cause the upsets to diminish. But if such scenes are repeated often, you'll need to have further talks with your children. If the consequences you've agreed upon are reasonable, you need to get at the cause for the failure.

Perhaps, at such a time, a show of anger would be appropriate. That might be all your children need to prove to them that you really *are* concerned with what happens between you. Children understand emotion. They have a hard time relating to cold, detached, unemotional behavior.

If, under unusual pressure, you get very upset and forget all about consistency, don't be too surprised. None of us is perfect. We can only try our best. And even an explosion, if you later explain it to your children, can result in a teaching situation that may turn your human inconsistency into a valuable lesson.

Give Each Child a Special Time

It's often difficult to make close, intimate contact with your children when you're busy and occupied with your own life. But the frequent use of special close times is essential to establishing a healthy relationship with them—one that can weather the changes that might occur if you meet a new person who becomes important to you. Try to find activities that you and your children enjoy together, and then put aside regular time for them.

Janice and her son, Greg, bowled together every Tuesday afternoon when she got home from work. For supper they had hotdogs at the bowling alley, staying there until just before Greg's bedtime. Janice had only one child. That made it easy for her to set up a regular time just for him.

David, on the other hand, had three children, a boy and two girls. He couldn't devote a full evening to each one, especially since he often had to work late. Therefore, he made Sunday their family time together. They began it by going to church together in the morning and from there striking out on a special outing. They'd visit the zoo, swim at the beach, or go biking. During the course of the day, he'd make sure he spent some time with each child, talking about the small triumphs and disappointments of the past week. At day's end there was always a family conference. David found himself looking forward to these outings as much as his children did.

As the years passed, the children began to develop individual interests that made the outings less regular. But, whenever possible, all four of them went someplace together. After David met a woman and they decided to marry, he explained to his children that he wanted her to come along on their outings, too, and asked how they felt about it. That was the right way to introduce her. The special time he'd set aside for them proved to be special for him and his new partner, too.

Special time can serve to bind parent and child together. Even after they were grown, David's children remembered their outings and, though their marriages were not upset by divorce, used the same idea to give themselves an opportunity to enjoy their own children.

Set Aside a Family Talk Time

David combined his special time with each of his children with what might best be described as family talk time. But for you, a separation of the two periods might be more feasible. If you work, you and your children are apart a good portion of every day. There should be some regular time set aside when you can all talk together about what has happened to each of you. This is a time when disagreements between your children can be ironed out and when you can plan for vacations or discuss weekend activities.

You might consider these discussion periods, as well as the special times with each individual child, as preventive maintenance. You can deal then with problems that *might* develop and discuss ways of avoiding them. During one of these sessions, you may want to introduce your family to another adult with whom you've formed a close relationship. Especially if you think you're on the verge of establishing a permanent bond, you may find that this is the easiest way to let your children get to know your new partner.

However, if you follow this procedure, be sure not to include your friend in the family time on a regular basis until you get your children's consent. They'll need time to talk with you about this new person in their lives. If you've established a regular period for such discussions, and if your children know they can say what they feel, you'll get a lot accomplished in the sessions that follow that first gathering of what you hope will be your new family.

What If You Did It Wrong?

Have you been kicking yourself as you read this book, aware that you got started on the wrong foot with your kids after your divorce? If you have, don't despair. You're not alone. Most adults aren't perfectly skilled parents. We all tend to act first and think later. All you have to do is watch television or read the papers to realize that many parents seem to be at the mercy of their undisciplined children.

But you shouldn't accept such a situation without trying to repair it. There *are* things you can do to reestablish your authority. First, you need to realize that if you've lost control of your children because of their persistent sabotaging of your social life you've probably lost control in other facets of your parent-child relationship as well.

You should also know that, if your children are defying you, they're living in a constant state of anxiety. Children realize that they aren't equal to the task of caring for themselves. They realize that they're dependent upon you for food, clothing, and shelter—for all the aspects of material security. They know they have years of schooling ahead of them before they can be in charge of their own lives. They recognize the fact that they aren't yet ready to earn a living.

But it's a heady thing for children to get an adult to give up control to them, even briefly. Ultimately, however, you, as parent, do have the power to correct any undesirable behavior your children may engage in. They need you. If they're behaving erratically, it's probably because you haven't given them enough guidelines—or haven't enforced the ones already laid down. If you've let them take over, they're experiencing mixed emotions. They may have a temporary feeling of triumph, but they're also aware of their own vulnerability.

Right now it may be hard for you to accept the fact that your children need—and want—you to assert your authority. Only when you do will a sense of security be restored. But the longer you wait to reestablish your control, the more difficult the task will be.

Many single parents (and parents of unbroken families as well) find the prospect of tackling the job alone too unpleasant. They seek professional help. But if you want to try on your own, first ask yourself two important questions:

1. Do I have any control left?

2. Am I willing to put up with quarrels and protests and remain firm until things get straightened out?

If the answer to the first question is yes, then you have a chance. There is, at least, something you can build on. If you answered yes to the second, you're ready to start.

Your first step must be to clarify in your own mind just how you want your children to behave. Be definite. A wishy-washy concept will destroy your program. Anticipate how they may react if you take a lover and prepare for any objections.

Now have a conference with your children. Lay down the cards. Make it clear that you know the dilemma they're in. Explain that you intend to make things right again.

Angela had lost practically all control over her twelve-year-old daughter, Lisa. The girl defied her mother's wishes on almost every issue that arose. She invariably stayed out past established curfew hours, spent much time with friends her mother didn't approve of, and insisted on dressing in strange, unorthodox attire. Her mother was especially irritated by Lisa's rude, boisterous behavior when Angela's lover stayed over. The only thing Angela could be sure Lisa would do properly was go to school. But that was enough to use as a basis for the reestablishment of parental authority.

After Angela decided where she wanted changes in attitude and behavior, she sat down with her daughter. She spoke calmly. "Lisa, I know you don't want to do anything I ask you to do."

Lisa didn't respond, so Angela continued. "I have to admit something. I love you very much. I want you to grow up to be a happy person. I want you to be happy now. But I can't have things continue the way they are. I won't fight with you anymore. It's over. I know I've let you take control of what goes on in our family, and I know it isn't right. So things are going to change."

She then produced a list of activities and attitudes that couldn't continue. Beside it was another list—the good things that would result from better cooperation. At first, Lisa responded with a tantrum. Angela simply waited. She didn't react as she had in the past, with a flurry of concern. When her daughter paused for a breath, she spoke again. "When you calm down, we can talk some more." Then she continued to wait quietly.

When Lisa realized that things really *had* changed (in the past, when she threw a tantrum, her mother was very upset and did anything to calm her down), she quieted down and the talk was resumed. Now Angela made it clear that she wasn't angry. This wasn't a vendetta for revenge. It was a correction made for the benefit of them both.

During the changeover period, Angela enlisted her lover as an ally. She met him away from her home because she didn't want to reactivate some of the problems she was only beginning to solve. Since he had teenagers of his own, and had a good relationship with them, she went to him for advice when she was frustrated or unsure of what to do next.

More important than the advice, however, was the moral support she got from him during a time when she was fighting her own instinctive wish to avoid confrontations with her daughter. He kept her on target many times when she felt weak. And, in the end, she managed to get her relationship with her daughter back on the right path. What surprised her most was that when the change was completed her daughter seemed happier than she'd been since before her father died.

Of course, the transition from chaos to order may not be this simple or take this particular form. A child who's been allowed too much freedom of choice may scream defiance, stalk from the room to sulk behind a locked door in some other part of the house, and even refuse to eat for a time. But a parent does have ultimate control if a persistent firmness is maintained. An attempt to talk through family problems should continue at every opportunity until a child realizes a tantrum won't accomplish anything and that a meeting of minds is the only possible solution. It may sometimes take days or weeks before reaching that goal. But if a parent remains resolute, a point will be reached where compromises can be made if necessary and a reestablished set of guidelines can be agreed upon.

When to Seek Professional Help

Angela was fortunate. Things had gotten out of hand, but not so far that she couldn't reestablish her authority. Before you try to remedy a chaotic relationship on your own, look for any of the following symptoms in your child. Experience has shown that children with these conditions need more guidance than can be given by an amateur—no matter how loving and caring.

Seek professional help if your child has repetitive sleeping disorders, asthma, allergy attacks, vomiting, frequent headaches, tics, or eating disturbances such as a loss of appetite. Bedwetting after the normal age for self-control is another problem that may need special attention.

If your child resumes thumb-sucking after years of not doing it, that act may be a cry for help. Clinging behavior, withdrawal, and daydreaming (or any other appearance of detachment from the real world) may also be signs of a serious problem. So too are overly aggressive behavior, frequent crying spells, poor school performance, and poor relationships with peers.

If your children have passed through some of these stages and have gone on to self-destructive behavior such as drug or alcohol abuse, the problem is more severe and indicates the urgent need for expert help. If they appear to be acutely accident prone or sexually irresponsible, you also won't be able to cope with the difficulty alone. Neither will you be able to handle depression in your adolescent or preadolescent children without some professional assistance.

If you encounter any of the above problems, don't delay in getting assistance. Failure to act promptly will only result in unnecessary pain for both you and your children. Also, if a damaging behavior pattern becomes too well established, the family begins to revolve around that condition. Then it becomes far more difficult to intervene professionally and achieve success.

These problems transcend the sabotaging of your relationship with any one partner. They're caused by a variety of circumstances that are often beyond your control. Before you blame yourself or give up entirely, find help. It *is* available—and it can make the difference between happiness and despair.

Where Can You Find the Help You Need?

I recommend that you seek help from a licensed psychotherapist who has skills in working with families as well as with individuals. If you have more than one child, and one of them is deeply troubled, the others will be affected, too. The problem then becomes a family issue. Many families get trapped in a rut, much as a needle can get stuck in one track of a record. An experienced therapist can help the family reestablish good relationships by opening up channels of communication.

When seeking a psychotherapist, I suggest that you speak to your friends or your family doctor. Some of them may know a professional to recommend—one you'll feel comfortable with. If you're unable to get help in this way, contact your pastor or rabbi. Religious leaders are often trained as counselors and may know of some good therapists in your area.

Most states have provisions for the licensing of psychiatrists, psychologists, clinical social workers, and marriage, family, and child counselors. The individuals in each of these professions generally belong to associations that are registered within the state. If people you know can't recommend a psychotherapist you can trust who deals with family issues, call the appropriate association and ask for a list of people in your neighborhood. There *is* help available. Don't give up until you find exactly the kind you need.

In the Resources section you'll find a list of books that can help you deal with your family problems. The important thing is not to give up hope. You *can* effect a change. And when you do, you and your child will be happier for your persistence.

6 *Are the Birds and the Bees Enough?*

Sex-Education Issues

Gladys, seven, and her younger sister, May, five, were on the back porch playing with their dolls. Their mother, Marie, preparing dinner in the kitchen, was barely aware of their conversation until Gladys's voice rose slightly.

"Daddy and Mommy didn't do that. Mommy says Daddy's gone to be with God. God doesn't like people who do things like that."

"You're sure, Glad?" Suddenly, May's voice sounded shaky.

"'Course I'm sure. Mommy wouldn't ever do things like we saw in those pictures."

Marie smiled. How charmingly innocent Gladys was! But her amusement didn't last. Her thoughts raced on. What pictures? Where?

She knew it had to be at her brother Joe's. She had warned him that she didn't want his pornographic material left out when the girls visited. Why hadn't she checked first thing when she and the girls arrived for their regular Sunday visit?

In the year since her husband died, Marie had lived in dread of just this happening. She depended on her brother for so much these days. If only he and his wife were a little more conventional. They didn't seem to care what their children read, or what pictures they saw.

She strained to hear something more from the porch, but her daughters' voices had dropped below audible level. Then, suddenly, May let out a howl.

"I'm not a baby!" She subsided into sobs.

"Yes you are. Babies cry at nothing."

Marie stepped out in time to prevent any further fighting, wondering uneasily if they battled more often since Allen was gone. Or was she just more sensitive?

After Gladys and May raced off to play jump rope with some friends, Marie stood studying their doll house, her mind in a turmoil. It hadn't been easy for her since Allen died two years ago, but she had managed. She felt very lucky to be able to stay home with her daughters, even if she was busy some of the day at her sewing machine.

But had she been aware enough of her children? Had she neglected their sex education—of all things? What did kids of seven and five know about sex? What did they need to know?

Marie is typical of many single mothers, especially widows, who have devoted much of their time to caring for their children. It's not uncommon for a woman who has lost her husband to shy away from seeking regular employment if she's financially able not to work permanently. There's a feeling that as long as she's able to remain a housewife she can pretend that her life has not changed appreciably. This is, admittedly, a way of hiding from reality, though it isn't necessarily a disastrous one.

However, Marie has allowed herself to accept other pretenses as well. She believes her children are not interested in sex, and that they don't need to be taught about it. In this she is not unique. Many parents are afraid to talk about sex, hoping their children will not think of it by themselves.

This head-in-a-barrel approach to sex education is especially prevalent in the United States, though it does exist to a lesser degree all over the world. Many parents believe that their children will remain sexually innocent until "polluted" by information they get from someone older.

But this concept of the innocence of children is tragically wrong.

Dr. Mary Calderone, a pioneer in sex education, makes the point that sex education begins at birth in terms of the influence of a parent's attitude and behavior. She states: "It's not a question of educating or not educating. You're educating whatever you do. And you owe it to your child not to do it blindly and unconsciously, but with knowledge and a positive attitude."

Another educator, Dr. Lee Salk, described the problem in this way: "Not telling your child about sex is like not teaching him about traffic rules."

Any parent who wonders at such a simile needs only to consider this: No parent sends a child off to school who doesn't know how to cross streets safely. A child who gets a bike is taught bike traffic safety rules. And a teenager who is ready to drive a car legally is given driving lessons, either in school or privately.

If children never experimented sexually, the comparison used by Dr. Salk would be meaningless. But we know that today one in five teenagers has sex before the age of fifteen, and a little more than half of them will be sexually active by the time they finish high school. We also are informed statistically that, at the present time, the annual teenage pregnancy rate is 1.1 million nationwide.

So the attempt many parents make to keep their children sexually innocent is doomed to failure. Children *will* learn about sex—and they'll develop attitudes toward sex along with that knowledge. If you want to be influential in teaching your children sexual morality, you'd better also be involved in giving them sexual information including knowledge of contraceptive measures.

Dr. Jay Gale, author of *A Young Man's Guide to Sex*, stated, during a verbal interview, that "sex education starts with a pink blanket and a blue blanket." He believes that there is no such thing as not communicating regarding sex. If children don't get acknowledgment of their need for sex education, they'll get their education in the streets, and "it won't be good." He emphasizes that "if you don't fill in the blanks, someone else will."

The fact is that most children learn about sex from their peers or siblings. Often what they learn isn't only pure fantasy—it's dangerous, as well. For example, an occasional teenaged girl may become pregnant because she honestly didn't know that intercourse caused pregnancy. Boys who try to avoid impregnating their partners fail, even though they use a condom. They don't realize that condoms are not 100 percent effective as birth-control devices.

Sex education is important not only for those children who are sexually active, but also for those who aren't, who sometimes live in fear because of their misunderstandings about sex. Alicia, the six-year-old daughter of Len, a single father, abruptly stopped a practice that had given them both much pleasure. From the time she was very small, Sunday mornings had been special for them. She'd climb onto his bed and sit beside him as he read the funnies aloud. Then they'd talk about everything that had happened during the week just ended. Now, Len couldn't get her to sit closer than on a chair near his bed.

After some questioning, Alicia finally admitted that she was disturbed by something her fifteen-year-old baby-sitter had said. He felt a rush of panic. He'd been careful to let Alicia gradually become acquainted with his lover, Joyce, but he had never told his daughter that Joyce sometimes stayed with him after the sitter left. Had the sitter, a teenager, made some comment that made Alicia uncomfortable?

Dreading the next response, Len persisted. "What did she tell you, Puddin'?"

Alicia's voice grew very quiet. "She said if a person was in bed with a man, she could get siflus."

Repressing a smile, Len responded, "Did she tell you what syphilis is?"

"No."

Fortunately, Len had talked with Alicia about sex before. He was able to give her an explanation that soothed her fears and allowed her to resume the tradition that meant so much to him. But if he'd been less understanding, or if he'd jumped to a conclusion without asking questions, his relationship with his daughter could have been impaired.

Let's return to Marie and her two young daughters. Gladys has decided that her mother and father couldn't have been sexual, since her mother doesn't approve of Uncle Joe's pictures, and has, in fact, made it clear that she thinks they're disgusting. Yet the child's conclusion is obviously false and may affect her sexual development later. At least at present, this belief only indirectly affects Marie, since she's still devoting all of her time to her children and hasn't begun to date.

But if Marie follows a normal mourning period, she'll soon feel the need to resume a normal life-style. At that point, her daughter's amusing idea may be far from funny. What will happen to Gladys when she realizes that her mother is doing with a stranger something that she has been allowed to believe never took place between her father and mother? What about Gladys's attitude toward sex? Is it good for a child to believe that her parent categorically disapproves of it?

Obviously not. Children need as much sexual knowledge as possible so that they'll be able to make the right decisions for themselves and so that they'll understand their own sexual needs and the sexual needs of those they love. Children need to learn to accept their own parents' sexuality before they can accept their own. Misinformation—or no information at all—can severely warp children's sexual development. If children are being raised by a single parent, they need sexual knowledge even more, since misinformation could cause a child to become extremely upset if that parent becomes sexually active.

I have noted that, for sundry reasons, a number of my clients who are single parents seem to fail to provide their children with the sex education they need. I feel it is most important for single parents to place emphasis on sound sex education for their children. What is taught at home can profoundly influence how the children develop, and also has an effect on how they relate to their custodial parent's social-sexual life.

That can be very important to you. You can't expect your children to understand your sexual needs unless you first make certain that they have enough knowledge of sex in general.

Most Learning Is Gradual

To return to the earlier analogy between sex and traffic: You would never expect your teenagers to drive cars successfully down a freeway until you first taught them how to handle a car. You would expect to teach them the rules of the road and the local laws governing driving. You'd also expect them to understand that cars are basically a form of transportation, used to get from one place to another—on streets. You wouldn't want them to take your new Camaro onto back-country jeep trails. They need to understand that with the right to drive comes responsibility—for safety of oneself as well as of others.

Yet, you actually teach these things over a period of years. Your children are passengers in your car. They hear your comments about other drivers. They watch you and observe how carefully you obey the traffic laws. If you zoom through yellow lights, they probably will, too, when it is their turn to drive. If you're considerate of others, they will be, too.

Sex also has rules and requires knowledge on the part of participants and some understanding of what function it has in our society. Your children need to know that sex is one way of expressing love between adults. They need to know what happens during sex so they'll understand how women become pregnant. They need to understand that the rules of sex, like the rules of the road, impose responsibilities along with the privileges. They need to appreciate your sexual needs.

It takes time to transmit all this knowledge. You can't expect your children to handle a sudden appearance of your date in your bed any more than you would expect them to be able to maintain the safety of themselves and your car if they were suddenly put at the wheel in the middle of a busy freeway.

Sex education, like all forms of education, takes place slowly. Some of the information must be given much as a history lesson or an arithmetic lesson is taught—with an adult explaining and the child asking questions. But other lessons are learned subliminally. Your attitude toward erotic art or a neighbor's liberal sex life tells them how you value sex. Your willingness to let your children see you kiss your date lets them know that you feel that such a kiss is good and acceptable. Everything you say about some sexual occurrence, and every reaction you have to it, teaches your children.

You Need to Be Comfortable with Sex, Yourself

The best advice on how to talk to your children about sex has little value if you're too embarrassed and uncomfortable with the subject to face it. If you act overly nervous and uneasy whenever sex is discussed, your uneasiness will have more effect on your children's attitude than will anything you say.

Bill, twelve, wanted to understand why his parents were divorcing. But when he asked his mother, Betty, she had difficulty answering. She felt guilty about the entire affair. She recognized that she'd married George, Bill's father, more out of fear of being unmarried than from love. And now she was in love with another man.

Bill picked up on his mother's guilt and gave up on his questions. But when his father later accused Betty of "whoring around," Bill had no way of defending her, even though he desperately needed to do so.

An outsider could recognize that Betty had little reason for feeling guilty. She had married young, during a period when all of her friends were marrying. And George was, at the time, an imposing figure—a star on the high school football team. She thought that what she felt for George was love. But in the subsequent years she matured and George didn't. She was no longer the young woman who'd fallen for a football star. Now she needed more from a man than George could give her.

If Betty had been more at ease with herself—if she'd come to recognize that she could neither stop her own mental growth nor demand that George grow with her—she might have dealt more calmly with Bill's questions. As it was, he was angry at her for years after the divorce. Only when he married was the rift repaired.

Clarify Your Own Sexual Values

It's important to remember that your attitude toward your sexual behavior can be colored by many other aspects of your life. One young mother, Karen, dealt well with her sex life and with her two daughters who were placed in her custody after her divorce. "I reminded myself that Gina and Jill would be adults for far longer than they'd be children," she explained. "Whenever I realized I was getting embarrassed about talking to them, I thought of how long it had taken me to feel good about my liking sex. That was all I needed to steady myself. I didn't want my kids having all the hang-ups I'd had to overcome."

Karen was fortunate in that she was able to separate her room from her children's, so she was able to bring a lover in without waking them. As long as she was interested only in one-night stands, she kept her sex life removed from her children. At the same time, she was relaxed when sex was discussed. She made sure her two daughters were comfortable with their own sexuality.

When Karen met Don, whom she thought she might marry, they decided to live together first. Then she had to tell her children. It was easy for her, since she'd always been able to talk with them. She was justifiably pleased at their response to Don's presence in the house.

The easy, casual manner in which Karen let Gina and Jill become aware of what was happening in their mother's life allowed the girls to accept her without automatically taking her behavior as a pattern for their own. They know their mother married very young. They have no wish to subject *their* children to the possibility of a divorce that might result if they act without a full understanding of their own needs. Whatever they do, they'll reflect their mother's easy acceptance of herself. Karen has managed to teach her daughters that each individual must establish personal values, for life in general and for sexual behavior in particular. She's taught them that adult acts are accompanied by adult responsibility. This understanding is critical. It isn't easy for children to be held accountable for one set of sexual values while observing their parent's acceptance of an entirely different set for themselves.

Karen was consistent in her treatment of her daughters. They understood that until they were old enough to make their own choices, to earn their own money, and to manage their own mistakes, they had to accept their mother's judgments in any major area of their lives. Yet, at the same time, Karen was teaching them how to make decisions with which they could live.

Listening Helps

Besides being consistent in her treatment of Gina and Jill, Karen also knew how to listen. She talked to her children about her problems, remembering to keep them simple enough for a child to understand. But she also listened attentively when Gina and Jill talked about theirs. She paid attention to what the school they attended taught about sex, so she was prepared to have her daughters express different viewpoints.

Dr. Jay Gale emphasized in a verbal interview that "a lot of sex education has to do with listening. It may be helpful to share some of your own feelings, but it is very important not to cut off a kid's feelings. Parents need to be aware that their child may have feelings that are different from theirs. Their values may not match up with their parents' reactions to masturbation or to whether a kid is going to sleep with a girlfriend or boyfriend. Think about what are the advantages of their values, as well as what are the advantages of your own."

There's a difference between lecturing and discussing. When a parent falls into the trap of lecturing, other opinions are cut off. In a discussion, everyone has the right to voice ideas. A lecture is a power struggle won by the parent. A discussion is an open airing of values that acknowledges the right of each individual to differ.

Yet, if you acknowledge your children's rights to their own opinions, is there any guarantee that you'll have the same results as Karen? Won't your children simply act on their values and toss yours aside?

There's no easy answer to this question. There are no certainties in life. But the probability of your children rejecting you completely is diminished if you've established a rapport with them. If you've shown respect for their opinions, there's a better chance that you'll receive respect in return.

How can you establish rapport if your children never seem to have any questions? There is a way. If you find that your children aren't bringing up the subject you want to deal with, there's no reason why you can't be the initiator.

Raymond, a single father with a thirteen-year-old son, realized that he needed to have a talk about sex with his boy. But Frank seemed to avoid the subject. So Raymond took his son camping. As they sat beside the campfire, he started talking about the interesting changes animals and humans pass through as they mature.

This opened the subject. Because Raymond kept the approach light, Frank didn't shy away from it. Instead, he dared to ask some questions that had bothered him and tell his father what his friends had told him.

By the time the evening was over, Raymond had helped Frank see that humans couldn't have intercourse as casually as did animals. Humans had to prove themselves responsible before they risked the possibility of becoming parents.

When Frank asked why Raymond had never remarried, Raymond was able to explain that he felt he had a good home for him even without a mother, since the same nursemaid who'd cared for Frank when his mother died had stayed on. Raymond added that he'd known a few women in the past, but they just hadn't been special enough. Now he had met a woman whom he liked very much, and he wanted Frank to meet her. He expected to see a lot of her, and she'd probably stay overnight with him sometimes.

Frank had a lot of questions, all of which Raymond answered honestly. This helped to prepare Frank for his father's sexual involvement. It also helped him to accept Louisa when she did stay over.

The close talking helped Frank realize that he wasn't threatened by the new situation. So when Raymond did introduce his son to Louisa, Frank wasn't upset. But if the conversation hadn't taken place, he might not have been so pleasant. Also, because of their new understanding. Frank now felt free to bring his sexual questions to his father, since he knew that Raymond would not be angry or upset no matter what was said.

Special Problems of Single Parents with Opposite-Sex Children

Even in two-parent families, many adults have difficulty talking about sex with their children. But they have one advantage. They have each other to serve as "sounding boards" when ideas about how to do it are considered. Also, a child may hesitate to talk about sex to Father, but may find it easy to do so with Mother. It may work in the opposite direction. There are alternatives when both parents are available.

At present, the majority of single-parent families are headed by women. This situation is changing, it's true. However, in divorced families where the man is not actively involved with his children, the mother must provide her sons with some sex information that they would normally get from their fathers. She often has to struggle with sexual problems alone. This can be difficult, especially if she's not at ease with the subject.

Ruth had trouble dealing with her son Jason's beginning puberty. She was afraid that if she talked about sex with him, she might be accused of being seductive. Part of the difficulty lay in her own reactions. She knew Jason resembled his father, and though John was remarried and living in another city, Ruth was still attracted to him.

Every time she tried to talk about sex with Jason, she became so uneasy she had to stop. Finally, she asked a neighbor to help. This man was very friendly with Jason and often had Jason assist him in work around the house. Ruth first told the neighbor what she wanted Jason to hear, and since the neighbor agreed with what Ruth wanted, he found it easy to communicate with the boy.

Dr. Gale emphasizes that, even without a neighbor's help, such a situation isn't hopeless. A mother can explain that she's a bit nervous because she hasn't done anything quite like this before. She can tell her son that she really wants to know if he has any questions about the changes that are taking place in his body. By admitting at the outset that she's uneasy, she can minimize the effect her nervousness will have on her son's responses. They can even tease about her reactions—thus making her son an ally in "getting through" the discussion. If things work out well, she can use the same technique to get her son to talk about his feelings toward her dates, especially if she has a man stay over.

A single father faces the same problem with a daughter. It is important that such a father be honest about his uneasiness with the situation, so his nervousness doesn't keep his daughter from asking questions or from voicing her honest opinions.

What's important is that parents allow their opposite-sex children an opportunity to ask questions and talk about their feelings and concerns. Then, if the communication has been real, the children will be more willing to listen to their parents when they talk about *their* feelings and values. They'll have more respect for the information they get. In such a discussion, it's important for the opposite-sex parents to admit when they just don't know an answer or when they're puzzled. Nothing discourages a child's willingness to talk faster than the feeling that a trusted parent is not being honest.

If a single mother doesn't know the answers to her son's questions or a single father is unsure of what to tell his daughter, and they don't know anyone who might help, they can suggest that they read books. In the Resources section you will find a list of books that give accurate pictures of children's sexuality and help them see their parents as sexual beings who may want the companionship of an adult of the opposite sex.

This latter point is very important. We often forget that our relatives are sexual. The fact is that even in parent-child relationships there are sexual feelings. In the course of any discussion about sex erotic feelings may develop. In themselves, they are not bad—they are simply normal human reactions. But it's important for the adult to make certain that these emotions and feelings aren't acted upon. This is, in fact, an excellent example for the child, since he, too, will react to a charged situation. If parents in such situations keep things under control they will be demonstrating sexual responsibility—and teaching it to their children.

There may be many pitfalls surrounding the sex education of a child, especially in a single-parent family. However, if you remember your aims, you'll find most of the traps easy to avoid. Take time now to write out the goals you have for your children's sex education. Below are a few suggestions. Add as many more as you want.

1. I want my children to understand my need for sex without expecting to have sex themselves.

2. I want my children to understand that becoming sexually involved demands responsibility. I don't want my sons getting any girl pregnant. And I don't want my daughters to get pregnant.

3. I want my children to be able to talk about sex with me without feeling embarrassed.

4. I want my children to know the truth about sex and not to accept the myths and fables that are circulated on the street.

5. I want my children to recognize the danger of sexually transmitted diseases, and to avoid promiscuous behavior that might put their health in jeopardy.

When you have completed your list, you'll be in a position to decide how best to carry out your children's sex education. Find out what is taught in their school. Get books from a library, or buy some. Just be sure you read them before you give them to your children, so you know that the ideas they present coincide with yours. Take responsibility for teaching your children about sex. You'll gain their respect, for they'll know then that you consider their education important enough to give it your personal attention.

7 Arrangements

Common Dating and Sexual Dilemmas

Today, there are more single parents with the need to date and have sexual gratification than ever before. Just as your circumstances affect the kinds of problems that confront you as a dating single parent, so do the various arrangements you may make. You may be widowed or divorced and the custodial parent of one or more children, or you may be an elective unmarried parent, or a single homosexual with the custody of children. You may be interested in anything from a one-night stand to remarriage. The variety of single-parent situations and potential dating arrangements is greater now than it has ever been before, and the attendant problems are more confusing.

Fortunately, there are now some articles and books available that can tell you how others have solved problems similar to your own. Many single custodial parents have dealt with their dating problems successfully, and some acquaintance with their decisions and judgments may help you, too. But another's solution may not always be the one for you. You probably need to find that delicate blend of what others have done and what seems right for your unique situation so that, when you apply the cure, it works.

Of course, no problem can be solved until it has been identified. Begin by asking yourself a few questions.

1. Do you approve of one-night stands? If so, how do you handle them?

2. Can you enjoy a casual relationship with someone you don't seriously consider as qualified to be a marriage partner?

3. How do you answer the question, "Your place or mine?"

4. Is it all right to have a person who's a stranger to your children sleep over?

5. How do you feel about establishing a personal, intimate relationship with someone who isn't the parent of your children?

6. What if you decide to live together? How will the kids react?

7. Do you have any reason to believe it will cause emotional problems for them if you bring a new partner into your family circle and show that you love him or her?

8. What happens to your arrangements if you and your ex-spouse each have part-time custody of the kids?

Your answers to these questions are the only ones that are valid for you. If you carefully consider your reactions to each of the above queries, your decision making will be easier.

One-Night Stands

Most single parents agree that the so-called one-night stand is generally unsatisfactory. However, many also admit that there comes a time after divorce or bereavement when they find themselves confronted with a clear choice—one-night stands or nothing. Perhaps you're already faced with this situation, and the feeling of desperation it brings, and wonder why you've decided to use this route to sexual gratification anyway.

Maybe you've been isolated with your children for some time, and you're beginning to be afraid you've forgotten how to relate to an adult intimately. Maybe you're just feeling terribly lonely, and someone has come along who seems to soothe the ache. Or maybe your spouse ran off with another person, making you feel very unworthy. These are all negative reasons for accepting a one-night stand, but they can be powerful.

There can be positive reasons, too. You may be reveling in your new freedom, feeling eager to taste all the forbidden fruits that have for so long tempted you. You may just want to indulge your senses for a while. You may feel that a variety of experiences with a number of partners will help you grow. Or you may just want to let off steam after a period of feeling bottled up.

Whatever your motivation, it's important that you protect your children in these situations. This phase of a parent's life should be private. Children are only confused when they have to deal with a string of different "uncles" who appear in Mother's bed, or a series of "aunts" who show up in Daddy's room.

The typical response of a child who becomes aware of this phase of a parent's life is to become very anxious. Some children respond to this anxiety with anger. Others, unable to accept what's happening, deny what they see and try to protect themselves from further unpleasantness by distancing themselves from their offending parent.

Whatever a child's reaction, it results in unnecessary stress. You have the right, as an adult, to experiment as much as you need to, but you also have a responsibility to protect your children from the stress and anxiety that will follow if they become aware of every partner you entertain.

Karen, whom I mentioned in chapter 6, was able to design her home so that she and her partners could enter without disturbing anyone's sleep. It was an ideal solution to the question of how to indulge her need for varied sexual experiences without upsetting her children. She lived in a house, not an apartment. Her children slept on the second floor. Her bedroom was on the first floor beside the kitchen and adjacent to the garage. If she brought a man home for a one-night stand, she could bring him in without the children knowing. These lovers left before the children got up for school. A next-door neighbor sat with her children when she was out. Karen would come in, pay the agreed fee, and watch out the front door until her neighbor was back in her own house. Then she'd invite her one-night lover in. It was simple—and it worked.

But perhaps you live in a small apartment with paper-thin walls, and your children share the bedroom right next to yours. If anyone came in for the night, the children would wake up. Besides, your baby-sitter comes from five blocks away, so you can't just stand at the door and see her home. She's a teenager and needs to be in by 12:30. That puts a definite limit on your free time.

You feel you can't go to a motel, at least not very often. You'd get home too late. It seems impossible. Is there any solution to your dilemma?

There may be—especially if you're determined enough. First decide how you expect to meet your one-night stands. If you go to a singles club, you may have time for an hour or two at a motel before you have to get the baby-sitter home. If you need sex enough, you'd prefer that to a movie. You might just decide to leave the meeting early, so that you can extend your time together.

Lois found this a solution that worked as long as she felt interested in one-night stands. She met her partners at a singles meeting once a week, a different man each time. She wasn't sure why, but after one time with a man, she had no desire to see him again. If he was at the next meeting, she tried to avoid him.

It wasn't that the sex was always bad or unsatisfying. Some of her partners were quite skillful. But she was desperately afraid of being tied to one person again. Her ex-husband had hurt her very much when he ran off, and she didn't trust any man who tried to get close to her. Besides, since her ex-spouse had deserted her, she was feeling very unworthy. Somehow, it bolstered her ego to have a different man every time.

Only once did she miss getting back to drive her sitter home on time. But her sitter's parents were out even later, and so they never learned about her slip. She felt lucky that this one offense didn't result in her losing her sitter, whom she trusted.

Craig, another single parent, refused to let himself be hampered by a deadline. He found an elderly woman in the condominium complex where he, his son, and his daughter lived. He paid her to stay overnight and to fix breakfast for the children. He chose Saturday as his regular night out, and he knew he didn't have to worry about his children until late Sunday morning.

Singles groups didn't interest Craig. He wanted a wilder kind of recreation. Three different nightclubs were his favorites, and he alternated between them, picking up someone from whichever place he visited. Occasionally, he'd drop in at a disco or a comedy club, just for variety. Because the clubs were all rather close together, he chose a motel where he felt safe and reserved a room for every Saturday night.

Even when his children grew old enough to do without the sitter, he kept her on. He felt it was important that they have an adult available to them if they needed one on his night out. Besides, they'd developed a good relationship with the woman, who served as a surrogate grandparent (his own parents were dead, and his ex-wife's family lived in another state).

Maybe you don't have the money Craig obviously had and you can't afford a weekly hotel room or an overnight sitter. Then try Lois's solution. It does mean you have to go places where you can meet partners early in the evening, since you must usually be home by an agreed-upon hour, but it doesn't necessarily put an end to your social life.

One hopeful thought. Most single parents who go the one-night-stand route find their interest in it doesn't last. They seem to need a period of profligate sexuality to prove to themselves that they're okay. Once the need is satisfied, they go on to more durable relationships.

Casual Lovers

Even when you've had your fill of one-night stands, you may continue them for a while longer simply because not every relationship can be *the* one you're hoping for. But the day will most probably come when you find one partner who seems to have many of the characteristics you've been looking for. Still, you don't want to jump into anything. You see this person more than once. You may even establish a regular date night. But neither of you is ready to commit yourselves to a long-term relationship.

Then you meet another person who seems even more desirable. It's okay, you know, since you're not committed to the other partner, so you date this person, too. It's common for a single parent to have many close yet casual relationships before finding one that takes over and fills his or her life.

These short-term, casual relationships may be sequential or simultaneous. Some people are comfortable dating a number of partners with whom they have sex. Others find that they can handle only one relationship at a time.

Generally, something tells you, during such relationships, that this person isn't the one, after all. However, you may still enjoy the companionship and the sex. You feel good because you know you're appreciated. Often a real friendship develops and you continue to see the person even after you are no longer sexually involved.

You feel somewhat ambivalent about these relationships. Since you like each one of your casual partners, you realize there's a possibility you might make the bond permanent with one of them, and this makes your decision more difficult. Your children should have a chance to meet each person you're seeing and are serious about. However, you need to consider every aspect of each relationship and decide how willing you would be to make it permanent. Then you need to consider whether the individual with whom you're involved is the kind of person who isn't very stable and is likely to disappear from your life. You'll probably want to avoid introducing such a person to your children, no matter how much fun you have together, since children who have gone through divorce or death have a difficult time adjusting to the loss of a new friend.

Even if you're not contemplating permanence, your children may not necessarily be harmed by getting to know a temporary lover, especially the sort who likes young people. Such a person can be very helpful to your children. If you detect a true fondness for children in a lover, you may want to expand your relationship to include your entire family. Sometimes, these friendships are strong enough to endure even after you cease to be lovers. This kind of relationship may be very important to your children, for they need adult friends of both sexes.

If you have frequent contact with one individual, even though you're not planning on permanence, your children need not be excluded. It's important for them to have a sense that they're recognized and accepted by someone who's special to you. Otherwise, they may begin to feel excluded, not only by your lover, but by you as well.

Marsha and Dennis began to date casually after meeting at a singles club. The first time they had sex, it was more as a lark than because of tremendous attraction. But they had fun together, both in bed and out, and so their relationship grew. For a while, they both believed this was it, that they had at last found the answer to their hopes. They began to spend some nights at her place and some at his.

Marsha's two children, Ricky and Joan, six-year-old twins, met Dennis one afternoon when she took them to the zoo. It was a prearranged meeting that allowed the children to get better acquainted with Dennis. The first time he stayed overnight with her, Dennis took Marsha and the twins out to dinner first. The children knew he was going to stay over, and they accepted it because they liked him.

From then on, Marsha and Dennis usually went to her place. Ricky and Joan began to fantasize that Dennis was their new daddy. They protested when he was absent for a number of days at a time, and they began to make plans for things they'd do with him in the future.

Fortunately, Marsha picked up on the cues. When she realized that her relationship with Dennis was casual and would not develop into a permanent thing, she sat down with the twins and had a family talk. She wanted to prepare them for the change.

"Dennis is a good friend, isn't he?" she began.

Both children agreed. Ricky and Joan launched into descriptions of how Dennis had helped them repair their toys. It was clear that they loved him.

"Dennis and I are good friends, too. We enjoy each other's company. But good friends aren't part of our family. They visit us. Sometimes they spend a long time with us. But sooner or later they go away again."

Marsha listened while her children responded to this idea. Joan was the first to understand. "Isn't Dennis going to be our new daddy?"

"No, he isn't. But we're still good friends, and he'll come over and visit us sometimes. I hope he'll see us a lot. But he won't ever live with us all the time."

Again, she waited while the twins expressed their feelings about what she had said. Then she continued. "Maybe some day we'll meet someone who'll be just right as your new daddy. That would be nice. But even if we never find a new daddy, it won't be that important as long as we have good friends like Dennis."

Ricky voiced the fear both children had. "Dennis won't go away, will he?"

"I don't know. I don't think he will, at least not right away. He's our friend. But if he did, we might be angry for a while, but we'd still love him, wouldn't we? And we'd have fun remembering the good times we had together. Like we do when we think about Daddy."

The children were sad for a time, remembering their father, whom they saw very seldom because he lived in another town. Marsha gave them time to accept what she had said. Then she smiled. "Who wants to go sledding?" This day, only the three of them would be on the weekly outing. The children had to be reminded that they had fun even when Dennis wasn't along.

Your Place or Mine?

If your relationship is still a casual one, and you have a choice of "your place or mine," I recommend that you not choose your place. As long as you have the choice, there is no reason to confuse your children with your sex life. The issue, however, is more complex than the question implies.

Are you the only one who has children? Maybe you both do. Then which children are of an age to best weather the possibility of discovering that their parent has a bed partner—if only for a night?

Which of you has to get up first for work? Maybe you have an early check-in time but your new partner can arrive at the office late without causing comment. Then, for practical reasons, you may choose your place.

If you decide to take your lover home, it may be better if he or she leaves after you're through with sex, or at least before the children wake up in the morning. Don't assume, however, that because your lover leaves late at night or very early in the morning your children won't know someone has been there. Children do stir in the night. They wake, are briefly aware of their surroundings, and then go back to sleep.

Joe, an attorney, told me of his dating a woman who had two children, ages nine and eleven. Whenever he stayed over, he would rise early and leave before the children woke. Or so he thought. But later he learned that when the children were older they told their mother they would awaken when he started his car and say to each other, "There goes Joe. He slept with Mom again."

Joe felt as though his attempts at secrecy were wasted. This is not necessarily true, though, even if the children did know he was leaving. Since his relationship with their mother was casual, it was just as well the children didn't have to deal with his presence when they got up.

This is not to say that the children should have, at the time, felt hesitant about speaking with their mother about what was going on. It isn't good for children to feel they can't talk about things that confuse or trouble them. If you always keep your dating and your lovers secret from them, they can't help but get the wrong impression about your relationship.

If it's necessary for a single parent to bring a lover home, especially if it's done often, that parent probably should assume that the children are aware of what's happening, even if some attempt at secrecy has been made. Under this circumstance, it may be wise to broach the subject to the children. This can be done without a great deal of confusion simply by remarking the next morning, "Did you hear something last night? Just before we were supposed to get up?" If the children say yes, you can explain that you had someone staying overnight with you who had to hurry home to go to work. Add that you're sorry if it disturbed their sleep. That might be all you need to say. But if your children ask for more information, give it. You might conclude by saying that, if they'd like, you can arrange to let them meet your friend.

The problem of adding another element to the morning tasks of getting ready for school and work may offer the best reason of all for many overnight lovers to leave early, as Joe did, even if the children do know what is going on. You, as a working single parent, will be less fragmented if you don't have to deal with a lover at the same time you're preparing to leave for work and getting your children ready for school. Your time with your children is limited, especially if you have to work, and mornings can be important for both you and them. Children are leaving you for the day. It's best if they go off to school or to the sitter without the added confusion of seeing you with a lover. They need to feel that your attention is focused on them.

The other consideration concerns your partner. The night before there were only the two of you. Your entire attention was centered on this person with whom you were having sex. Now, with the morning, comes the truth. You're a parent. Your children are more important than this person with whom you've shared the night. The result may be that your lover loses self-esteem. If you are busy with your children, your lover may feel excluded entirely from your attention, and guilty for being there at all.

Sarah, an attractive woman in her midthirties, described her discomfort when she dated a man who had custody of his ten-year-old daughter. After several dates and a beginning sexual relationship, he invited her over to have dinner at his house, even though both he and Sarah realized that their relationship was a casual one. His daughter was polite but cool when she was introduced to Sarah.

Her lover encouraged her to sleep over, which she did. But in the morning, when she again encountered the child, she was uneasy. She felt certain the girl had been faced with other women in similar situations, and that made her feel cheap. Also, she found that she liked the girl, but she didn't want to become attached to a child with whom she knew she would never have a lasting relationship. She wished she had not consented to stay. She also regretted that she had been prematurely introduced to the child.

You may be fortunate enough to have more options than just your place or his, children included. Maybe you have a brother or sister who can take your children for a night so you don't have to worry about them when you plan to date someone with whom you're having sex. Your children's grandparents can be helpful in this way, too. They may love to have the children for more than a few hours, at least occasionally.

If you have a good friend who also has children, you might arrange to have yours stay there overnight. Your children, too, may have friends whose parents would accept a one-night visit. Explore these possibilities before you consider the more expensive one of hiring an overnight baby-sitter.

Particularly if you are having a casual affair and don't want to involve your children in it, such solutions are ideal. If you have no relatives or friends who can help you out, then I advise you to take your date to a motel, even though you will not stay the entire night. This is particularly important if you know your children will be upset or if you have not had time to prepare them for the introduction of your date into their lives.

Sleep-overs

When the relationship with your casual lover grows serious, you both begin to hate getting up and going home. You find it painful to separate and want to spend the entire night together as often as possible.

But before you open your bed to a partner on a regular basis, I suggest you explain to your children what is happening. You can tell them that this is a very special person with whom you want to share your time, someone who will be sleeping over as often as possible. What's important is that you keep your children at the center of your thoughts while you're speaking. They need you very much. They can accept having another adult around who will give them love and attention, but they cannot endure losing *your* attention and seeing it lavished on another.

Be alert as you talk to them about your plans so that you have a better opportunity to recognize the cues they may give you. Children are usually transparent enough so you can tell what they're thinking. If you pick up on their cues and answer their worries, you will help them to accept this change in their lives without anxiety.

Remember, you do not have to abandon your plans just because your children object. Their disapproval simply means that you should try to answer their objections so they can be put to rest. If this isn't done, problems may develop that could have been avoided.

Jonathan, the father of two boys, described to me how he handled the dating and sexual relationship with a woman he has since married. She is the mother of two teenage girls. During their dating period, he often slept over at her house. And sometimes during the day, even when the girls were at home, he and their mother would spend time in the bedroom, having sex. He realized the girls knew what was going on, but he chose to pretend he didn't. When remarks were made that clearly indicated their awareness, he let them pass without responding. Even though it was evident to him that they were upset, he would not acknowledge their right to be irritated by his and their mother's obvious sexual behavior. As a result, his relationship with the girls was awkward. A barrier of unspoken anger kept them apart.

Jonathan rationalized that it was their mother's responsibility to deal with the situation, and yet, despite his awareness that she did not know how to handle the situation alone, he offered her little support. He now regrets he was so insensitive. He realizes he should have helped her deal with what was going on and should not have been so demanding of her sexually, especially in the presence of the girls. He's aware that there's still some resentment in both his wife and her daughters because of his thoughtless behavior.

He reasons that he dealt with the situation as he did because he really didn't know how to relate to teenaged girls. He believes that had his wife-to-be been the mother of two boys he would have been more comfortable with them, since he is a man and has sons himself. Then he might have been able to talk to them about the sex he shared with their mother, even though she was still hesitant to do so.

Fortunately, his awareness now may enable him to overcome the mistakes he made in the past. He recognizes that he and his wife-to-be were not communicating as well as they should have, and he's working to improve that situation.

The fact is, however, that the girls' mother had a responsibility that she didn't accept. The girls were her children, and even though Jonathan behaved insensitively when he pressured her into having sex during the day when the girls were present, she had the right to say no. She also should have spoken to her children so they would understand what was going on. It's appropriate for Jonathan to acknowledge his share of the responsibility for this unpleasant situation, but the greatest part of the burden still lies with the mother.

Remember that you are responsible for your children. If you begin a relationship that is serious and long-lasting, it is your obligation to explain things to them. Don't push that duty off on your lover. If you do, you may sour your relationship, for you will show that you are not as mature and capable as you're pretending to be.

Getting to Know Your Lover

In a continuing relationship, there comes a stage when the two lovers are almost living together, but not quite. They may each feel a bit fearful of a total commitment, yet are very attracted to the notion of being together all the time and, perhaps, even marrying.

This can be a time of great stress for the two adults, but it can also be difficult for any children involved. They feel they're in a sort of limbo. They don't know what their relationship with the lover should be. Is this still just a friend of their parent? Should the lover be considered a stepparent? What expectations and rules does this new situation demand?

If the parent doesn't take the time to explain what is happening to the children, they may act out their dilemma in front of the adults, being either rude or overly attentive to the newcomer. This behavior is an attempt on the part of children to force the issue. They want to know who the new adult is and where they stand in the relationship.

During one otherwise ordinary family dinner, eleven-year-old Kevin behaved in an angry and insulting way to his mother in front of her lover, who was now spending most of his time in their home. Fortunately, his mother was aware that this was unusual behavior, so she remained calm. However, she later spoke to him about it.

Kevin responded by asking if "that man" always had to be around. His mother was puzzled. She knew that Kevin and her lover got along well. She didn't realize what the problem was until she came to me to discuss it. I helped her to see that it was the ambivalence she and her lover felt, and unconsciously revealed to Kevin, that was contributing to his behavior.

Armed with this new information, she was able to deal with the situation. She told Kevin that she and her lover were thinking about living together all the time. They just hadn't made up their minds yet. She made it clear that she understood how difficult it was for him to know how to act, and she expressed a hope that Kevin would be patient a while.

This didn't stop the behavior entirely, but it did provide Kevin with an understanding that released some of the stress with which he had been living.

Living with Your Lover

It's common these days for many couples to forgo marriage altogether—choosing instead the less formal arrangement of living together. But even if marriage is anticipated, two people often live together for a while. They claim that this period of uncommitted closeness can be a time for finding out how it feels to have this special person nearby on a day-to-day basis.

Many couples just drift into living together. While this may be ideal for two people who do not have responsibilities, it can be dangerous if one of them has children. What often happens is that important issues are not settled before the living together begins. Issues like child discipline, who does what chores, and how money is handled all remain unresolved.

In some isolated instances this may not be a disaster. Some couples are able to work out these questions as they arise. Some children are capable of living with a limited amount of uncertainty without becoming apprehensive and troublesome. But, generally speaking, little is gained by leaving these issues to be resolved by chance. Fuzzy planning is seldom beneficial in a relationship.

If your lover unexpectedly begins to live in your home, your children can be confused. You need to sit down with them and explain what is happening. The explanation must be appropriate to the ages of your children, but the general idea should be the same.

Tell your children that you and your lover have decided you want to live together, and you'd like to know how they feel about it. If your lines of communication are open, your children may voice a considerable amount of opposition. They may be fearful that they'll be displaced in your love by this new person. They may announce that they "just don't need anyone new around."

Not all children resent the arrival of a partner for their single parent. A sixteen-year-old girl expressed relief when her mother announced she was remarrying. After the death of her father, she had been aware that her mother felt overwhelmed. Her response had been to assume responsibility for her mother's happiness. The arrival of a new husband for her mother took that burden from her shoulders. The girl also came to recognize that she was gaining another friend, for her mother's new husband was a loving, sensitive man who did a great deal to fill the emptiness in his new daughter's life.

This can happen, especially if the custodial parent has not been adequate to the problems he or she faced alone. Whether the child anticipates the arrival of a new parent with pleasure or uneasiness, the end result is that the child experiences a major change in life. For some children, this is an expanding experience. Others may feel that their lives have contracted. How your child feels depends partly on how well you have considered everyone concerned in your plans.

Every aspect of your new merger will be improved if you and your lover discuss possible problems beforehand. You especially need to agree on just how much your lover will participate in disciplining your children. This can become a sore spot in your relationship if it's left unresolved, especially if you and your lover decide to marry.

Rhonda married Tom after they'd been living together for some months. During that period, when Rhonda was living in, Tom began to turn over the responsibility for his daughter, Julie, to her. He never said anything directly, but in many subtle ways he made it clear that he didn't expect to make any more decisions regarding his child. That was Rhonda's duty.

The problem was magnified because Tom also never spoke directly to Julie regarding his expectations. So Julie would seek her father's support when she didn't want to accept Rhonda's decision on some subject. Sometimes, and especially when he was annoyed with Rhonda for any reason, he'd support his daughter. Another time, when the issues were the same, he'd back Rhonda.

After a time, Rhonda sued for divorce. She hated to lose Tom, but she couldn't stand being put in the middle this way. She admitted afterward that she should have insisted on solving the problem before she agreed to marry Tom, since she was aware of it almost as soon as she moved in with him. But at that time she was most concerned with keeping Tom. She foolishly believed she could take care of that "little difficulty" later.

According to statistics, there are estimated to be twenty-five million stepparents in the United States, and the number is growing. Janice H. Nadler, who has worked extensively with stepparents, has found that "stepmothers experience more feelings of anxiety, depression, and anger regarding family relations than do natural mothers. Stepfathers also experience greater emotional dissonance, less psychological adjustment, and less satisfaction with the family than their natural counterparts."*

In her group work with stepparents, Dr. Nadler places particular emphasis on relieving a stepparent of the "frequent, self-imposed mandate that they uncritically love their stepchildren despite the stepchildren's ambivalent or even hostile feelings toward them." A stepparent is also helped to eliminate feelings of low self-esteem that can develop because they have lost control over their emotions.

Dr. Nadler notes that stepparents often describe their position in the family as "peripheral." They feel alienated from the natural parent-child relationship. In an effort to correct this, they often overextend themselves and attempt to act the "super-stepparent." This results in an exaggerated type of parenting, usually motivated by a desire to gain the children's affection. If the children don't respond, the stepparent frequently begins to withdraw.

The natural parent, typically, feels caught in the middle, being aware of the conflict, and attempts to support the new

*Janice H. Nadler, "Effecting Change in Stepfamilies: A Psychodynamic Behavioral Group Approach," *American Journal of Psychotherapy*, Vol. 37, No. 1 (January 1983), pp. 100–112.

spouse while simultaneously indulging and overprotecting the children. Often this splitting of loyalty arises because the natural parent still feels guilty about the divorce that deprived the children of their other natural parent.

All of the child-stepparent confrontations described by Dr. Nadler, which are a common part of second-family relationships, can exist to an even more intense degree in a family composed of children, a custodial parent, and a live-in lover. Here the difficulties are compounded by the lack of formal commitment between the two adults. The live-in lover not only has to deal with the recalcitrant children, but also with his or her own feelings of insecurity.

Difficult as these conflicts may be, they can be eased by honest confrontation of the issues. To start, never enter a live-in arrangement without first clarifying who will be responsible for the children. When you and your lover have reached an understanding, bring your children into the discussion. You may want to do this when your lover is not present, unless a good rapport between them has already been established. Let your children voice their feelings in the matter, then tell them what you have decided.

Maybe you will conclude that both you and your lover will act as equal parents, and your children accept this. For a while, things may go smoothly. But, sooner or later, there are sure to be times when you disagree about how to deal with the children. When that occurs, wait to criticize until you two are alone. Remember, if you expect your children to honor your lover's decisions, you must not undercut his or her authority with them.

There is one other important consideration. Remember that even in natural families there are disagreements about discipline. If you and your lover find yourselves at odds because of your children, don't assume that you're unique. It's difficult enough for just two people to get along together without quarreling. When the number is increased, the possibility of discord multiplies.

Natural families face the same problems. When they succeed in finding solutions, they do so by remembering that their love for each other is greater than any difficulty they might face. You can follow their example. Hold on to your love for your new partner *and* for your children. Let your love, and your desire for whatever is best for all, govern your decisions. Be patient. And never hesitate to seek help if the difficulties seem insurmountable.

Part-time Custody Issues

Many divorces today result in shared custody of the children. If none of the children is in school, this problem is generally easy to solve. But if there are children of school age, complications arise. Sometimes the children spend their winters with one parent (so schooling will be uninterrupted) and summers with the other. This, however, is not usually satisfactory. The school parent becomes the disciplinarian—the summer parent the one with whom the children have most fun.

If the divorced parents live close to each other, the children can maintain consistent schooling and still alternate weeks with each. If they are separated by a little more distance, the best arrangement may be to let the noncustodial parent have the right to evening visits and to have the children on alternate weekends. The final decisions regarding joint custody have to be designed to suit both parents and to disrupt the lives of the children as little as possible.

If you're divorced, and if you and your live-in lover will be having the children only part of the time, some of the pressure you feel will diminish. You will have times alone together that will allow you to renew your personal relationship.

This periodic breather may enable you to face the conflicts the presence of your children may incur. However, it can also create new difficulties. Your lover may have trouble adjusting to the occasional presence of children in the house. If you don't have a live-in lover, your more casual lover or lovers may find it hard to put up with the on-again, off-again relationship you offer—especially if, when your children are with you, you devote most of your free time to them.

Your children, too, may have added problems. After all, they have their own adjustments to face. Your ex-spouse may be settling in with a new companion, too. If neither of you takes time to discuss these changes with your children, they cannot be expected to emerge unscathed.

For that reason, you are well advised to anticipate what might happen and plan ways to avoid problems. Even though you've discussed discipline, is there a danger your lover may intervene between you and your children? Know in advance how you will deal with this problem. Are your children very loyal to your ex-spouse, and might they resent your lover, maybe even be rude or sullen? You've talked to them already, but have a procedure ready to follow if they still cause trouble. Maybe your plans won't ever have to be used. But if you need emergency measures, they'll be ready.

Another conflict may arise if you have small living quarters with no separate room for your children. Verne, the father of a teenage boy and girl, lived in a one-bedroom apartment. He was unsure how to handle sleeping arrangements. When he came to me, he explained that he had his sixteen-year-old daughter share his bed. He made it clear that he never touched her. There was no incest. But he still knew that this wasn't the best thing for her or his son, who slept on the couch.

I agreed. It wasn't good for him to share his bed with his daughter. If he felt uneasy about letting her have the couch, and having his son share his bed, there was a solution. The two children could use foldaway beds that are kept in a closet when they aren't in use.

This is a solution available to any single parent who has living quarters too small to accommodate the occasional visits of children. With high rents, few single parents can afford to pay for rooms that aren't needed all the time. Another solution is to have sleeping bags, which can be spread out on the floor. Especially in very small apartments, this may work best.

Sleeping bags can also be used when a single parent travels with children, in motels where extra cots are not available or when the two double beds usually provided in motel rooms are not enough. Motel rooms are expensive. If each child has his or her own sleeping bag, the journey can be a fun adventure, and the costs can be kept down.

A good point to remember is that most children can adjust to any change if they're given some help—and if they're prepared in advance. Whatever your situation—whether you're still enjoying one-night stands, are involved in a casual affair, or are planning to live with or marry your lover—it's important to communicate with your children.

If you're divorced and can include your ex-spouse in the discussions, all the better. You can't keep your children in the dark and expect, somehow, that they'll still understand what you're doing. Talk to them. Let them talk back. Only when the channels are open can you hope for your children's cooperation as you plan your life.

Perspective of the Lover

Each level in a relationship between a single parent and lover has its own specific problems as far as the children are concerned. It's easy to become so centered on the children's reactions that one forgets that the lover may have special difficulty with certain behavior patterns. Often, a single parent's lover is also a single parent. This can serve to compound the problems that arise when the age-old question "your place or mine?" is asked. There's a need, in such a situation, to discuss these issues early in the relationship.

I have worked with and visited many singles groups, and I find it interesting to note how often people are surprised at others' reactions. Yet it would be helpful to many single men and women for them to understand each other's points of view, and to realize that the questions and objections raised by any individual in a specific group meeting tend to reflect serious problems faced by many. The problems that arise when a single parent dates can be summarized in six questions that affect almost all.

1. How do you feel about meeting your date at a location other than one of your homes?

There were a variety of responses to this question. Men seemed to have strong feelings on the matter. Those who prefer a slower pace to their relationship generally want to know as much as possible about their date. It appears important to them that they know how the woman they date lives and whether or not she has children. Those few men who expect sex on every date also have strong objections to a rendezvous in some neutral location, but their reasons are not the same. They seemed to feel that meeting on a first date at the theater or a restaurant is a poor way to start the evening.

One man who hoped for sex whenever he dated said he didn't like meeting his date at a restaurant or the theater, since it put the entire affair on too practical a basis. He made the assumption that, because of the way she avoided having him come to her house, she wouldn't consider letting him go there with her after the date ended. He felt such arrangements were most often made by women who wanted to avoid sex with him. This made him feel resentful. It was clear to him that such a date wouldn't turn into a romantic evening. This is an assumption many men make. When they find the woman they've dated is a mother, they feel that some of the casual fun is gone. Some men even believe that every single mother is actively searching for a man who will be a substitute father for her children.

Many women prefer to meet elsewhere than at their home, at least the first time they go out with a man. They give several reasons for this. First, they feel safer when they don't bring a man to their home until they know him better. Second, they want to keep their dating separate from their children until they have established a relationship that they feel has value. And third, some women fear that their children might scare off their date. They'd rather not have a new man pick them up at their home. They're not trying to deceive a man who's interested—only to avoid having him walk away before they have a chance to get acquainted.

There are many single mothers, however, who prefer to have their dates pick them up, since it makes them feel special and cared for, and they get far too little attention of that kind. But this doesn't mean that they are totally unaware of a man's need for similar consideration. Occasionally, a single mother dating a man who also has children may alternate with him, meeting one time at his place and the next at hers. This avoids putting either one of them in the position of always driving home late at night. One woman who prefers this scenario remarked that she feels it is only fair. Men shouldn't always be the ones to bear the burdens of driving, especially when they, too, are single parents.

2. If the children are home when you call for your date, how do you feel about talking to them?

Most of the time, it is the man who calls for the woman, and so this question applies primarily to men who are dating women with children.

Many men object to having to spend time with children who obviously resent any intrusion into their family by a stranger. "The conversation is monosyllabic and very awkward," one man remarked. But awkwardness isn't the only thing that bothers them.

One man didn't like to find that his date couldn't control her children. His reaction was the same whether he was very interested in the woman or just considered her as a temporary date. "It says something about a person when she can't control her kids."

Occasionally a woman may indicate an interest in being the one to pick up the man in her car, especially if she is dating a single father. One woman said she preferred to see the men she dated with their children at least once in a while. "If I see how a man treats his children, I have a better idea of what kind of person he is," she stated.

3. Do you want to know about a date's children before you go out together?

Generally, the answer is yes, but the reasons are as varied as the people who respond. Most men simply want to know as much as they can about their date. Especially if a man is considering a serious relationship, he wants to know about her children and her life before he met her. Women have the same reaction. Neither men nor women want to feel manipulated, and when they are not informed that their dates have children until after the evening ends, they feel they have been tricked.

There were a few men who insisted they didn't care one way or the other unless their dates expected them to pay for the sitter, or unless the children were used as an excuse to avoid sex. One man was very adamant about this. "I took a woman out once who didn't tell me she had kids until the evening was ending. I asked the old bromide, and she froze. 'I can't stay out much longer. My baby-sitter has to be home by twelve,' was all she said. I know I was crazy, but I pushed the issue. 'So let's go to your place.' I tried to sound romantic, but I was already pretty turned off. Of course she said no. By that time, I expected it. But the nerve of her, not letting me know about the kids from the start."

Women often don't approve of this attitude. They cite many examples of men who seemed turned off when they learned about the children. Others agree with the man who complained. They felt that not to talk about the children in order to get a date was a form of deception and a bad way to start any relationship. They also felt that any man who would be that rejecting of children wouldn't be a worthy partner, and probably couldn't establish more than a casual relationship, at best, with any woman who had children.

4. Do you feel comfortable going to your lover's place if there are children there?

Some men indicate very little reluctance about going to a woman's place if she has children. However, most seem to prefer it if the children are small and sure to be asleep. They also prefer to leave early. "Gives me time to get my day together," one man explained.

Women seem to be less comfortable going to a house where children are sleeping. This applies to going to their own homes as well as to a lover's place. One woman, who feels most at ease at a motel, was even willing to share its cost, just so she didn't have to worry about children interrupting their lovemaking.

Many women object to this, since they just don't have the money for such luxuries. They prefer to have their lovers come to their homes because they know their children will be sleeping. Also, they don't like to drive home alone after midnight.

5. What about motels? Are they okay to use instead of either of your houses?

Men's reactions to this question vary. Some prefer motels. Others feel they should not be required to pay the entire expense if one is used. But women's incomes are often too low to permit many luxuries, and many women are unwilling or unable to share the expense of a motel.

6. What particularly in the single-parent relationship turns you or your date off?

Both men and women are turned off by a single parent who can't stop talking about the children when they're on a date. They feel that such a person isn't interested in them, and hasn't any energy left for a relationship with them. "When I'm out with an adult, I want adult conversation," was one man's explanation of why he didn't date women with children.

Most men back off when women ask them to assume any semblance of responsibility for their children, whether by giving advice or by paying for child care, before they've established a relationship. "I want to know about her kids," one man explained, "and maybe I'll want to meet them eventually. But first I want to know that the woman's worth going to all that trouble. I know I'll be getting involved with the kids once things begin to gel between us."

Women seem generally to share that feeling. They want to know that the relationship that exists with a lover is valuable in itself. Only then do they feel it is logical for them to spend much time with a man's children or assume any share of their care.

Sometimes a man seems to lose interest even though it appeared that he and his lover still felt great affection for each other. One such man explained that he's no longer dating a woman he liked very much. "We couldn't stay at her house because of her kids." But if she stayed with him, he had to drive her home when they were sexually exhausted and both would have preferred snuggling down for the rest of the night. Then he had to drive all the way home again. "I finally just stopped asking her out, without telling her why. I never gave her a choice. But if it hadn't been for her kids, we'd have had something great going. I still feel bad about it." The solution to such a problem? He should have discussed the problem with her, especially since he obviously was fond of her, and she of him. Maybe they could have worked out another solution. The woman might have been willing to drive home alone, at least some of the time. Or, if the relationship was sound enough, he might have been able to sleep over at her house, at least some of the time.

Women have different objections. Many aren't happy with men who are too arbitrary with their children. "I feel he's showing a hardness that can't help but affect other aspects of his life," one woman explained to me. "I might enjoy a few dates with him, but I wouldn't ever let things get serious. I'm sure I'd regret it if I did."

Neither do women like men whose attitudes about childrearing differ widely from their own. "If I find that a man I'm dating treats his children very differently from the way I treat mine," one woman remarked, "I become alert to other ways we may disagree. I really get upset when I see a man acting very bossy with his children."

All of the complaints, whether from men or women, have similar themes. They don't want to be deceived or manipulated. They don't want to be taken advantage of. They want to be valued for themselves. They want to feel that the person they date is open and willing to communicate. They recognize that it's impossible and inappropriate to discuss every possible area where problems might develop before the first date. They understand that this can't even be done in the early stages of a relationship. Yet, if single parents are aware of the issues concerning their children that will come up as relationships develop, they can anticipate and avoid many of the problems that have been discussed in this chapter.

Undeniably, single parents have special problems when they begin to go out socially. The need to juggle all the different considerations can make even a simple evening out a complicated matter. However, if you, a parent seeking a chance to date, consider the points discussed so far, you will find that some of your decisions will come more easily, and your relationships with your dates and your children will improve.

8 Are They Reliable?

The Baby-sitter Problem

It would be comforting for single parents as well as for parents in a nuclear family if there were a general rule regarding the age at which a child could be left alone without a sitter. Comforting—but impossible. Most parents know that children differ too much to make any such rule of thumb practical. It would be illogical for a court to decide that all children of any one particular age are mature enough to be left by themselves.

Some youngsters are very responsible and capable of managing not only themselves but younger children as well—often working as baby-sitters for neighbors and relatives. Others—ranging from very young children all the way to those beyond the age of legal consent—are too unreliable to be given anything but minimal responsibilities.

In many states, laws on the subject are understandably vague. The decision that a parent has neglected his or her children is often made only after the fact. If a child gets into trouble or is injured, then a charge of child neglect can be made. A parent leaving children alone is like someone playing Russian roulette with a gun. If the chamber is loaded—that is, if any mishap occurs or the child gets into trouble—the parent may face legal action. But most of the time, if good judgment is used in deciding whether or not particular children are responsible enough to take care of themselves, everything is fine.

When you consider whether or not to leave your children alone, you need to ask yourself the following questions. How emotionally mature are your children? How secure do they feel when you're away? How safe is your home? Your neighborhood? Is a concerned adult quickly available? If your children have an older sibling living nearby, is he or she there to help if the youngsters, left alone for the evening, need someone? If you decide to use a baby-sitter, what kind should you choose? How much does a good sitter cost? Are there any other alternatives?

How Old Is Old Enough?

Official statements regarding the appropriate age at which a child might be left alone are rare and often unspecific. The National Center on Child Abuse and Neglect provided the following explanation: "While the need for adult supervision is, of course, relative to both the situation and the maturity of the child, it is generally held that a child younger than twelve should always be supervised by an adult or at least have immediate access to a concerned adult when necessary."* In a limited survey of a number of parents, married and unmarried, many of whom are also my professional colleagues, I posed this question. All agreed that age should never be the sole consideration. Yet, they did reach a consensus as to how young is too young. None believed that a child under the age of nine should ever be left alone. This age, nine years, coincides with the developmental point noted by Wallerstein and coworkers as a critical changeover in the latency period, when a child's coping skills increase.

**An Overview of the Problem*, U.S. Department of Health, Education and Welfare, Office of Human Development, Office of Child Development–Children's Bureau, National Center on Child Abuse and Neglect, Vol. 1, No. 75-30073 (Washington, D.C.: 1975), p. 8.

Most of these professionals also believed that nine-year-olds, or even children up to eleven, should never be left alone except when a parent makes a quick trip to the store or runs an errand that takes no more than a couple of hours. But during such short parental absences, it's important that there be immediate access to an adult—a neighbor or an older sibling—in case of emergency. These brief periods without the parent can then allow children to learn to be alone, giving them a sense of mastery at being able to care for themselves.

May, a teacher and single parent, worked out a comfortable arrangement for her two sons, Bill, ten, and Walt, eight, during most weekdays, since they ate lunch at the school and arrived home only shortly before she did. But, one evening a week, she left directly from the school where she taught to spend the evening with a male friend, going out to dinner and then to his apartment for sex. This necessitated some form of care for her children from the end of their school day to the time when the sitter arrived to stay with them and prepare dinner.

Fortunately, May had a next-door neighbor, another single mother with one boy, who agreed to be available to Bill and Walt during this time if they needed help. The three boys usually played together at her home after school anyway, so it was a satisfactory arrangement.

Since Walt, the younger of May's boys, arrived home about fifteen minutes before his brother, it was his job to open the house. But he often felt apprehensive about doing this alone. He talked to his mother about his feelings and she reminded him that, if he wanted to, he could go next door and wait for Bill, but he rejected the idea. He wanted to solve his problem himself.

May helped him set up a schedule that would keep him busy during the short time before his brother arrived. She'd been considering purchasing a dog, and she now did so. This kept Walt from feeling lonely when he entered the house. The short period of being by himself and his responsibility for the dog gave Walt a feeling of pride.

The question of whether to leave a child alone for an evening raises other issues. The professionals I spoke with disagreed as to the age when that would be safe. Some felt that a child of twelve years would be capable of being left alone. Others felt that a youngster should be sixteen or more before such a move would be justified. Many noted that children of twelve and thirteen often baby-sit, suggesting that if a child of that age could be trusted with other children, it would seem safe to trust him or her alone. The word *alone* is the key to this issue. Baby-sitters aren't alone. What's more, they feel a sense of maturity and responsibility because of the younger children entrusted to them.

Many adults are not able to endure solitude, and the problem is intensified for youngsters. Children who are afraid of being alone, or who've shown poor judgment in the past, should not be left by themselves for long periods, regardless of their ages, especially in the evening or overnight. The dark can be frightening, even to adults.

This decision may be affected by the availability of an adult. If a child who's left alone knows that right next door there's a kind man or woman who will help if any trouble arises, the situation is eased. If that neighbor agrees to drop over once or twice during an evening, just to make sure everything is okay, the fear a child faces when alone for a long period might be alleviated. An emotionally mature child of twelve or more might be allowed to decide that no more visits are necessary, and arrange to phone for help if there's a problem.

In anticipation of a child's need to use the phone, I advise that you give instructions on how to dial, making certain that the essential numbers—like those for the available adult, the police, the fire department, and where you can be reached—are readily accessible. Some parents set up practice drills, so that a child has actually gone through the motions of calling for help before it's really needed. This gives both the child and the parent confidence and reassurance.

If you can't find a neighbor or relative who'll be available to your child while you're gone, or if you know your child would refuse to ask for help, then you may need either to have an adult stay over while you're out or to arrange to have your child stay with a relative or a friendly adult. I also advise that you establish a stable of baby-sitters, so you aren't ever dependent on just one person. This will avoid the possibility of your having to make a choice between canceling a date or leaving your children home alone, neither of which is desirable.

It's difficult for a parent to decide just how age and temperament affect the issue of leaving a child alone—or for how long. Children the ages of Bill and Walt, who have demonstrated emotional maturity, for example, may be allowed to feel that they're staying alone for an hour or two during the day if a cooperative neighbor is close and available. But a child of thirteen is still too young to be alone overnight and, unless emotionally mature, is not old enough to be left all evening without an adult to call on.

Fay had often left her daughter, Karen, alone during the day as long as her neighbor was available if needed. But the success of this arrangement made Fay overconfident. When Karen was thirteen, she was once left alone while her mother went dancing. Fay had told her daughter she wouldn't be back until morning and for Karen to go to bed and not worry. The neighbor had been asked to be available were Karen to need her, but because her mother seemed to expect her to manage, Karen didn't voice her uneasiness at being left alone. This led to unexpected complications.

Fay hadn't considered Karen's inability to stand up to her peers or to manage alone for a long period of time. When a girlfriend "just dropped over" with two boys, one fifteen, and found Karen alone, she insisted that they all stay with her. The two younger children (both around thirteen) phoned their parents to say they were staying overnight at Karen's house. The older intruder got on the phone when the parents of the younger two asked to speak to one of Karen's parents and managed to allay any suspicions, since none of the parents was acquainted.

Once they were assured of privacy, the three intruders began to play sex games. They insisted upon involving Karen. Her protests were weak. But when the older boy began to disrobe, Karen became frightened and screamed. Fortunately, the neighbor heard the commotion and hammered on the door.

Her arrival put an end to what could have turned into a traumatic experience for Karen. She might even have been raped had she continued to protest. The older boy was sex-wise. He'd planned the visit when he heard Karen brag to a friend that her mother trusted her to be alone overnight.

Karen's experience points up the need to recognize the difference between leaving a child alone for short periods and being absent for extended periods of time. Also, it emphasizes the fact that, if a single child is left alone, he or she is much more isolated than if a brother or sister is present. Walt and Bill had each other for company. But even then, their mother didn't leave them alone for long. Karen was all alone. At thirteen, she didn't have the judgment or maturity to assume that responsibility.

How Secure Do Your Children Feel?

Karen was uneasy about being alone. So was Walt. But Walt was willing to talk about his fears. It's very important that your children be able to communicate easily with you, especially if you're planning to discontinue having a baby-sitter and expect to leave your children (or child) alone when you go out. Whether your absence will be short or long, whether you'll be gone during the day, the evening, or overnight, you need to have a good talk with your children about your plans so you know their feelings and don't ask of them what they can't handle in maturity and responsibility.

Greg was planning a date with a new friend. He assumed that Kirk, his twelve-year-old son, was capable of staying alone until he returned home. But before he confirmed his date, he sat down with Kirk and told him of his plans.

"I'd like to leave you alone, if you think you can manage. Mrs. Jones isn't available, and I know you don't like Brad to be your sitter. What do you think about it?"

Kirk hesitated before speaking up. "I dunno, Dad." He hesitated again. "Whenever I'm alone in the house, it's creepy. I know there aren't any real ghosts, but . . ."

Greg knew about Kirk's preoccupation with ghosts. It had started with a spread in the Sunday paper some weeks earlier, and then a television movie he'd seen at a friend's house had added to his fears.

"I know how that is, Kirk." He kept his voice low. "We've talked about that before. Ghosts aren't real. But it's hard to get over a fear like that. Is it any better than it was?" He'd been working with Kirk to overcome that fright. "Maybe, tomorrow, we can talk more about any other worries you have."

"Yeah." Kirk was shamefaced. "When I'm alone . . ."

"Okay. I won't ask you to stay alone then. Maybe you'd like to spend the night at Jack's."

Kirk felt very safe with his father or he wouldn't have dared to admit his fear. Greg's response to his son's admission reinforced the child's trust. He knew his dad wouldn't make fun of him because he was afraid. He also knew Greg would never force him to do something that terrified him.

Greg's concern for his son was also shown by his interest in talking more about his fears and worries. A child of twelve who is afraid of ghosts may also be dealing with other underlying fears.

Ghosts and goblins are very real to children. They hear the creaking sounds that occur in an empty house, and they visualize monsters lurking behind every door. But these aren't the only fears a child may have. Whatever frightens a child when alone is very real—even though common sense says it isn't. Logic provides no comfort. Take your child's fears seriously. Often, you can help overcome them. But only if you accept them as real fears.

Only you can answer the question as to when your child can be left alone. A child who is insecure or immature can't be expected to exhibit independence and self-sufficiency. But if your child is emotionally secure, is accustomed to making good decisions, and has shown an ability to cope when alone, it's far more possible that you might dispense with the services of a baby-sitter.

How Emotionally Mature Are Your Children?

There is one possible difficulty. Some children just grow up faster than others. A child who has already shown emotional maturity may appear to do very well alone. There is a problem, however, if your child seems *too* mature. Often, maturity beyond one's years is the pseudomaturity of a child who's caught in a role-reversal situation. Such a "little grown-up" may be hiding fears that are too overwhelming to express.

If you have more than one child, and most of them show emotional maturity, they may get along well even if the eldest is not much over twelve. However, it is very easy to allow your desire for them to be capable of staying alone overnight to influence your assessment of their abilities.

If you believe your children are emotionally mature enough to be left alone, you might test your conclusion over a period of time before you stay away from them for an entire evening. Try leaving them alone during the day while you go shopping. Make your absences brief at first, gradually lengthening the time you're away. Then, when you do decide on an evening out, you'll have good reason to believe that your children will be safe alone. Even then, however, I suggest you provide them with the phone number of a nearby adult they can call in an emergency.

A word of warning here. Some parents tell their children, "You can call Mrs. Jones if you need help," without first checking with Mrs. Jones to see if she's agreeable to the arrangement. This isn't facing up to parental responsibility or responsibilities to your neighbors as well. Be sure—if you tell your child to call a specific adult—that you've first checked to make certain that person will be home and is willing to be available to your child.

How Safe Are Their Surroundings?

Television cop shows periodically deal with children who, left alone at night, get into trouble. One story was about a five-year-old boy who was shot when a policeman, investigating the report of a prowler, fired at a shadowy figure crouching behind a chair in the dark and holding a gun. The gun was merely a toy the boy had been playing with. As a result, the authorities considered arraigning the mother for child neglect.

As is so often true with these stories, the child lived in a tenement. Crime was common in the neighborhood. Police were alert to danger when on patrol, and adults were quick to call in about prowlers or break-ins. In such a high-crime neighborhood, a small child alone is in more danger than the same child would be in a more stable area.

No five-year-old should ever be left alone. But if you're in a safe neighborhood, you may dare to leave your older children alone far sooner than if you live in a high-crime area. Generally, you may expect your decision to be sound if you've considered all the factors discussed in this chapter. However, even the safe suburbs have danger spots. A swimming pool, a flight of steep steps, a balcony, a poor electrical connection, or inadequate locks and safety arrangements may pose dangers to a child left alone.

Dorothy, two years old, fell into the family's unfenced pool while her mother was shopping. Her sixteen-year-old sister, Lisa, was on the phone at the time and came out to see her baby sister struggling feebly in the water. Neighbors rushed to the child's aid and called paramedics.

This particular accident was the result of an unfenced pool and the older daughter's lack of awareness of the danger it presented. Unfortunately, when a parent hasn't shielded all dangerous areas, she or he can hardly be surprised if children don't recognize them as hazardous.

Is a Concerned Adult Available?

This matter has been mentioned before. Dorothy's near-drowning and countless similar incidents emphasize the need for some responsible adult to be nearby, even if older children are left alone or in charge of their younger siblings. Lisa might not have thought of the paramedics in time to save Dorothy. Often, in an emergency, adult judgment can make the difference between safety and disaster. There is a large element of danger in entrusting a young child to an older sibling without first determining that the older child is capable of assuming the responsibility.

Does a Baby-sitter Just Sit?

It's easy to think of the time your children spend with a baby-sitter as nonproductive time. But for the children, this isn't so. Especially if you are gone during the day, your child is alert and in need of guidance.

Children are social beings. They constantly react to their environments, learning from the people around them. A sitter who actually does just sit, especially in front of the television set, will not only be teaching your child that this is acceptable daytime behavior but will be neglecting your child's physical needs as well.

Infants require both physical care and mental stimulation. They accumulate knowledge by interacting with the people who care for them. They can't learn in this way if they're left to play alone for hours on end. Make sure your sitter will enrich your baby's mind with interesting play and much attention. Provide toys that build perception and help develop an infant's coordination. Urge your sitter to talk to your infant and to take walks that will provide a change of scenery.

Older children also require mental stimulation and social activities. They need to engage in group play such as that provided by the Cub Scouts or Brownies. And when they're alone with a sitter, they need guidance, too, just as they would were they in their parent's care.

As children approach the ages of nine to twelve, their social lives expand. Your sitter should be in a position to bring them to Little League, to Girl or Boy Scout meetings, to the Y, or to any available school activities. Peer relationships are very important to preadolescents.

Alice worked during the day and arranged for her youngsters, Doris and David, to stay with Katherine, a neighbor who also had children. Katherine ferried David and Doris about as if they were her own. As a result, they were able to participate in many activities that would have been denied them had they been in the care of a baby-sitter who wasn't concerned with their growth.

By putting her children in the care of a neighbor who was herself a parent, Alice was taking into consideration their developmental needs. When she and her neighbor sat down with the children and planned the week in advance, she was adding to her son's and daughter's growth. They began to feel they had some mastery over their lives.

Especially on those occasions when Alice dated, this preplanning was invaluable. Because she took the trouble to help her children do something interesting while she was on a date, she demonstrated to them that even when she was out with another adult she was concerned with their happiness.

When this sort of planning is part of parent-child cooperation, children often make an easy transition from dependency to independence. They gradually learn to assume responsibility for their own lives. There isn't any sudden change to which you and they must adjust. This kind of growth can come about only when constant attention is paid to their developmental needs.

If the only sitter available to you is one who seems to prefer just to sit, you will need to enlist your children and the sitter to create situations that will be stimulating to their growth. Arrange for your children and their sitter to go to a museum or the zoo. Provide them with games they can play together that will increase their knowledge. Remember, you don't have to abdicate your responsibility for their mental development just because you aren't around all day, or because you take an evening out.

Be Accessible

If you will be leaving your children alone while you work, or if you plan a night out, balance your absence with some special time you spend just with them. Other adults—such as teachers, neighbors, and friends—can give your children a great deal of help as they grow, but no one can take your place. You are, after all, the source of your children's security. They need to know you care for them and are concerned for their development. And they will weather your absences far better if they know that, when you are around, you're ready to consider their needs.

Especially if you're out on a date, your children need to know how to get in touch with you. They'll feel safer, knowing you're available, and you'll feel more at ease knowing that in an emergency you can be reached. This should always be in addition to having a nearby adult who can be called. If an emergency arises, quick action may be necessary.

Alternative Arrangements

Some single parents, having no neighbors or relatives nearby to furnish backup care for their children, seek other arrangements that will provide a supportive environment. If money is not a problem, a live-in housekeeper to act as a surrogate parent may be ideal. Unfortunately, money isn't always available for such a convenience.

A good alternative is to engage a college student to care for your children in your absence in exchange for free room and board. If you can find someone who is mature enough to take the job seriously, this can be a very satisfactory arrangement. In effect, it provides your children with a surrogate older sibling.

Networking: The Buddy System

If you find neither of the above suggestions appropriate to your situation, you might try to establish a buddy system in your neighborhood. This can also be described as *networking*. Occasionally, such a system develops accidentally, in a rather haphazard manner. But it can be approached systematically, and, if it is, its efficiency will be greatly enhanced.

I suggest you take paper and pen and begin organizing your approach to developing such a network. Start by listing any single parents who live nearby. Add any couples you know who are both working and have children. At the bottom of your list, write the names of organizations that might be tapped for ideas and assistance. These will include Parents Without Partners, Fathers' Rights of America, your children's school, and any church or social groups of parents to which you might have access.

Now list the goals you hope to achieve through your networking. The following items may serve as the basis for further ideas.

Networking will:

1. give every participating parent some extra time alone, including some evening hours free from child care;
2. increase the growth-giving activities in which your children will participate;
3. expand your children's experiences while maintaining or increasing their feeling of security.

Obviously, the potential for networking is great. What's important is that you find people who live near you who share your need for intermittent child care. To start the process working, all you need do is go out and talk to your neighbors. Bring your list of ideas to your single-parent friends and to those couples you feel might profit by cooperating with you. Let them add their own ideas. Keep the group small enough so it remains manageable, and so the children involved will be able to reach any one of the participating adults if necessary.

It's probable that everyone will already have made arrangements for child care during working hours. But many are sure to be in need of time they can spend alone with a date or a lover. Even if you have married couples in your network, they'll have the same desire for occasional time together without their children. You might work out an arrangement that gives each of you a weekend free once a month. Or, if a full weekend away from your children would upset them, you could make it one day—or even just overnight, or one evening.

In considering potential members for a network, observe the quality of care these other parents give their own youngsters. You don't want someone in the group who lacks the necessary concern for children. If you exert a reasonable amount of caution in choosing those people with whom you network, you can be rewarded with more time to yourself and the expectation that your children will be well cared for during any periods they're left with others of the group. Your children will benefit, too. They'll have a broader vision of the world. They'll increase the number of their friends and learn about facets of life you might not have recognized as being important to them.

But try to keep a good balance in the arrangements. While taking into account the quality of child care donated by each person, try to make sure each participant contributes about the same amount of time and effort. This avoids disagreements.

One other alternative exists: that of two single parents with children sharing a home and the responsibilities of child care. However, explicit conditions need to be written down and agreed upon before such an arrangement takes place. Each parent should know when free time would be available—what nights each could have off. The same balances needed in networking exist here.

Either of these arrangements has the same big advantage. Both the child whose single parent is a member of a network and the child whose mother or father has decided to share a home with another single parent have the certainty that they will never become unsupervised, vulnerable children, whom society has labeled "latch-key kids."

Baby-sitter Checklist

Below is a checklist you might find useful when looking for someone to sit with your children. Some points apply mainly to situations lasting overnight or longer. Others deal principally with short-term sitters.

1. How old are my children? How mature are they?
2. Do they feel safe with this person?
3. Do they like this person?
4. Is this person emotionally mature?
5. Does this person demonstrate good judgment?
6. If the sitter is an adolescent, is there a concerned adult or an older sibling of my children available, if needed, for consultation or assistance?
7. If no other adult is available, can I be reached by phone in an emergency?
8. Are the physical surroundings in and around my home safe?
9. If the sitter will be needed for a short time during the day:
   Have I provided a list of activities my children are involved in and has transportation to those events been arranged?
   If this includes a mealtime, does the sitter know any diet preferences of mine that may apply?
10. If I will be absent for one evening:
    Is the sitter aware of my bedtime rules?
    If my children are accustomed to bedtime stories, are there books available to be read to them?
    Does the sitter know my preferences regarding any personal visitors while baby-sitting? (Most parents prefer that sitters not have any friends over, but if this is not clarified, a young sitter may use your home as the locale for a party or as a private place to entertain a girl- or boyfriend.)
11. If the sitter will be needed overnight or longer:

Have I hired someone who is dependable and capable of managing children for a long period of time?
Have I provided a list of the many activities my children engage in, and prepared transport for them to the places they are to go?
Have I provided my sitter with a comfortable sleeping place and access to money for food and emergencies?

12. Is the sitter capable of providing my children with opportunities for growth?
    Have I talked with the sitter long enough to know we share the same or a similar philosophy regarding child development?
    Have I made my expectations in this area clear?
    Does the sitter know my pediatrician's phone number? That of the police? The paramedics? The concerned adult who lives nearby?

13. Are there any legal aspects to consider before I leave?
    If my child falls ill, does the sitter have the necessary power of attorney needed to authorize medical treatment? If not, does the sitter know who does?
    Has the sitter been informed of any special medical problems my children have?

Add any unusual items that might pertain specifically to your children and then use this list whenever you engage a new sitter. You'll feel safer if you've answered some of these questions in advance, and your sitter will be more confident and better able to deal with emergencies.

9 *Don't Leave It All to Chance*

Underprotection of Children

Children, as they grow up, are faced with a variety of situations and influences that can, at the very least, puzzle and confuse them—or, at worst, traumatize and psychologically injure them, sometimes severely. Even in the safest and most affluent neighborhoods, there may be dangers ranging from an unfenced pool to a cruising child molester. And the home—any home—has been found to be the location of a majority of severe accidents.

Most parents and relatives try to protect children from physical harm and abuse originating outside the home—try to keep them, for example, from playing in dangerous areas, fighting with other children, carelessly crossing streets, going anywhere with a stranger, or, in the case of older children, getting involved with alcohol or other drugs. Similarly, parents usually do their best to guard children from physical dangers within or around the home—dangers like playing with matches, getting locked in an abandoned refrigerator, pulling scalding liquid down from a stove, or ingesting some harmful household substance.

Even in the area of psychological or emotional hurt, parents are generally very protective of their offspring outside the home environment. They'll go to school and confront a teacher they believe has somehow treated their children unfairly or unkindly. Or they may do battle with neighbors or their neighbors' children for the same reasons.

However, within the family itself, many children are under-protected and abused, often unknowingly, by the very parents and grown-up relatives who are supposedly there to guard them from harm. Unfortunately, children living with only one parent are even more likely to be emotionally and psychologically damaged. Single parents have greater vulnerabilities and weaknesses because of the heavy burdens they must carry alone. As a result, there are certain special dangers that arise, or normal ones that are exaggerated, solely because only one parent is present.

Susan was such a parent. Because of the dependency she had had on her ex-husband, she now overcompensated by being completely intolerant of any need to be taken care of. She displayed excessive independence and refused all assistance, including emotional support. She was equally unable to accept dependence in her children, a boy, ten, and a girl, thirteen. She wanted them to grow up to be self-sufficient. But her attitude was causing them much psychological harm. In an attempt to prevent her children from making the same mistakes she had made when she married a man who mistreated her and then stayed with him because of her fear of being on her own, she overreacted and denied them the right to experience normal childhood dependency.

A single parent may insist on a pattern of behavior for a child that will, it's hoped, help the child avoid the mistakes and pitfalls the parent has encountered. Usually such insistence is detrimental. Or a parent will make a child the scapegoat for his or her own feelings of guilt or inadequacy. Or create a role reversal and look to a child for the solace and comfort no longer provided by an adult spouse. Or make a child the target of a secret exercise of power, as compensation for the lack of control he or she had over the mate that left. Or subject a child to extremes of stimulation by behaving in a seductive manner, or even indulging in incest.

Why do these things happen? The reasons are many and varied. Usually adults behave in some of these ways because this is how they were treated by their parents.

Some single parents have had inadequate role models to guide them. They're simply confused and bewildered when faced with situations for which they're completely unprepared. They don't know what to do, so they often do the wrong thing. Others have the basic knowledge but are just overwhelmed with their own problems and are unable to muster the strength to carry out what they know needs to be done in the best interests of their children.

Sadly, there are single parents who have such poor self-images that they subject both themselves and their children to harmful situations and stimuli. Feeling frightened and lonely and unworthy of another adult relationship, they often turn, usually without conscious thought, to their own children to meet some of their adult needs.

For others, there simply aren't enough material resources to pay for certain normal services like baby-sitters and day-care centers, and so, because it seems as if there are no other options, they place unusual and unnecessary burdens and responsibilities on their children. With some single parents, underprotection occurs because they are angry and bitter toward an ex-spouse. Consciously or unconsciously, such hostility winds up being directed at the nearest available target—the innocent child.

Furthermore, children may suffer because of a single parent's need to exercise power. A parent may have had no opportunity to do so with a former spouse, so the outward manifestation of this need to feel important and in control falls on the children. This wielding of power by an adult over children is a condition generally considered normal by society, and therefore tolerated. A child is regarded, more or less, as a parent's personal property; and while there are many restrictions on an adult's physical abuse of a child, there are few, if any, regarding what parents may do to a young person's emotions and spirit. The excessive use of power by adults over youngsters is likely to continue as a normal aspect of our culture until we become more aware of the suffering and anguish it brings to our children—who will, in turn, pay it all back to their own offspring in the future.

Regardless of the cause, both single parents and their children suffer when underprotection and the resulting abuses occur. Children suffer because they're unable to care for and protect themselves and can consequently feel overwhelmed, and parents suffer because they're left feeling guilty and inadequate. Examining some of these factors in more detail may be helpful in understanding and changing the patterns.

When Guilt Makes You Blind

People who feel too guilty about something they've done, or not done, usually try to avoid thinking about it, sometimes denying the very existence of facts, feelings, or insights that might make the pain of guilt even stronger. It upsets them greatly to recall the circumstances of their wrongdoing.

When a person in this situation is a single parent with guilty feelings about the breakup of a marriage and home, and his or her children are in some kind of distress for any reason related to the breakup, the parent often can't or won't face the problem at hand because of an unwillingness to admit it exists. To confront the issue might increase the feeling of guilt and the subsequent pain.

It's ironic that a parent who may feel the most guilty also contributes the most to children's problems because of a need not to see, recognize, or face the youngsters' distress. Such a parent may distort reality in order to deny the guilty pain that would result if the children were perceived accurately. The situation then becomes a vicious cycle. The parent is unable to comfort or reassure the children adequately, which only heightens the problem.

It isn't easy to discover this problem in yourself. But you may be aware that your child is in trouble at school. You may have a good friend who'll level with you if you ask for an opinion of your child's emotional health. Or your pastor or rabbi or some other spiritual counselor may tell you that your child seems to be overwhelmed by a heavy burden of guilt.

The problem, then, is to discover the origin of that guilt. It may be related to your own reactions to certain aspects of your life. If you recall, in chapter 1, I emphasized that children often reflect the feelings of the adults around them. You may not yet have reconciled your attitudes toward sex to the reality of your life. You may be using your child as a surrogate spouse. Or you may be making demands that force your child to assume the parental role. If you suspect any of these, or if you just can't put a finger on the cause of your child's heavy guilt feelings, I advise you to take your child and see a therapist. These are problems you can't easily solve without skilled help.

When There's No One Else to Blame

It is, unfortunately, quite common for people, including parents, to deny responsibility for any unpleasant situation they become involved in. They need to see a problem as existing outside themselves and then to find someone or something on which to focus the blame.

Do you find yourself blaming a child for your inability to establish a good relationship with a lover? It could be that you're putting onto your son or daughter the responsibility for your own shortcomings. A child is so available—and so defenseless. If you find that you're accusing your child of interfering with your dates, or of chasing dates away by being too dependent, look first at yourself.

In single-parent families, children are often assigned the role of scapegoat. The burden of guilt (as mentioned above) being already too heavy for some parents to bear, whenever there's a problem, large or small, they tend to project the blame in the nearest convenient direction—at the children.

In order to halt this unjustified abuse of children, to stop making scapegoats of them, it's necessary for parents to assume responsibility for their own behavior. If this should come about as a result of therapy, a parent's personal problems—which had been masked by projecting blame onto a child—often emerge and the real issues can then be confronted.

It may be that a particular parent harbors unresolved rage toward a former spouse. If a child of the same sex as the spouse also possesses similar characteristics or interests, the single parent may find it irresistible to cast the child in the role of the former spouse and heap feelings of guilt, frustration, and rage on his or her head.

Try now to observe your relationship with your children. Is there one child who is bearing the brunt of your anger? One child who always seems to be in the wrong? If there is, you might do well to ask a friend if you seem to treat that child differently from the others. Does that child resemble your ex-spouse to a greater extent than any of the other children?

In many such cases, just recognizing this problem serves to diminish it—or eliminate it altogether. But if you find that you aren't changing, even after becoming aware of what's happening, you may find the best solution is to seek professional counseling. Then, if it still seems necessary, let the child live with your ex-spouse, where the resemblance will not be detrimental. The habit of avoiding blame by pushing it onto another is insidious. There always appear to be good reasons to sidestep the responsibility for what's happening. And that makes it difficult for any person to change without help.

You're Such a Comfort

There was a time in our history when, if a father died, his eldest son was told, "You are the man in the family now." And the son did, in fact, have to assume a man's role. In those days, small boys became wage earners so their mothers could stay home as was the custom.

Today, we know that such a situation is bad for both mother and child. It's appropriate for children to do their share of chores and to take charge of their own personal routines (bathing, being on time for school, and so on), but it's not appropriate for any child to become a full partner with an adult parent, sharing in money decisions and monitoring younger children in the family.

When this happens, generation boundaries become fuzzy for both parent and children. The eldest child withdraws emotional energy from appropriate developmental tasks necessary to growing up, and becomes overwhelmed by the gratification derived from being special and equal to a loved adult. And the attitudes that develop, both in the child and in the single parent, can wreak havoc when that single parent begins to date.

Ted's wife, Joanne, had never been an emotionally stable person. She was always joining some cult or other. She left home to "find herself" when her daughter, Monica, was ten years old. Ted was devastated, but he refused to face his feeling of rejection and his belief that no woman was reliable. Instead, he concentrated on the tasks that needed doing. He turned to Monica for companionship and support, secure in the knowledge that she wouldn't leave him.

With her mother gone, it was quite natural for Monica to assume full control of the household. She made her father's breakfast and packed his lunch, just as she'd often done when her mother forgot her "duties." She dropped her little brother, Greg, at a neighbor's house on her way to school. When she came home, she prepared dinner for herself and her father. Then, together, they picked up Greg.

Everything went well until Ted finally overcame his feeling of being abandoned. He began to desire adult female companionship—and sex. The first time Ted brought a date home, he expected no difficulty. Monica and Greg were, supposedly, asleep. But shortly after he climbed into bed with his date, Monica began to moan. He stopped what he was doing and went to her side. For that evening, he had no interest in sex. His daughter's welfare came first. But the episode was repeated the next time he brought someone home, even though Monica had been well in the interim.

The pattern continued each time he had a date. He became

very angry with Monica, scolding her when the incident was repeated. When it still continued, he solved the problem by taking his dates to a motel. He wouldn't admit to himself that he had a responsibility for his daughter's behavior.

The bouts with upset stomach that Monica experienced when her father brought a date home were cries for help. Monica had been used by her father during the period when he was hesitant to let any woman close for fear she, like his ex-wife, would desert him. During that time, Monica was substitute mother to little Greg and housewife and companion to her father. However, he at no time took sexual advantage of her.

As Ted recovered from his wife's desertion and felt better about himself, he began to experience a normal male need for adult female companionship. But he made no attempt to help Monica understand this change in him. Instead, he refused to admit that he'd ever taken advantage of his daughter. He felt that all she'd done was just her job.

Monica felt she was being pushed aside. She was afraid of being left alone when he finally chose a replacement for her. She was also jealous of the women he saw, since they were, in her eyes, rivals for his loyalty and affection. She saw his behavior as unpredictable. When there wasn't an adult woman available, he returned to the warm comradeship they shared after her mother's departure. But when he got a date he left her alone again, with little concern for her feelings.

Ted had a difficult time seeing that he had failed to protect his daughter. But he did finally begin to understand that he had used her as a shield to keep women away after his wife left. During that period, Monica's availability had been a barrier behind which he hid to avoid another close relationship. Only when he saw what he'd been doing to Monica was he able to help her adjust to his new attitude toward life and women.

Boys can take over this adult role, too, with similar results. Eric, twelve, the oldest of three boys, assumed the triple role of big brother, daddy, and husband after his parents were divorced. He was intrusive and bossy with his two younger brothers when he took care of them while his mother, new in the role of real estate agent, was out showing a house to a client. But he did keep the younger two in line, and his mother, Sally, frequently praised him, saying that he was the man of the house.

Because she wasn't accustomed to making decisions for herself, Sally often consulted Eric about financial matters. She shared her triumph with him when she made a sale and came to him for comfort when she didn't. She needed constant reassurance from him that she was doing a good job.

In a drawing of the family made by Don, the youngest boy, Eric and his mother were pictured together in the upstairs of the house while the two younger boys were downstairs. Even in his brother's eyes, Eric was the man in the family.

On a more personal level, Eric had ceased to function as a child. Like Monica, he had assumed the role of equal adult in the family. In school, he was too good, too much in alliance with his teachers. Fortunately, his teachers were able to recognize his behavior as a sign of trouble.

It was difficult for Sally to see that she was giving Eric more responsibility and authority than was appropriate for a child of his age. Like Ted, she had used her child for comfort without considering what that did to him. But when she gradually assumed her proper authority, being careful to help Eric recognize the shift as beneficial to them both, Eric once more began to behave in a manner normal for a boy of his years.

Had Sally started to date before the role confusion was cleared up, she'd have run into severe problems with Eric, who, like Monica, would have been jealous of another person taking his place.

This is a good time for you to list those areas in which you've allowed your eldest (or only) child to take your absent spouse's place in the family. This might be the most difficult list you'll make, especially since much of this transfer can occur without conscious awareness. Take time now to look at the actual tasks your children are performing and the responsibilities they have assumed. If your eldest child displays an intense sense of responsibility for the household and for any other children you may have, you can be almost certain that you've unfairly turned that child into an equal partner.

Little Parents

Sometimes a child does more than assume the equal partnership position vacated by an absent spouse. If an overly dependent woman is a single parent, and if she's unwilling to recognize that she's the one who must provide security for her family, she may force the role of surrogate parent onto her child—she, in effect, becoming the child in the family and her eldest becoming the parent.

An immature father, too, can indulge in role reversal and put a child into the position of parent if he feels unequal to the task. The sex of either parent or child is not the issue. The problem is one of dependence and of an unwillingness on the part of the remaining parent to accept a role that has been called for by the departure of a spouse.

It's rather remarkable to see children as young as four or five attempting to reassure and comfort their parents—at the same time masking their own needs for fear of overwhelming an adult from whom they're receiving messages of helplessness. Most children in such parental roles perceive, accurately, that they cannot make it on their own without adult help, so they're placed in the unenviable position of having to console and prop up an insecure parent.

Marilyn had never had to deal with the mundane affairs of life, such as earning money or handling bank accounts, until her husband, Rollin, deserted her. She immediately got work but had trouble keeping a job as a secretary, since she often used her child as an excuse for needing time off. Eventually, she took a part-time job at a restaurant, where she barely managed to earn enough to keep herself and Ann, her nine-year-old daughter, fed, housed, and clothed.

Ann seemed to rise to the occasion. Tiny as she was, she filled in all the empty places for Marilyn, especially during that first difficult year. She slept with her mother, cuddling and comforting her when she cried.

But the effect on the child was devastating. Ann's innate awareness that she couldn't survive alone made it essential that she bolster her mother and keep her functioning. She could no longer function as a child.

When they came to me for counseling, I noted that Marilyn was spontaneous in her speech, reacting emotionally to what she said and to what was said to her. Little Ann was just the opposite. She sat quietly beside her mother until Marilyn began to cry. Then she rose, walked to her mother's side, and comforted her.

The problem they brought to me dealt with parental dating. When Marilyn began to meet men, Ann resisted this change in her life. Marilyn assumed Ann was jealous. But it became clear as we talked that Ann wasn't as resentful of the intrusion of a new person into her family as she was fearful that this new man might desert her mother, too. If that happened, she'd have to endure the comforting period all over again. She was also afraid of developing a relationship with a new daddy who might leave her as her real father had.

Marilyn had difficulty seeing what she'd done to her daughter. She resented Ann's meddling in her new romance, refusing to recognize that she'd been taking advantage of the child. Yet Marilyn's behavior was at the root of the whole problem. If she'd perceived her own strengths more accurately, she'd have been able to accept *her* role as parent instead of forcing it on her child.

If this is your problem, you, like Marilyn, may have difficulty facing it. Again, the best way to see what's happening is to look at your children. If your eldest child is too much an adult and has taken on the role of comforter, trying to protect you from further hurt, then you need to recognize this and prepare to make the necessary changes. You may need outside help, however. This is not an easy situation to face or to alter.

More than They Want to Know

Children cannot handle and should not be exposed to adult conduct they don't understand. Certain behavior that adults take for granted has other meanings for children and can be overly exciting, confusing, or even frightening. Being exposed to blatant displays of a parent's sexuality, for example, can result in overwhelming stimulation for a child.

It sometimes happens, unfortunately, that parents act seductively toward their children. Occasionally, this occurs with intentional awareness, but more often it happens through unconscious or misguided behavior. And it can take place in families of all income and social levels that otherwise appear to be respectably conventional.

The seductive activity can range from subtle caresses to actual incest. It may include the fondling of a child's genitalia in changing or bathing; permitting a child of the opposite sex to sleep in the parent's bed, with accidental and not-so-accidental touching and caressing (even, in some cases, genital stimulation); and a mother's allowing older children to fondle her breasts.

Some parents display their own nude or partially nude bodies when their children are around as a form of exhibitionism. They behave seductively when they are partially undressed. One mother, who was quite inhibited about her sexuality with adult men, was in the habit of being nude in the presence of her two sons, aged eight and eleven. She permitted them free access to her bedroom or bath, whether she was clothed or not, and she posed seductively when they were around. Such experiences can be stimulating to a child and can arouse sexual excitement. This may frustrate a child and lead to intense anger, which a child does not know how to handle. Some children subjected to this exhibitionism become physically aggressive and abusive. Others regress to the greater safety of earlier, more childish behavior patterns.

And there are parents with a similar disregard for the emotional welfare of their children who—in a misguided effort to counteract the repressive sexual upbringing they had and to be more modern in their attitudes and behavior—allow excessive nudity for all members of the family in any part of the house. No privacy is provided for anyone—anywhere.

It is, admittedly, important for children that parents be comfortable with their own bodies and not be overly concerned if a child and parent see each other undressed. On the other hand, it's not good for children when parents make it a point to exhibit themselves simply for their own gratification. This is especially true if the children are at a developmental stage where they're dealing with Oedipal issues (ages three to six or in the teens), during which period they are even more vulnerable to a parent's seductive behavior.

Of course, seductive behavior by parents can and does occur in intact families as well as in those headed by a single adult, even where there is an appropriate sexual outlet. Therefore, it becomes even more important for single parents to be alert to their own behavior with their children so as not to turn to them for surrogate love in any form. Because of the danger of doing just that, there's even more reason for single parents to seek out and secure relationships and gratification with other adults.

When dealing with any emotional issue, self-awareness is difficult. Yet, you need to consider your relationship with your children in as clear a light as possible. Do you let them sleep with you? If you're nude before them, what are you thinking at the time?

Like some of the other issues in this chapter, this is a difficult one to recognize. It can be done, though. If you feel any uncertainty as to your motives, and you are sharing your bed with a child or possibly asking your child to reassure you regarding your own sexuality, you might do well to at least visit a therapist for an evaluation. If you need help, that's where you can get it.

Incest: The Ultimate Taboo

Once considered too shameful, and rare, even to discuss, incest is now openly acknowledged to be a growing problem in our society. It's estimated by some professionals in the field that incest

—usually defined as sexually arousing physical contact between family members who are not married—occurs in one out of every one hundred families. This is an incidence ten thousand times greater than expert estimates of only twenty or so years ago.

While incest is considered a crime, until recently it was seldom brought to the attention of police or other authorities. But even when it's publicly exposed, the offender (about 90 percent of the time a father or father figure) is rarely convicted, since the evidence for prosecution is slim at best. There's usually little physical sign of abuse, no eyewitness, and doubt on the part of jurors as to the credibility of the child involved.

If an adult male initiates the incestuous relationship, and he's discovered, prosecuted, and convicted, punishment really falls on all members of the family. The offender may go to jail for a time, but the others are made to suffer as well. Most, if not all, of the family's income stops. The daughter who's been part of the relationship may be openly or subtly blamed by the mother for causing the problem, which can easily lead to her becoming bitter, guilt-ridden, and sometimes self-destructive. Even if the mother truly recognizes her daughter as a victim, the girl can still feel confused, guilty, and self-reproachful. This is one situation where everyone loses.

Incest is usually thought to mean just illicit sexual intercourse between family members (usually an adult and a child), and in many cases that's true. However, even when instances of incest are brought to light, authorities have discovered that it has almost always been preceded by a series of less explicit actions.

A father who has grown up in a family where even the discussion of sex is frowned upon, if not actually forbidden, may be so inhibited in his marital relations that the first time he dares to look closely at a vagina, play with it, or become aroused by it is when he's giving a bath to his small daughter. Or a mother who, as a small girl, is shocked by the sight of an erect penis may develop an unreasonable dread of the male organ. But she may be able to allay her fears and attain a normal attitude toward the male genitals by examining and massaging her small son's penis.

The resulting erection is not threatening to her and is undoubtedly pleasurable to the child. This kind of sexual exploration of children by their parents may sometimes continue into puberty, occasionally resulting in sexual intercourse between parent and child.

One case that came to my attention provides an excellent example of how subtle this transition may be. Parent and child may be trapped in a sexual relationship that the parent did not deliberately choose but rather drifted into.

When Matthew's wife died at an early age, he was left to raise their two-year-old daughter by himself. After a time of sadness and mourning he began to date again, but he never seemed to find another woman to take his wife's place. He rationalized that none of them would be a good substitute mother for little Linda. He had learned to enjoy taking care of Linda in every way. He took great pleasure in bathing her, dressing her, and consoling her when she was sad. If the suggestion had been made then that he might someday sexually molest his child, he'd have been shocked. And had he been told that some of the things he did, like carefully washing the child's genitals after she used the toilet, could be the first step toward incest, he'd have been outraged.

In fact, it was this wish to comfort her and dry her tears that prompted him to let her crawl into his bed with him one night after she had a bad dream. She was only three at the time, so he felt there could be no harm in it. She cuddled against his warm body and was soon asleep.

Linda obviously enjoyed sleeping with him, and he found it pleasant, too, so the practice continued. At first there was only some accidental physical contact between them, which he found strangely stimulating. But after some months, he found himself deliberately touching and fondling the little girl during their time together in bed.

Either because of her obvious inability to deny her father anything or her own enjoyment of the caressing, or both, Linda made no protest. Even then, however, Matthew would have been angered had he been accused of seducing his daughter. He convinced himself that he cuddled and fondled her only to give her comfort. He would not acknowledge that his actions comforted and excited him.

He did, however, impose a common restriction on their relationship. From the start, he made Linda promise she'd never talk about it to anyone. Had he been more aware, he'd have known that this secrecy in itself was harmful to his daughter, because it implied that something bad was happening. She was a quiet child, withdrawn and overly compliant. In school, she was often teacher's pet, since she never got into any trouble and always did as she was told.

When Matthew took the step from fondling to oral contact, it seemed only an accident that wouldn't happen again. Still, he felt guilty and ashamed, repeating his injunction that what happened must remain a secret between them.

This time, however, he added that if anyone knew he'd have to go away. Linda was ten at that time. She was aware of the unnatural relationship between herself and her father, but the knowledge only increased her timidity. She knew her father could go to prison if he was exposed, and she was terrified at the thought of facing life alone. Yet, her guilt about letting the relationship continue made her even more withdrawn and depressed. Her school performance deteriorated.

The relationship did continue. The oral contact was repeated periodically, especially when Matthew had had too much to drink. He was, in fact, drinking more all the time, and so the occurrences became more frequent. As Linda entered her teens, she wanted to participate in some school functions and be with her peers, but Matthew was very restrictive of her activities. He refused permission for her to attend parties and, especially, to date. Linda began to sneak out to be with her friends.

Then, one day when her father had been drinking especially heavily, he forced her to have intercourse. When it was repeated, Linda took a few belongings, a little money, and ran away from home. Several months later she was picked up for prostitution in a distant city. After being returned to her father, she ran away again. It was only after a suicide attempt brought her to the attention of a city welfare department that she began to receive counseling and therapy. Linda is presently adjusting well but may carry the scars of her early sexual abuse for life.

Oddly, and unfortunately, there's another aspect to the incestuous relationship that is seldom considered. It's the harm that may come simply from the *fear* of incest. A single father may find himself extremely reluctant to show anything but the most cursory display of affection for a female child because of his fear of falling into the "incest trap." He fears that hugging or kissing his little girl may lead to incest, or may, at least, give the wrong impression to observers.

Such a man's understandable reaction is to be less affectionate, less physical with his daughter—who may then interpret the apparent aloofness on the part of her father as a sign of dislike or rejection. In this situation, both father and daughter lose. The father will always suffer the feeling that he hasn't been a good parent, and the daughter will probably never understand why her father showed so little love for her.

The area of incest is very sensitive, and most difficult to assess. If you have any feeling that what you're doing with your child may have incestuous overtones, you need to seek help. For your own sake as well as for the welfare of your child, you should not delay. Fortunately, children are resilient. If damaging behavior stops, and the child still feels supported by loving, caring adults, even the horror of incest can be overcome.

If Your Lover Harms Your Child

Many a single mother restricts her own social-sexual life out of fear that she may unwittingly begin a relationship with a man who turns out to be a child molester. It's a fear that certainly has some foundation. Sexual offenders who are attracted to small children may seek out mothers of little ones in order to get close to those children.

This fear creates a problem for any single mother. She wants to trust and be close to her lover, but she also wants her children to be safe. There are some precautions that a single mother can take that will minimize the danger.

Be alert to the possibility of trouble if your lover or a casual date:

1. shows a premature interest in your children and not very much in you;

2. fondles your children too much, or kisses them on the lips;

3. wants to spend time alone with your children before you have established a good, meaningful relationship;

4. makes seductive remarks with sexual overtones to your children, especially to your teenagers (comments about how a child is "stacked," or how she's sure to "knock the boys over," fit into this category);

5. drinks a great deal or is involved with drugs.

Most important is that you take seriously any complaint or remark your child may make indicating that your lover may not be behaving properly. Many of the children who finally receive treatment have tried to get their parent to listen to them for some time before they finally are heard and something is done.

Remember, not all child molesters will attempt actual intercourse. Though that act may cause a child the most damage, other less overt forms of sexual harassment still can cause great distress. One thirteen-year-old daughter of a single mother protested when her mother's live-in lover began to compliment her excessively. He'd tell her how sexy she looked in a particular dress, or remark on how her breasts were filling out. These comments made the girl uneasy, but she didn't dare voice them until she came to therapy. She was afraid her mother would get angry at her and accuse her of flirting with the man.

It's difficult for a single mother who recognizes her own need for companionship and sex to have this concern added to her many worries. But it must be faced. One single mother who married a man she'd known for over two years later divorced him because she realized he was making sexual advances to her fifteen-year-old daughter. If she'd been able to recognize his interest in the girl before they married, she'd have saved her child from a very traumatic experience.

You Can Overprotect, Too

In light of all the dangers that may disturb a child's physical, emotional, and mental health, it seems odd to speak of overprotection. Yet, too much shielding of a child can be as damaging to the family life of a single parent as any of the hazards mentioned thus far. Overprotection is usually caused by the parent's needs. It's a reflection of concern about personal problems projected onto the child.

The world seems, and often is, cruel and lacking in concern for the individual. The judgments of would-be employers and friends can sometimes be harsh and devoid of understanding. An overprotected child, when reaching maturity, has no defense against the onslaught of reality, having been denied appropriate opportunities to develop independence and the necessary skills and inner strengths needed to cope with life.

There appear to be two major causes of overprotection—unthinking acceptance of a prior generation's method of childrearing, and an ambivalent feeling on the part of the overprotective parent toward the children. Though these seem very different, the result is much the same. Children subjected to overprotection either become passive or overreact against authority, or both, in their attempt to obtain autonomy.

Some present-day parents who were themselves overprotected as children blindly follow the role models of the past in dealing with their sons and daughters. In doing this, they're displaying an emotional connection with, and a need to please, their own parents that should have been overcome as they matured.

Such insistence on maintaining their children's dependence and discouraging independent actions can infect the new generation of children and interfere with their process of growing up.

Nancy, an articulate thirty-seven-year-old divorced librarian, was still very attached to her mother. There were daily phone calls between them in which she reported in detail recent events in her life. Her mother then advised her on how to deal with the most minute facets of every issue she faced.

In her own parenting of her thirteen-year-old daughter and fourteen-year-old son, Nancy emulated her mother's behavior. She tried very hard to be a good mother. But this striving actually translated into her being intrusive, controlling, and infantilizing in her dealing with her two children.

Although she'd been divorced several years earlier, Nancy made no attempt to establish a social life of her own. She rationalized that her children needed her constant supervision. She also accepted her mother's notion that it was her maternal duty to devote all of her free time to her children.

In her determination to be a good parent, Nancy listened in on all of her son's and daughter's phone calls. She read their mail and her daughter's diary, and she anxiously supervised and nagged them about homework and school responsibilities. A perfectionist about her housework, she insisted upon performing most of the chores herself, yet bitterly complained that her children took advantage of her since they didn't help.

She was fearful of losing control and felt very threatened by either child's attempts to become autonomous. Her daughter reacted by becoming passive and withdrawn. Her son actively rebelled against this stifling overprotection and rejected all her efforts to regain the upper hand. When Nancy and her children came in for a therapy consultation, the boy was in conflict with all authority figures.

Nancy needed first to let go of her dependency on her mother. Then she began slowly to build a life separate from her mother's control. After lengthy therapy, Nancy was helped to understand and accept her own right to independence. Only then was she capable of recognizing what she had been doing to her children. It took further therapy before she understood how to give them the freedom they needed to develop lives of their own.

Parents who have ambivalent feelings toward their children (that is, loving and hostile feelings simultaneously) often handle the conflict by either underprotection or overprotection. In some cases, a parent blatantly acts out conscious or unconscious hostility by underprotection in the form of actual abuse. In other instances, antagonism may be handled by turning it into its opposite—overprotection. When this is done, the parent is able to deny the hostility. Then, overprotection acts as a compensation and cover for the hostile feelings.

We're beginning to face some of the behavior patterns that are most damaging to a child's growth, but we still have a long way to go. Yet our goal is critical to making important changes in society. When we do finally learn to help our children develop lives that are freer than their parents' or grandparents' lives were from guilt, unnatural responsibilities, unhealthy dependency, and inappropriate sexual stimulation, we'll find that they will be able to rear their children to be closer to the ideal. Then, finally, we may begin to see adults who no longer carry with them the burdens of mishandled childhood problems that continue to be passed from one generation to the next.

10 They Saw Us Together—in Bed

Handling Children's Exposure to Parental Sex

Some of our greatest joys can be found in our adult sexual behavior. Once we're mature, we recognize sex as a wonderful means of sharing love and pleasure. Many of us look back with regret to an early relationship, perhaps to an ex-spouse with whom we were sexually incompatible, and wish we had been better informed. We recognize in ourselves a sexual ignorance we'd like to overcome, so we read books and do other things to improve our knowledge.

Yet, despite our realization that correct information and a proper attitude toward sex are important, many of us don't apply this point of view to youngsters. Even though our children must have proper instruction and practical knowledge relating to their sexuality so that they're prepared for *their* future adult roles, our need to protect them from exploitation often causes us to deny them this learning experience.

For example, studies have been made which prove that masturbation is not only natural but serves as an efficient method of teaching the body how to respond sexually. However, despite these findings, many people persist in believing masturbation to be harmful, warning their children to avoid this and all other types of sexual behavior. Even those enlightened parents who accept the naturalness of masturbation still teach their children that they shouldn't let others touch their sexual parts. They want their children to be safe, and the ever-present danger of child molestation inspires caution. For this and other reasons, great numbers of adults do everything in their power to keep children entirely ignorant of sex in any form. (No one is completely successful in this effort, of course. If children of whatever age fail to learn about sex from their families, they'll learn—usually untruths—from their peers.)

This is unfortunate, for children do need to be regarded as sexual beings and to be given proper information according to their ages and abilities to absorb it. On the other hand, the sexual education of children can sometimes be taken too far in the opposite direction because a few misguided individuals believe that they can make up for their own ignorance in these matters by encouraging children to experiment sexually or by letting children watch the sexual activities of grown-ups.

Most mental health professionals agree that the exposure of children to the sight of adult intercourse is likely to be harmful. They recognize that very young children can misinterpret what is happening and assume it's an aggressive act which may harm the parent on whom they depend. This is true even when both adults are the children's parents, but it's especially frightening if one of the sexual partners isn't known or isn't yet trusted by a child.

What is it about the sex act that can traumatize a small child? First, children are frightened by any display of violence between their loved adults, and the various positions of the sex act may make it appear that the participants are wrestling. Second, the sounds adults may make during sex, especially the cries of a woman, may give the impression that they're in pain. This, too, frightens a child observer.

What about older children? Mental health professionals believe that, if older children are exposed to overt parental sex, other problems may develop. Older children may intellectually understand what is happening, but they may be upset at being forced to accept a parent as a sexual being. Moreover, the sight of adult copulation can be overly stimulating to those older children who have some knowledge of what's occurring, since they may respond by becoming aroused themselves, or begin to think of their parent as an available sexual person.

Yet, when children's natural curiosity about sex is made to appear bad, they may easily conclude that all sexual activity is bad, too. For example, as noted earlier, children who have been taught that masturbation or letting another person touch their genitals is bad might logically conclude, if they see their parents or a parent and lover touching those places they've been told to avoid, that these adults are also bad.

The conflict this stirs up can be very damaging to children. It may begin by children deciding that the people they've trusted are hypocrites. Everything else those adults have told them is then open to question. They may feel betrayed and begin to question and dispute everything they previously accepted. They wonder, since their parent lied about how bad it was to touch certain places of the body, what else that was said is also untrue. The parent or parents who were the children's ideal models now become less than ideal. Depending on the age of the child, this may be very destructive. Young children, who are not yet able to understand human frailties, may suffer. Older children who have already internalized their social standards and are close to the age where they would normally begin to recognize their parents as equal human beings may not be affected as much, or at all.

There is, however, a double-pronged defense that seems to protect against this scenario: information and communication. If children who have been given adequate information about sex, preferably by adults they trust, accidentally observe a parent in a sexual act, they'll have a perspective and a context in which to view it. At worst, such a well-informed child may be upset, but recovery will occur far more quickly than for one who's not aware of the role of sex in human life. And then, if there's good, open communication between a single parent and a child and they are able to talk freely—so the child doesn't think it's necessary to keep feelings in but can express them easily—any negative effect of this experience can be overcome.

Controlling Your Reaction

Despite the precautions most parents, single or otherwise, take to protect their children from exposure to adult sex, it does happen. Children may innocently walk into the adults' bedroom at just the wrong moment. Or they may hear unusual sounds coming from that room and rush to discover the cause. Or they may succumb to a natural curiosity as to what actually happens when Mommy or Daddy is alone with a lover and decide to investigate. Some children simply feel jealous of the attention a parent is giving another adult and intrude because they feel left out.

What's important when a child, for whatever reason, comes upon adult sexual intimacy is that the parent know what lessons might be learned from such an experience, for the child *will* learn something. If a parent is prepared, knowing that only positive things need come out of even this unexpected occurrence, then he or she will be ready with the proper reaction.

If a child suddenly appears in the room when you're unable to break things off and respond naturally, what should you do? The first piece of advice is *don't panic.* Any action taken in panic is apt to be wrong. All that is needed is a simple, "Jim and I don't want to be disturbed. Please leave us alone now. I'll talk to you later." This will center your displeasure on the intrusion. Your child can deal with having done something wrong, as long as it's clear what it was.

A parent who explodes in anger and accuses a child of spying pushes the blame for the incident onto the child. The child may also get the impression that something wrong was occurring, especially if the angry parent doesn't focus on the intrusion. Generalized anger at the child's appearance will surround the event with negative emotions that can only interfere with the parent-child relationship, since they will make it far more difficult for either parent or child to discuss what happened.

The second piece of advice is *don't ignore what happened.* You can be sure your child recognized that something unusual was taking place. Don't make the mistake of assuming that the child really didn't see anything. Such an assumption is often made by people who truly wish to avoid any confrontation dealing with sex. They decide that if they bring up the subject later, they'll only be making something out of nothing. But a parent who refuses to discuss what has happened not only misses an opportunity for educating the children about sex, but also conveys the clear message that it's wrong to speak about the subject at all.

A parent may feel overly protective of the relationship with a lover and hesitate to take the time to reassure a child, or fear that shifting attention from lover to child at a critical romantic moment might offend the lover and destroy a relationship that's still quite fragile. That adult shows insufficient parental concern, overloading the child with guilt out of fear that the accidental intrusion might scare the lover away.

If you consider the possibility of such an accidental intrusion, you will find it easier to control your emotions if and when it occurs. You'll recognize that it is your reaction that matters. You'll neither explode in anger nor pull away from your lover in shame or guilt. When you can approach the situation with self-control, you'll be ready to deal with all of the issues it presents to you.

Reassuring a Younger Child

Whatever the age of your child, it's important that you acknowledge what has happened. No child should be ordered away and made to feel bad. However, what you do depends on the age and maturity of the child involved.

If your child is very young, start by telling your lover that everything's all right but you need time to reassure your child and that might take a while. Promise to get back as soon as possible. Then take your child by the hand and lead the way back to bed. If the child has already run from your room, follow and offer as much consolation as you would have under any other upsetting circumstances. Offer assurance that you're fine—that you and your lover were just playing together.

You can ask your child to talk about what was seen. If reference is made to your fighting, reassure your child that everything you were doing was just fun and play. You can say that grownups like to kiss and hug and be close to each other. But even after your child realizes you aren't angry and weren't hurt, you might still need to sit nearby until sleep returns.

In the days that follow, be alert to any cues that may indicate your child has further questions about what was seen. Repeat the offer to discuss it. If more questions are asked, answer simply and honestly.

If your child shows specific curiosity about what was seen, you may respond that a grown-up man likes to put his penis into a woman's vagina. Explain that both men and women find this enjoyable. You should use the correct names for the sex organs, just as you'd call a head or an arm by its correct name. Assigning cutesy names to certain parts of the body tells a child there's something very different—and possibly shameful—about them. And it is not wise to give that impression.

If your child inquires further, you may add that this is how babies are made, but (if you're practicing birth control) you aren't making a baby now. You can explain that both you and your child owe your existence to sexual intercourse. It's helpful to purchase a book on the subject that's designed to facilitate sex education for small children and read it with your child. A list of such publications can be found within Resources. But don't push the issue. Your very young child may be satisfied with limited information. Don't load on more knowledge than can be absorbed.

Children of any age may become anxious that you and your lover are trying to make another baby, and that they will be displaced. If this, in fact, isn't the case, comfort them and explain that you were just enjoying being together and were not making a baby. But, at the same time, reassure them that, even if you might some time in the future want to have another baby, their place in your love will be as secure as ever.

Sometimes, after an accidental intrusion, small children may push back worries and fears for a time, act as if nothing happened, and make no attempt to get the answers they need. If your child seems to withdraw after such an intrusion into your room while you're having sex, I suggest you repeat the offer to discuss the matter. You may simply say, "If you want to talk about how you felt when you came into my room the other night when I was with Jim, it's okay. I'll be glad to talk about it."

If your child responds with relief, follow the advice given in the previous paragraphs. But don't push. Just be alert for future cues. What's important is that your child be reassured that you aren't angry and that you're not ashamed to talk about what you were doing.

Reassuring an Older Child

If an older child accidentally sees you involved sexually with your lover, you should respond initially much as with a younger child. Without any show of anger, say that you want your privacy. Say "Please leave the room and close the door." What you do next depends on the reaction of the child.

If your child is visibly upset, it's appropriate for you to offer reassurance within a short time. But if you recognize the child's reaction as only surprise and not dismay, you may wait until later to talk. You don't want to establish a pattern that allows your child to interrupt your privacy at will, knowing that an intrusion will destroy your time with your lover.

Depending on the age of the child, and how much you've discussed sex in the past, you probably won't have to give as full an explanation of the occurrence as was necessary with the younger child. This is a situation where consistent, organized sex education has value.

Nevertheless, even with good prior sex education, most children like to maintain the fantasy that their parents aren't sexual people. So, if you've already discussed sex, your child will understand what was happening but will need assistance in accepting it. You can help by saying that, even though you were expressing love for your partner and didn't like being interrupted, you still love your child.

This is also a time when you need to show by your behavior that you aren't ashamed of what you were doing. Make it clear that you don't feel you did something wrong. What's important is that you and your older child reach agreement that this is something adults do, preferably in privacy. Help your child work out some procedure that will avoid a recurrence of the intrusion, keeping in mind, of course, that had you locked your door before the interruption it wouldn't have happened at all.

Don't let yourself become excessively apologetic. Recognize, however, that you are responsible for your own privacy. Don't put that duty on your child. Find out what it was your child wanted and, if possible, take care of that need. If you've interrupted your lovemaking to speak to your child, this first discussion should end with your explaining that now you want to return to your lover and that you'll be available afterward.

You may face some criticism later. Adolescents often have a very rigid picture of right and wrong. They're dealing with their own sexual development, and the confusion created by the sight of a parent having sex may cause them to prefer to drop the issue entirely.

In any event, be available for discussion and make it clear that you aren't angry, even though you don't want such an intrusion to occur again. The important thing is that your child not be laden with guilt because of this unplanned invasion of your privacy.

For children of all ages, a special time together, within a day or so after such an accidental intrusion, might provide an opportunity to reassure as well as to talk about what happened.

Soothing Your Lover

Your lover may be as troubled as your children by the interruption. This is why it's important that you leave with a kiss and the reassurance that you'll be back. If you feel guilty because of what's happened, it's vital that you not displace any of these feelings onto your children. But you need to give the same consideration to your sex partner. If you show excessive guilt, you can convey the impression that you're ashamed of your relationship—and maybe also of your lover.

There may also be a need to reassure your partner that this incident has not affected your relationship. Explain that you can handle what has happened and make it right with your children, especially if this is an ongoing relationship. In addition, it may be necessary to provide reassurance that your lover's position in the children's affection hasn't necessarily been damaged.

Your lover will have reacted to your children's unexpected appearance, and will need to recognize and accept those reactions in the weeks that follow. You both need to discuss what happened so you will be consistent when you talk to your children. It's best if you both respond in a similar manner to the situation. This provides each of you with an opportunity to increase your understanding of the other's feelings. It also lets you clarify your attitude toward your children and assist in strengthening the relationship that exists between them and your lover.

In an ongoing relationship, it's important to remember that your lover should share some of the responsibility for helping the children adjust after such an intrusion. The key word here, as in many aspects of the interaction between single parent, lover, and child, is *communication*. The greatest damage will occur if a blanket of silence is drawn over the episode. If you and your lover both show your children that you don't feel guilty and don't expect them to feel that way either, you'll help them put the event in its proper place. Talking will also help you clarify your expectations regarding future times when the same thing could happen. Your children need to accept your right to privacy, but you and your lover should also use common sense in deciding when to have sex, and when to lock the door.

Turning It into a Learning Experience

Much as you might wish that private time with your lover never be interrupted by your children, it could happen. If it does, you may be able to turn an unpleasant intrusion into a learning experience, as in the following example.

Effie was in bed with Saul late one Saturday morning when David, her twelve-year-old son, burst into the room. He stopped in alarm when he saw that his mother and Saul were in bed together and that Saul was crouched over his mother in what appeared to be a fighting posture.

Saul saw David first and stopped what he was doing. Effie, aware immediately that something was amiss, glanced toward the door just in time to see David rush out. She waited for Saul to disengage, but she showed neither anger nor distress. Instead, she kissed him lovingly. "You okay?"

Saul settled back on the bed. "I guess so. What about Dave?"

"He might be upset. I think I'd better talk to him. Don't worry if I'm gone for a while." Effie pulled on a robe.

David was in his room, face down on the bed, when she entered. "Dave?" Effie sat down beside him. He shrugged when she touched his shoulder. "I know you're upset. You've never rushed into the room before when my door was closed. Did something happen?"

Relieved that his mother was concerned about him, and eager to give her the news that had occasioned his unexpected entry, David sat up. "Yeah." He was surprised that he no longer felt excited and happy. "We had tryouts at Little League. I'm going to be pitcher." He slouched down. "I guess it isn't so important."

"But it is." Effie put her arm around his shoulder, and this time he didn't resist. "We both know how hard you've practiced. I'm delighted. You must be, too."

His nod was still halfhearted.

Effie turned so she faced him. "Saul and I didn't expect you to come in so suddenly. Do you want to talk about what just happened? You looked so shocked when you ran out."

David's answer was unintelligible, but she could see he was still upset.

She touched his shoulder gently. "Maybe I can help you understand. Remember when I told you about how grown-ups show that they love each other? Remember I said the man puts his penis into the woman? Well, that's what we were doing. It's a very private thing. We didn't expect you home yet. You know Little League usually lasts until after noon. I'm sorry. We just lost track of the time."

"Didn't he hurt you?" David was feeling braver. "You were making funny noises."

"No, he didn't hurt me. When something feels very good, people sometimes make strange sounds. If you hear me making those sounds again, you needn't worry. I'm all right. And remember, if my door's shut, even if it isn't locked, you should knock before you enter."

"Why?" He seemed suddenly resentful, as if he were being pushed away.

Effie had a sudden inspiration. "I guess the best way to explain it is this. You know I don't object if you masturbate. I know you do it. And you know I know. But if you're doing it and I tap on your door, what happens?"

David lowered his head. "I stop. It doesn't feel right if you see me."

"That's it. Well, it doesn't feel right to Saul or me if you see us having sex. It's kind of personal between us." She kissed David's cheek. "We have our private things, too, you know. When you and I talk about how things were before Daddy and I broke up, we don't include Saul, do we?"

"No." David was feeling better. "Are you going to have sex again now?"

"Probably not. You know how it is. You can't always get back into masturbating if I've just left the room, can you? We'll probably want to be alone together after bedtime. What are you planning to do now?"

David was fine again. "I was going to ask if I could go and play with Roger. His mom said I could stay for supper if I liked hamburgers."

When David left, Saul and Effie did resume their love play, but they both felt more relaxed. David now knew that his mother cared for him, even when she was having private time with her lover. Effie knew that her son was no longer as upset by what had happened. And Saul knew that Effie was capable of taking care of such an unexpected intrusion. An incident that could have been traumatic turned out to be a learning experience for all three of them.

11 One Big Happy New Family

Including Your Lover in Your Family and Social Life

We've discussed how you can avoid premature meetings between your lovers and your children, especially if you're choosing to have a series of one-night stands. Now it's time to clarify the questions of *if*, *when*, and *how* it's possible, or even desirable, to bring your children and your love life together.

If you've known a single parent who consistently keeps the two isolated from each other, you may recognize the great personal danger in that practice. If the attempt is successful, the single parent often begins to feel fragmented, burdened by the problems of maintaining two separate lives to the detriment of both.

This is not to deny the fact that such parents usually believe they have good reasons for exerting the effort. Some are convinced that their children's welfare depends upon keeping them innocent of adult relations. They're convinced that the introduction of a new member into the family would create conflict and unhappiness. Others hesitate to introduce their children to a lover because they fear the children might wreck a relationship that's become important to them.

One forty-year-old client of mine, Peter, had reason for such fears. He had waited over a year after his divorce before he began to date, hoping his wife, who'd left him to "find herself," might return. But, by the end of the second year, he no longer wanted her back. It didn't occur to him to discuss his disillusionment with his eleven-year-old daughter, Paula. For her, the hope still lived.

He dated actively during the third year after his divorce and had sex with a number of women, but he didn't bring anyone home until he found Louise, with whom he had more than a casual relationship.

He was proud to introduce his daughter to Louise, but was stunned by Paula's reaction. The child first smiled, but then turned a troubled face toward him. "Daddy, aren't you going to marry Mommy again when she comes back?"

Peter tried to ignore the question, but it bothered Louise. When incidents like that were repeated, Louise began to observe Peter more carefully. She noticed his unwillingness to talk about his previous marriage in Paula's presence.

When she began to see that Paula was actually voicing what had, in the past, been her father's dream, too, Louise questioned whether or not she should break off the relationship. She recognized Paula's wish to have her mother back and understood how it could reflect Peter's earlier wishes. But his unwillingness to discuss his change of mind with his daughter troubled Louise. She wondered if he might still be ambivalent about remarrying or having a close relationship with a woman. Maybe, she decided, when Peter was ready to deal with Paula's open expression of longing for her mother, they could have a life together. However, when no progress was made in that direction, Louise and Peter began to drift apart.

When Peter saw what was happening, he tried talking to Paula, but his words seemed to fall on deaf ears. He was unable to bring up the subject without getting angry at the child. Soon, Louise disappeared from his life.

After a while, he began to date Grace, a coworker in his office. When the same scenes with Paula were repeated, Peter was forced to admit that a problem existed. In therapy, he recognized his remaining ambivalent feeling toward his ex-wife, at which time his fears about remarriage became clear to him. He finally understood why he had failed to convince his daughter that he no longer wanted her mother back. Only after he'd done this was he able to establish a relationship with Grace that his daughter didn't try to disrupt with ill-advised questions.

Many single parents hesitate to combine their family and social lives simply because they aren't sure how to go about it. For them, I suggest a few preliminary steps that can help smooth the road. They include some preparatory work and some self-examination.

You must prepare yourself, your children, and your lover for that critical first meeting. Then, with an awareness of how all of you are reacting, you can assess your own gut-level feeling about the approaching encounter. This will help you decide when and where the introductions should take place. It will also help you develop realistic expectations regarding your first experience with this new togetherness.

If all goes well, there will be a period of change during which you should be aware of any influence exerted by your ex-spouse, who—even if life is running smoothly—may resent any happiness you achieve. Your ex-partner may make a direct effort to destroy your new relationship. Part of that effort may be an encouragement of your children's fantasies about getting the two of you back together.

You need to remember that you're in charge of your own life and what happens to this particular phase of it. If you and your lover approach this get-acquainted period with the right attitudes and proper preparation, you'll be able to deal successfully with introductions, even if both of you have children.

Preparing Yourself

When you're developing an adequate social life for yourself while at the same time continuing to be a good parent, approach the problems you encounter slowly. Before you act, mentally rehearse the steps you'll take. Visualize your new "family" in happy communication. Get the feel of the satisfaction you'll experience. Then keep that sense of peace and happiness as you seek to balance your needs with those of your children and your lover.

Approach this changeover period with an understanding of your own needs and dreams. Realistically face the situation in which you find yourself. Do some soul-searching. Are you still clinging to the relationship with your ex-spouse? Do the two of you still have unfinished business that needs to be attended to? If you do, work it out now. If allowed to hang on, these unresolved problems can destroy a new relationship.

If your ex-partner is causing you trouble, deal with it in whatever way you must. If you can't win the right to a life of your own by discussing the matter, you may have to resort to the law. But whatever is necessary must be done.

Consider, also, your expectations for this new relationship. Clarify your dreams and reconcile them with reality. Anticipate troubles that may develop and consider possible solutions. The better prepared you are, emotionally and intellectually, for this changeover period, the easier it will be for all of you.

Preparing Your Children

The best way to prepare children for any important event is to develop—early in their lives, preferably long before any changes take place—an attitude and a social pattern that will make it easier for them to accept, or even enjoy, new experiences. But even if this has not occurred, it's never too late to help your children learn to cope with unexpected developments. If you haven't done so already, start as soon as you can.

Whether you're divorced, widowed, or an elective single parent, you need to create a social pattern that includes many friends. This is not only good for *your* mental health, but it makes your children aware that you have interests separate from them. It also eases their adjustment to the new lover you may someday meet.

It's important not to surprise your children with the sudden arrival of a special person, such as a lover you expect to begin living with. Prepare them for a newcomer in your family circle as carefully as you prepared them for your dating.

Before any meeting, clarify your feelings about the person being introduced. If this is just a casual friend, let your children know. It'll save them from getting too emotionally involved with someone whose relationship with you isn't established. But if it's a person you're very fond of, tell your children that this is a special person. Just make sure they understand that, no matter how much you love this new adult, you still love them, too. They can hardly be expected to accept with open arms someone they believe is a threat to their security.

This point must be emphasized. Parents sometimes take it for granted that their children recognize the constancy of parental affection and realize how much they're loved. But children don't know this. They need repeated reassurance, especially if the parent contemplates bringing a lover into the family.

An excellent example of how to handle this matter came to my attention when I met Helen at a singles gathering. When Helen was twenty, she had a child without marrying. The beginning years were wonderful. Helen accepted them as a special period in her life, devoted to mothering. She and her little daughter, Irma, were together a great deal.

However, Helen managed to maintain contacts with a few adults who were not parents. From early on, Irma was told there would be times when her mother wanted adult companionship. She accepted "Mommy's night out" as being a natural part of their routine. By the time Irma was ten, the pattern was well established. Helen went out regularly, sometimes with women friends, sometimes with men. But only if her companion was a friend as well as an escort did she arrange to be picked up at home. She wanted Irma to feel that the people in her life were important to her. One-night stands or casual acquaintances were kept away from her daughter.

Helen met Sam at a restaurant the first few times they dated, and when the question "your place or mine?" came up, she said "yours." But she soon realized their relationship was important to them both. It was time to introduce him to her daughter.

Sam was eager to meet Irma. He had no children of his own, though he'd been married before, and he looked forward to having an almost grown-up daughter. But Helen suggested patience. She wanted the two people she loved most to like each other.

Her first step was to begin talking to Irma about Sam occasionally, usually just before or after a date with him. She was careful not to let Sam seem more important in her life than her daughter was. She knew her child might be uneasy if anyone appeared to threaten her security.

Then one morning, after a date with Sam, she announced that he wanted to take them both to the wild-animal park. "How do you feel about it, Irma? Would you like to go?"

Irma hesitated. "Can't we just go alone?"

Helen was prepared for the question. "No, not this time. Sam asked us both. And Sam's important to me. I like him a lot."

"More than me?" Irma was accustomed to being direct.

"No, not more. I love him differently." She cuddled Irma in her arms. "I love you, baby. You know that. I always will."

She didn't discuss the outing again that day. But the next morning, at breakfast, Irma suddenly asked, "Is he fun to be with?"

"Who?" Then Helen realized Irma was talking about Sam. "Yes, Sam's fun to be with. I think we'll have a good time together."

Enough had been said. The meeting had been properly prepared. From there on, much depended on how Sam and Irma hit it off.

If you're divorced, or if your partner has died, your children may have a loyalty to their missing parent that can interfere with any possibility of friendship between them and your lover. They might be afraid their other parent wouldn't approve of their spending time with you and your new partner. This can be a special problem if your ex-spouse hasn't yet begun to socialize and appears to be abandoned.

This issue can't be dealt with superficially. Your children may be reflecting their other parent's sadness. If so, you need to help them see that they won't cheer up someone they love by being unhappy themselves. Remind them of some time when they were sad and you were able to help them feel better only because you felt good, yourself.

At the same time, you can help them recognize that they aren't responsible for another's happiness. Children can't be held accountable for what their parents do. Use any example from their own experiences to help them see that people have to accept responsibility for their own emotions. It's not easy, sometimes, but it can be done.

There are many good books dealing with this subject, which you can read with your children and use as springboards for these discussions. Many of them are written with great sensitivity. They deal with problems from loss through death to the arrival of a new baby in the family. A listing of some of these books is in Resources at the back of this book. You can get invaluable help in this manner.

During this premeeting period, your goal is to let your children fully air any fears they have concerning a new person in your life. Listen to them when they talk. Answer any questions they have. Be careful not to take expressions of insecurity lightly. At the same time, don't act as if you expect them to fall in love with your new partner immediately.

Though you shouldn't require a show of affection that isn't felt, you have a right to expect your children to act properly at the meeting. Since they're apt to feel uneasy with this new person in your life, they may misbehave. Therefore, you may want to playact the first encounter so they'll know just what to do.

Let one of them pretend to be the new person you're bringing for them to meet. Now introduce that child to the others, using your lover's name. Let them experiment with different ways of saying hello. You might even let them act out some wrong ways so they'll see how impoliteness makes everyone uncomfortable. End this little session with a run-through of the way you hope they'll act, so the right behavior is emphasized.

It's worth repeating that you should never ask your children to pretend an emotion they don't feel. You can insist on politeness in any situation, but don't demand effervescence and a display of happiness that aren't sincere. This can contribute to the development of a false self (the one shown to the world) and an inner self (hidden from everyone). Such dual identity can be very damaging to your child.

Of course, you may have a lover you know will never form a permanent bond with you. Nevertheless, this person may be someone with whom you have so much fun that you want your children to share it. If that happens, prepare them before the meeting for this person's probable disappearance later on. Help them recognize this relationship as being a fun thing in your life, and let them know you want them to share this temporary pleasure. Answer any questions they have with clarity, so they don't begin to fantasize a relationship that doesn't and won't exist between you and this person. They must understand the impermanence of your relationship with this individual so that they aren't devastated when it breaks up.

Preparing Your Lover

Once you decide it's time to introduce your lover to your children, you'll be wise to discuss with him or her all aspects of the meeting before it takes place. Certain decisions need to be made:

1. Where will the meeting occur? Is your home the best place? Maybe you'll prefer to introduce your lover and your children during an outing to some pleasant park or entertainment center.

2. How long will the meeting last? The ages of your children are an important factor. Young children tire quickly. If you do go to a park or the zoo, don't make it an all-day outing. If you want your children to behave well, you need to avoid fatigue.

3. Your lover may not know how to act toward your youngsters. Determine, beforehand, how much your friend knows

about the behavior of children. Prepare for the unexpected. Ask if there are any special concerns about the meeting and try to settle them beforehand.

4. Prepare your lover for any rivalry that might develop. Make it clear in advance that you'll have to give a good part of your attention to your children. A family outing isn't like your dates. Overt expressions of love between the two of you should be limited, at least until they accept your relationship.

5. Be aware that your lover may feel jealousy, too. Explain that your children are too young, no matter what age, to adjust to an abrupt change in your behavior toward them. You shouldn't be expected to treat them differently when your lover is around from the way you would when you're alone with them. However, your lover, being an adult, should understand what's happening and not be upset.

6. You may need to make it understood that you don't expect perfect behavior from your children, your lover, or yourself. You just expect everyone to try to behave well, act politely, and be considerate.

7. Decide in advance how this first family outing will end. If you and your lover want to go out alone afterward, the children will have to be prepared. But it might be better to plan the day so you end it alone with your children or all together as a new family.

Occasionally, a lover may resist all plans for this crucial meeting, and the single parent goes along with the delay. In that case, the motives need to be considered. Too long a delay in bringing the new family together may indicate problems neither lover nor single parent wants to face.

Recently, a woman came to me because she was troubled by the aftermath of such a long delay.

Verna had a regular relationship with Bert that lasted for almost a year. During most of that time, he behaved as if she had no children. In the beginning, Verna enjoyed her nights out because they were so different from her day-to-day existence. It was fun to play the role of a woman who had no responsibilities and an indulgent lover.

As the relationship grew more serious, however, Verna began to feel uncomfortable. If Bert phoned her and one of the children answered, he didn't even say hello but asked if Verna was in. The children began to resent his obvious refusal to accept them as being important in their mother's life—and her willingness to go along with his game.

Yet, despite their irritation and her awareness of its harm, Verna hesitated to make any demands on Bert that he include the children in any of their activities. She was fearful that if she did he'd reject her. Nevertheless, she felt increasing irritation with him because of his insensitivity to her dilemma. This anger was reflected in her gradual withdrawal from him sexually. The relationship deteriorated and finally fell apart.

She wished, then, that she'd made the effort earlier to bring her children into the relationship. She believed she might have persuaded Bert to accept her and her children if she had dared to stand up for what was important to her.

Smoothing Ruffled Feelings

It's important that you be prepared for some upsets when you plan a meeting between your children and a lover. Your children may get sick. Or they may, in spite of your preparation, behave badly. A lover, especially one with no children, may not know how to act, and may talk down to your teenagers or be gruff with your three-year-old. In spite of your premeeting discussion, you may be expected to be as demonstrative as if the two of you were alone.

If you encounter any problem, it's important to face it immediately. Don't expect time to eliminate incompatibilities. To the contrary, time may only make them more difficult to deal with.

If your children are the ones creating the problem, handle

their behavior as best you can at the moment, but then be sure to bring it up at your next family conference. Maybe the problem resulted from their feeling that you were neglecting them. It's possible you did ignore them at times. But maybe they resented *any* attention you showed to your lover. Find out the cause of their attitude. Your children's behavior will change when the reason for it is treated

A lover who is personally rather strict might have difficulty tolerating children's constant testing of rules. Yet this testing is a natural pattern for children. Do what you can to help your lover become more tolerant of normal childhood behavior. Talk about what it was like for you when you were a child. How were you disciplined? What were the fun things for you? How were you helped to deal with sadness and anger? Encourage your lover to join in and share childhood experiences. As you expose your vulnerability, you make it easier for your lover to do the same and to accept the child that we all carry within us.

One patient described to me how this worked for her. Her lover, Len, had a difficult time relating to Helen's two children until she engaged him in this kind of reminiscing. When he began to describe his own childhood, she understood why he was so strict with himself. His father had been a martinet, demanding complete adherence to rules that often made little sense to Len.

Only when they began to talk about fun times did she begin to feel Len's growing understanding of his problem and the behavior of her children. He'd appreciated Helen's more loving way of dealing with her children, but the child in him had been jealous and angry at the realization of all he had missed.

If, even after a number of such discussions, your lover still shows no ability to put up with your children, maybe you need to look at your relationship. You may not be comfortable with a person who's intolerant of behavior that is natural to all children.

There is one simple rule you'd be wise to follow: Avoid private, adult communications when your children and your lover meet. Your children may react by feeling threatened—excluded from the fun. Discuss this issue with your lover before the meeting so that it doesn't become a problem later. Then, if you're still bothered by little private asides to you that exclude the children, you can be justified in limiting your response to them. You'll need to talk about it later, so it doesn't happen again.

This is a touchy area. Your lover may feel it's important for your children to understand the special closeness of your relationship and may insist that private asides are one way to establish this. You'll need to make it clear that you see this kind of action for what it truly is: a ploy of the "inner child" to get special attention. It only engenders jealousy, which is painful to your children, and for which you'll undoubtedly pay later. This form of attention-getting establishes your lover as a competitor with your children—not a friend. It's also a cue that your lover may not feel secure in your relationship and that underlying issues need to be examined, discussed, and settled.

In therapy, Helen was helped to be patient with Len's inner child by becoming more aware of how her own influenced her behavior. She had many talks with him, slowly moving from the subject of his childhood to a more comprehensive discussion of how it affected his present expectations. Because she was loving and willing to listen and because he wanted to change, they gradually established ways of dealing with his inner child and with the behavior patterns he'd developed. Their relationship deepened as a result, and he felt a growing rapport with her children.

Choosing the Right Time

I've already mentioned your need to decide how your first outing with your lover and your family will end—and why that decision is important. It's all a matter of timing. You can assume that your lover is emotionally mature, and is therefore better able than your children to put up with being left alone at the end of a fun togetherness day. They'll profit from the reassurance this gives them that they're still important to you, even though you have a lover.

Timing can play a part in other aspects of this critical first meeting. If your children have recently lost a parent, you'll need to be especially careful. Such children shouldn't be subjected to a series of "uncles" or "best friends" brought in by you. They've already suffered one loss. They're apt to respond badly if they experience a series of losses, as your lovers move in and out of your life.

In fact, when children haven't had time to recover from the loss of a parent, whether through death or divorce, they shouldn't be forced to meet even a person you're very fond of. They may make an unfounded connection between your new lover and your divorce, for example, and conclude that this is the person responsible for your family breakup. Such an erroneous picture can result in a rift between your children and your lover that even time and much talking cannot repair.

This happened to one couple who otherwise had a strong relationship. Bette brought George to meet her sons five months after the divorce from their father was final. Her elder child, Louis, eleven, was still hoping his parents would get back together, and when he saw how fond Bette was of this new person, he decided that George had talked her into the divorce. He was resentful from the start. Ken, the younger son, reflected Louis's feelings.

Nevertheless, George and Bette married, even though the children didn't seem happy. As the years passed, the problems increased, despite George's attempts to be a good stepparent. When he was fifteen, Louis ran away from home and became involved with drugs. Only when the court demanded the boy get therapy did some of the problems surface. Fortunately, the younger boy was saved from many of the difficulties the older one faced. The family therapy that followed Louis's rebellion had brought out the deep-seated resentments engendered during those first months after Bette's divorce.

Problems of adjustment are different for the noncustodial parent. Since they have large blocks of time without the children, it might appear they could introduce a lover without causing much, if any, trauma. But in this situation, a new difficulty arises. A noncustodial parent whose visitation time falls on weekends and evenings when the lover is also more available may be tempted always to have the lover present when the children visit, without realizing the need for preparing the way for this change in their lives.

It's important that both parents devote some time exclusively to their children. If that doesn't happen, the children will react negatively. One child remarked that he could only see his dad on Tuesday nights and Saturday mornings. "Why," he asked, "does he always have to bring Ellen with him? He pays more attention to her than he does to me."

One good way for a noncustodial parent to deal with this problem is to bring a lover in for only a short time when the children are there. If the children arrive each Saturday morning, for instance, arrangements can be made so that on alternate weeks the lover meets them for lunch and then departs. The other Saturdays might be spent in family time, with everyone, including the lover, enjoying an activity together. It could even end with the lover staying overnight.

The benefit of such transition time is illustrated by the experience of a woman who came to me for a brief period. Janice was a professional woman who began dating Roger only a year after his divorce. After four months, they recognized the depths of their affection and decided to have her meet his daughter, Cindy, who lived with her mother. At first, Janice only occasionally went along when Roger picked Cindy up, so the child wouldn't feel too threatened.

Three months later, Janice and Roger were preparing to live together. Only then did Janice sleep overnight while Cindy was staying with her father.

The change, for the child, had been gradual, yet she still had some adjusting to do. In the year since her parents' divorce, Roger had devoted most of his time to her whenever she visited. Janice's presence made Roger's household more standard, and so not as exciting to Cindy. The feeling she'd had before of dating her father was gone. Nevertheless, she did adjust with few difficulties. The preparation Roger had made paid off.

One other important consideration for the noncustodial parent is that of the children's growing autonomy. When they're young, it's usually easy to set visiting days or, if custody is shared, to move the children from one home to the other. But as they grow, they have activities in school and with their peers that may intrude on the time that once belonged exclusively to the noncustodial parent.

Taking children away from a special birthday party or an important game to spend time with you and your lover may only aggravate the resentment children feel. This is particularly true for adolescents.

Usually, a little attention paid to your children is rewarded with smoother relationships all around, as Felicia, a recent client, learned. When Felicia's teenaged children visited her, they didn't want to be included in any special activities with her lover that took them away from their friends. If he dropped over and they were at home, they wanted to be included in the conversation—but that was all. Her children were healthy, normal adolescents, with many normal teenage interests. Fortunately, she lived close enough to their custodial father so they could continue with their own social lives even when they were at her house.

This acceptance of children's preferences is important. Many noncustodial parents feel shut out when their youngsters begin to develop social lives of their own. But they shouldn't feel rejected because teenaged children show a desire to spend a great deal of time with their peers. Children's relationships with their parents can't take the place of friendships they establish with others of their own generation.

However, an adolescent who isn't socially successful may make excessive demands to be included in everything a parent and lover do. This is not a healthy situation. Such a child may need special help to begin the separation from parental ties that should start during this period.

Avoiding Unrealistic Fantasies

One ever-present danger is that in preparing for your lover to meet your children you may have unrealistic expectations that can only bring you disappointment. It's easy to dream of the ideal situation where your children behave like angels and your lover treats them with just the right amount of respect and humor. But dreams and reality are seldom the same.

In that first encounter with your children, your lover might reveal characteristics that you find undesirable. Perhaps unable to accept normal childhood behavior, this person you love may make unreasonable demands on your children. You're wise to be prepared for such occurrences.

It's doubtful that you'll want to establish an ongoing relationship with someone who's too judgmental. During this get-acquainted period, it's advisable that you pay close attention to the interactions between a lover and your children. However, you shouldn't base your decisions entirely on the youngsters' reactions. But, certainly, how your lover behaves toward them during these first, more casual meetings can be an indication of reactions you might expect will be repeated after your relationship is solidified.

A word of advice. Don't make an optimistic prediction like, "You'll just love him!" It can build expectations and be the best guarantee that your children and your lover will be too critical of each other when they meet. We're all many-faceted. We can have friends that appeal to each of our different aspects, but that doesn't mean they'll all get along with each other.

If they just don't seem able to get along, especially if your children are in their teens, you may need to use your special family time to get to the root of the problem. Channels of communication between you, your lover, and your children need to be open enough so that this kind of problem can be solved. Even if they feel they just don't like each other and that feeling doesn't change with time, they can learn to get along if communication channels remain open and they are able to voice their attitudes in a way that is not cruel or vindictive.

You need to make some clear decisions with your lover regarding responsibility for your children. Your sixteen-year-old son may be all right if your lover lives with you, but he may resent any attempt on the part of this newcomer to direct his life. Settle such issues before you make any dramatic change. And be thankful you became aware of them before they turned into problems large enough to destroy your new happiness.

If the first encounter between your children and your lover creates a situation you can't tolerate, you need to find out why. Is your lover's behavior inappropriate? Are your children making judgments before they get well acquainted? If you can't seem to settle these questions, you may need professional help in reaching solutions.

"Daddy Wouldn't Do That!"

We tend to think of past friends and past experiences every time a new friend or new experience comes along. It's inevitable that your children should make such a comparison between your lover and the parent who's no longer a part of their lives. Sometimes this can be advantageous to your new relationship. If you're divorced and your ex-spouse was unkind to you and your children but your lover is sensitive and affectionate, the comparison will all be in favor of the newcomer.

It's probably wise to avoid trying to duplicate, with your lover, experiences you and your children shared with your ex-spouse, at least until a good relationship has been established, since that can't help but increase your children's tendency to judge one against the other. It's also important that you permit your children to remark on comparisons when they note them. Squelching these natural feelings could frustrate your children, causing them to act out any possible negative feelings in other, less acceptable ways.

Be alert for nonverbal behavior or indirect allusions that might indicate that your children are uncomfortable with the changes taking place in their lives. If they seem sad during a joyous occasion, like a big holiday they used to share with both you and their other parent, don't ignore the cue. Instead, sit down with them and talk about how they feel—and why.

One client who had come to me for guidance before divorcing an alcoholic husband handled her son's nostalgia for the past very well. Elsa noticed her son, Jeremy, sitting listlessly on the couch as her lover, Kirk, brought in the Christmas tree. "You look sad, Jeremy." She put her arm around his shoulder as she spoke.

Jeremy didn't answer, but his expression remained the same.

Elsa sat for a while without talking, waiting for Jeremy to speak. When he remained silent, she made an educated guess as to why he was downcast. "I feel a bit sad, too. I was thinking of how much fun we had last year when Daddy put up the tree. Remember? He didn't want to cut the top off. He told you he was going to cut a hole in the floor of your room and let the tree stick out next to your bed."

Jeremy nodded, tears welling up in his eyes. "Daddy phoned this afternoon and said he was all alone."

"I know. I wish he could be with us, but it just wouldn't work out. Remember he started drinking later, after the tree was up, and it wasn't such fun then." There was no need, she knew, to remind her son of his father's drunken rages. "I know Kirk isn't your daddy. But he wants to make Christmas as nice as he can for us all. Maybe we can tell him about the hole in the ceiling. I bet he'd laugh."

Jeremy brightened and began to tell the story to his new friend. Soon the sadness was put aside.

Part of Jeremy's unhappiness was the realization of a beloved parent's alcoholic retreat from society. It was almost as though his father were standing beside him, making him feel ashamed of any enjoyment in his life. This guilty feeling can easily affect children of divorce. Their own depression is increased when they are aware of an absent parent's isolation and loneliness.

If your children are also aware of this parent's disapproval of your new partner, they have an increased tendency to feel they're betraying a loved one. You should not ignore the symptoms, or you may find your children beginning to act out their unhappiness through unacceptable behavior. When Jeremy's mother spoke to him about his sadness, he did not have to resort to more extreme behavior, such as peevishness and disruptive conduct, in order to get her attention when she and her lover began to decorate the tree.

The solution, then, is to notice how your children react whenever they, your lover, and you are together, especially if you're involved in some activity they've enjoyed previously with their other parent. The earlier you become aware of their need for comfort and reassurance, the less disruptive the memories will be. And the comparisons may frequently show that their life in the present is at least as good as—and maybe better than—it was in the past.

Creating a New Special Time

By this time, you recognize that you and your children should enjoy some special time together, time when they're able to tell you their problems and feel your love and concern for them. But once you and your lover move in together, a new relationship is created. Your children and your lover need to develop a special communication of their own. There are a number of important reasons for this to take place.

1. Your children need to feel personal contact with any adult who becomes part of the household. If they don't, that person is almost a nonperson to them. This is why I advise you not to bring home one-night stands or casual lovers.

2. Children need to feel accepted in their own right, not just tolerated as appendages to their parent.

3. You can't continue forever as interpreter between your children and your lover. They need to develop their own relationship.

Special time for your lover to spend with your children may seem risky to arrange during those days prior to your living together, when this new partner is just a visitor in your home, spending much time there, but still retaining a separate residence elsewhere. You may feel it's too much to expect such an intimate relationship to develop until after the move together is finalized. But if it's worked out, even if the time spent is short, the reward for your entire family will be great. Special time is what binds you and your children together. It provides an opportunity for the expression of concerns and fears, and it helps keep fresh the bond of love. It can have the same effect on the relationship between your children and your lover.

Adjusting to the Change

The period just before the decision to live together is reached can be one of the most stressful, especially with regard to the children. The relationship is still not clearly defined. It's no longer just dating or a serious love affair, but it's not an openly acknowledged living-together relationship, either. The lover may spend most nights and weekends as part of the family and may still keep a separate apartment where clothes and personal belongings remain. You have a quasi-family, not yet solidified.

During this transition time, everyone involved feels added tension. Issues of discipline, finances, and familial responsibilities haven't been defined. Both children and the custodial parent may have the feeling that the lover is a guest who needs to be entertained. No one is totally comfortable about sharing work or responsibilities, even when the lover offers to help.

In this nebulous period, children may react by testing disciplinary limits. They act up to see if the rules they're accustomed to are still in effect.

It's important, during this time, to confront the uneasiness and testing, yet it's difficult for both the custodial parent and the lover to face these issues squarely. Both may fear that a too-early discussion of the matter might precipitate a decision neither one is quite ready to make, either rushing them into a move together or causing them to call the whole thing off. And this hesitancy only adds to the stress.

The situation can be discussed directly, in spite of the fear of precipitating change, if the point isn't overemphasized. Willa, who had come to me when her daughter had trouble adjusting to her dating, returned for advice when she and her lover, Jason, were on the verge of living together. Jason spent most of his time with Willa and her daughter, Lisa. All three felt the stress of this relationship in transition, but it was especially hard for Lisa, who didn't know quite how to act toward Jason.

I suggested Willa talk with her daughter, acknowledging the situation and its difficult aspects. She reported that she sat down with Lisa that evening.

"Lisa, I know it's not easy for you having Jason around all the time, even though I know you like him. It's kind of like having a permanent visitor, isn't it?"

Lisa nodded. "It used to be fine when he just came around sometimes."

"I understand." Willa went on to explain that Jason would probably be moving in soon, but neither he nor she was quite ready for that yet. "You don't have to act special toward him. Just remember that you like him, and that he understands that we can't entertain him all the time, like we would a real guest. I think he'll be more comfortable, too, if we just act natural when he's around. And remember, if you feel uncomfortable, or if there's any problem, just tell me. I'll listen and try to fix things up."

Knowing that she could turn to her mother for help if she felt uncomfortable relieved Lisa's uneasiness and lessened her stress. It helped Lisa to stop acting out her tension, which had been disruptive to both Willa and Jason.

I then urged her to talk to Jason as well. She did, explaining to him what she had told Lisa and adding that she needed this transition time as much as he did and didn't want to rush things. He admitted that he felt like a guest. Talking things over helped him to relax a bit and to act more as he had when he had come around less often.

They reached an understanding about what he felt comfortable doing, like making his own coffee or pouring his own water if he was thirsty, so he didn't feel and seem so much a visitor. They also agreed that, until they were sure they wanted to live together, Jason would not be involved in disciplining Lisa. Because she spoke only about the stress, and didn't urge any acceleration of the decision process, all three of them experienced a lessening of the tension. The remainder of the time before Willa and Jason actually began to live together was far more enjoyable for them all.

Who's in Charge?

If you're introducing your children to a new lover with whom your relationship isn't yet firm (and this may happen, even though it isn't the most desirable situation), you need to decide beforehand who'll be responsible for the children's behavior and for any correcting that has to be done. Even if you and your lover are close to establishing a solid relationship, this decision may be needed.

Nothing seems to upset children more than to be given orders and directions by someone they feel has no right to tell them anything. So if you recognize your responsibility to control your children and your lover keeps hands off except in an emergency, things will probably work out more smoothly.

It isn't advisable to make a big issue of the matter. Before an outing, just say to your lover that you hope the kids won't misbehave, but not to worry if they do, that you'll take care of things. Such a way of putting it shows your willingness to accept your authority in the situation, not in order to keep your lover from voicing an opinion, but rather to avoid having your children spoil a pleasant outing.

You may, at least at times, especially as you're approaching a live-in relationship, wish the burden of controlling the children could be shared. But this isn't the time to relieve yourself of that obligation. Later, either with the same lover or with another to whom you feel more committed, a shift or sharing of authority may take place. Rushing things may scare your lover away. Moreover, your plan to live together may fall through. If this happens more than once, your children may be subjected to too many secondary authorities. After a while, they may cease even a pretense of cooperation.

When You Both Have Children

If both you and your lover have children, some of your problems may be lightened while others increase in their complexities. Family outings can be more fun with more children present—but quarrels may develop, too, and your children may expect you to take sides with them. Both you and your lover need to be prepared for this so you aren't pulled into the children's disputes.

Be especially aware of each child's stage of development. For example, if you have an eight-year-old and your lover's youngest is eleven, you may both need to be prepared for possible conflicts. The eleven-year-old may be domineering and the eight-year-old too easily controlled.

Another possible area of trouble is discipline. You and your lover will need to agree on standards so that there isn't too great a disparity between what you each ask of your children. You need to agree on the importance of manners, too. If you teach politeness and your lover doesn't, many disagreements, especially between your children, will develop when you live together.

A client of mine recently dissolved what had at first appeared to be a nearly ideal relationship because of the different attitudes he and his lover had toward manners and discipline. Linda and Bob each had two children. When they decided it was time for their families to become acquainted, they arranged to have a big picnic. Each parent brought food to share as well as special treats they knew their own children enjoyed. They met at a park. Both informed their children of the planned meeting and prepared them by discussing how they expected the afternoon to go.

Problems arose almost immediately. Linda had never felt it necessary to teach her children special eating manners. Sue, the older, nibbled at her food, leaving much of it on her plate. Hansel, her younger, took food from his mother's plate. Both chewed with their mouths open and talked while they ate.

Bob, on the contrary, was strict with his children. They were expected to be polite to their elders and to eat properly. He was unhappy with Linda's indulgence. After lunch, Bob and Linda settled down on a blanket to rest, leaving the children to play alone. Arguments soon broke out that got totally out of hand. Both parents had to take their children home.

A few days later, Bob tried discussing the experience with Linda. But she refused to admit there was any problem. Bob, realizing that were they to move in together these conflicting attitudes toward raising children would become monumental, decided to discontinue their relationship.

Sometimes, when single adults both have children, things are simplified, especially if the children get along well. Dick and Joyce decided to live together, and to consider marriage, after dating for about a year. Each had three children, all between the ages of seven and twelve. They arranged for their first family get-together to take place at a picnic sponsored by their singles group. Fortunately, they knew they had similar standards of behavior for their children.

The picnic was a success. Dick and Joyce played shuffleboard with all six children. There were a few minor arguments, but they were settled reasonably. Both adults were convinced their plans had a good chance of working out to everyone's benefit.

The reasons for this satisfactory conclusion to their first family outing are clear:

1. They already knew they had common backgrounds and similar standards for themselves and their children.

2. They waited to introduce their families until they'd discussed most potentially volatile areas where disagreements might exist.

3. They knew their own emotions and minds.

4. Their children, when presented with the new family unit, were given proper guidance before the meeting and were supervised adequately throughout the first encounter.

All the suggestions made throughout this chapter apply with special emphasis if both you and your lover have children. Prepare your youngsters adequately for the first encounter with what you hope will be their new family. Be ready to help them overcome any nostalgia that may draw them back toward what can no longer be, and listen to their assessments of the new situation. Expect them to be polite, but don't force them to feign affection they might not yet feel for these potential stepsiblings.

One other point is made by the two examples just given. Before you attempt to combine two families of children, you need to discuss thoroughly your attitudes toward childrearing and discipline. If your concepts and those of your lover are too disparate, you may be better off if you keep your children apart and continue to maintain your relationship on a more casual level—at least until you're able to work out the differences.

Nothing points more directly to areas of possible disagreement than children who've been raised differently. A lackadaisical parent and one who believes children should have evenhanded guidance will find themselves at odds if they move in together. And their children are almost sure to resent each other.

If you anticipate problems and recognize that your children may confront you with conflicts you've overlooked, you'll face fewer surprises in the days ahead. And if you can handle at least some of these areas of disagreement before you and your lover actually move in together, your chances of successfully establishing your new family unit are greatly increased.

Bringing Your Lover into Your Extended Family

If your relationship becomes serious, and you feel you'll soon be living together, you may want to begin to bring your lover to family gatherings—Christmas at Grandma's or a backyard barbecue on the Fourth of July, for example.

If these are times and places you used to share with your ex-spouse, you may encounter new problems when you decide to bring your lover instead. For example, your parents may have a real fondness for your ex-partner, who is still invited to some of their gatherings; or, in the past, both of you may have used this time to discuss joint-custody or visitation issues in a neutral setting. Your children may look forward to those rare times when they see their parents together again. So, unless you and your lover are both very sure of your commitment, I recommend that you leave things as they are. See your lover some other time and give your family and children time to accept a substitute for your ex-spouse.

There are many such situations that can cause or rekindle issues of divided loyalty in your children. The presence of your lover in the extended family can emphasize to them the finality of your divorce and the certainty that you and their other parent will never get back together. This may be depressing to your children, causing them to feel sad when others are happy.

Because of the possible negative effects of including your lover in an extended-family situation, I suggest you not do so unless you are both reasonably certain that your relationship is going to last. Don't bring a casual lover to such important affairs.

Think ahead. What are the customs at these gatherings? Are photographs taken? What assumptions might your parents and siblings make regarding your present relationship if you bring your lover along? Do you want them to assume that this is a permanent relationship? If your extended family is close-knit, will your lover feel out of place? Will it appear that you're pushing toward a permanence in your relationship that isn't yet acceptable?

If you consider your children, your extended family, *and* your lover, you may decide that, for the present at least, you'll keep your love relationship separate. There'll be time for larger gatherings later, when you're more certain of the feelings and expectations you and your lover have for each other.

A Checklist

In summary, if you're getting ready to introduce your children and your lover, you'll do well to consider the following questions:

1. Have I prepared my lover? Have I explained my children's idiosyncrasies and what to expect of them at their ages?

2. Have I prepared my children for the meeting? Have I reassured them of my continued love while at the same time explaining how very special this person is to me?

3. Have we chosen a good time for the meeting?

4. Have we chosen something we'll all enjoy doing, so problems will be few?

5. Am I prepared to deal with my children's renewed regrets and new awareness that I'll never go back to their other parent?

6. If we both have children, have my lover and I already determined that our ideas on raising a family are similar? If we disagree on some subject, have we reached a settlement with which we can both be comfortable?

If you ignore some of these questions, your first get-together may end in disaster. If, on the contrary, you've considered the above six questions and reached satisfactory answers to every one, then that critical meeting has a good chance of being a pleasant occasion for everyone involved. You'll have taken the first—and probably the most important—step toward establishing a happy new family.

12 *Who Pays for What?*

Financial Issues

*T*he impact of money on dating and other relationships involving single parents shouldn't be underrated. People often have very different expectations of one another when it comes to financial matters, but a discussion of these differences seldom takes place. Assumptions made by either partner in a new relationship as to who will pay for what, and when, may often prove to be untrue. The result can be annoyance, hurt feelings, or anger—any of which can prematurely end a relationship that showed promise.

I find it interesting that most of my clients can talk more freely about their sex lives than about how much money they make and how they spend it. Other psychologists indicate the same reactions on the part of their clients. Carol Colman, author of *Love and Money*, interviewed hundreds of people in preparation for her book, finding that most of them had never really talked openly about their attitudes toward money and its impact on their relationships.*

All this is astonishing when one considers the importance of money in our society, especially in that most personal of associa-

*Carol Colman, *Love and Money* (New York: Zebra Books, 1983).

tions, marriage. Couples often disagree, sometimes violently, over money matters. Usually it's because there's too little. Frequently, it's because too much is spent for what one or the other considers to be the wrong things. Such disputes can even lead to divorce.

If communication regarding financial matters is so neglected by couples who are deeply committed to a relationship, it's not surprising that the issue of money is seldom dealt with when two people are just dating. And yet, money has an obvious and powerful impact on a relationship because, in addition to the practical aspects of it, money also deals symbolically with emotional issues such as dependence, independence, and the giving or withholding of love.

Why are we then, as a society, so hesitant to discuss it? Why are single parents and their lovers, who are certain to encounter some disagreements about money, still reluctant to bring up the matter until it's forced upon them? One possible reason is that the possession of money or its lack is often considered an indication of personal worth.

Despite all evidence to the contrary, many people continue to assume that anyone with a lot of money must be successful, powerful, and very self-satisfied. The opposite is suspected of those with meager resources. And since few people have enough wealth to be sure of how their financial status will appear to others, they prefer to avoid discussions involving money or how it's to be spent. They are afraid it might turn out that they aren't as well off in comparison to the others in the group as they thought they were. No one wants to be judged in this regard if they think they might come out second best.

In other instances, people just don't think ahead. They've always lived from day to day or month to month financially, spending money as necessary with little forethought. It's not surprising, then, that it is standard procedure to improvise without any clear knowledge of how things really are when it comes to the financial aspects of any relationship, from a simple date to sharing space with a live-in lover.

Be Clear About Your Expectations

Since money, or the lack of it, can have such an impact on a relationship, how and when it's spent, and by whom, should not be left to chance. Carefully examine your situation and determine what you expect in the way of financial help or sharing from a new partner. Don't assume certain financial matters will be taken care of unless you have a previous understanding. Disparity in expectations can't help but result in problems later.

Some people operate on the assumption that if a date or lover really cared, was thoughtful, sensitive, generous, and so forth, he or she would volunteer to share the expenses. That may be true. But it may be equally true that certain things aren't done because there's no real understanding of what's wanted. If you desire a particular action or response from a date or lover, it's a sign of maturity to discuss the matter and ask.

People who proceed on assumption rather than on mutual agreement always risk upsetting others. Misunderstandings occur because each of us has had unique experiences and role models and therefore has a different frame of reference. Even people who deliberately talk over their personal viewpoints, goals, and expectations with each other can fail to understand exactly what the other person means. After all, none of us is perfect in expressing our thoughts, for language itself is an imperfect method of communication. The best we can do is to be very clear in our minds about our own expectations and try to impart this information to others who need it.

One of the realities in the social lives of many single parents (especially women) is the question of who provides money for child care, such as baby-sitting. Not facing this issue from the outset can result in friction and misunderstanding between a single parent and a date or casual lover, and in some instances it can create a situation in which children are left unattended.

A parent is always the one responsible for a child's welfare and should be the one to initiate any relevant discussions. However, some parents feel too proud or embarrassed to bring up the subject and need help in dealing with this issue. In view of the fact that female single parents usually have a much more difficult time financially than their male counterparts, it's helpful, thoughtful, and responsible for a male partner to be sensitive to the pressures on a single mother concerning the costs of child care and a child's social activities. If he is aware that she is having financial problems, he can offer to help with these expenses, or at least not expect her to be available for dating as often if she decides to pay them herself.

If you're faced with a situation in which you can't afford to leave the children at home with a baby-sitter, and can't afford to pay their way if they go along with you and your date, think carefully about what can be done to solve the dilemma and then talk it over with your lover. You may need to plan more economical activities, so that money is available to help pay for baby-sitters—and make your family outings picnics rather than visits to expensive restaurants, and hikes rather than trips to amusement parks with expensive rides.

When Incomes Are Unequal

Kramer vs. Kramer notwithstanding, statistics show that in 90 percent of single-parent families it's the mother who has physical custody of the children—whether by default or by mutual agreement. If we were to agree that, ideally, the parent of a child should pay for any expenses connected with that child's activities or care, we'd have to look at some hard realities that can affect this position. Often, if the parent is a woman, her income just can't cover many baby-sitting fees.

Statistics reveal that the standard of living of mother and child usually suffers greatly following a divorce. The same holds true when a husband dies. In a comprehensive ten-year study of the impact of no-fault divorce, the California Divorce Law Project (headed by Stanford University sociologist Leonore Weitzman) found that divorce is financially profitable for men and an economic disaster for women and children.

California courts order, as a median child-support payment, an amount that is less than half the actual cost of raising a child. Yet despite this small obligation, "most studies indicate that fewer than half of the fathers comply more or less regularly with court orders to pay child support."*

The sharpest decline in awards for support of spouse under the no-fault law has been to mothers of younger children, only 13 percent of whom have been awarded any support at all. However, it's encouraging to know that new laws are being passed to enforce child-support payments.

Interestingly, the California Divorce Law Project didn't corroborate the expected stereotypical notion that many men are suffering from the burden of supporting both first and second families. It found that, while men remarry sooner than their ex-wives, they generally marry women who are working and who therefore contribute additional income to the amount earned by the men—increasing, not diminishing, the new family's standard of living.

Nationwide studies by federal agencies reveal that there are more poor women raising families by themselves than ever before, an example of the so-called feminization of poverty. Two out of every three needy adults in the nation are women. Therefore, families headed by women are generally poorer than those headed by men. While female poverty is greatest among blacks and Latinos, statistics indicate that an increasing number of former middle-class white women are now receiving federal welfare benefits.

When you couple these facts with data showing that women earn only 59 percent of what men are paid for comparable work, we discover a clearly inequitable situation. It's apparent that regularly leaving it up to the single mother to pay for the babysitter and other social costs can be, in many instances, an unrealistic and unfair arrangement. This is a women's issue as well as

*L. J. Weitzman and R. B. Dixon, "Alimony Myths: Does No-fault Divorce Make a Difference?" *Family Law Quarterly*, 14:141-185 (Fall, 1980), p. 180.

a cultural one. Until singles develop as a political force in order to obtain more and better child-care centers, the situation is unlikely to change.

It's not just single mothers who struggle with financial problems when dating. Men who have physical custody of their children can also be trapped financially. The same holds true with men of limited income who are paying child support. Though there aren't as many of them as there are financially strapped women, their problems are just as real.

Many men are caught up in the myth that only a man who is financially successful is adequate. One young male client, Larry, who has three children under the age of seven in his custody, told me he doesn't date at all because he can't afford to—unless his date wanted to spend an evening at the laundromat with him and his children. This attitude is not uncommon, yet men who share it are not examining all the possibilities. Some women, especially those with children of their own, would be happy to help plan outings costing very little money. By denying himself and his children on financial grounds, Larry was doing his part in perpetuating a double standard for men. He also limited his options, not only for himself but for his children. They could benefit from the presence of a woman in their lives and from an enjoyable social time.

The sexual double standard can be harmful to men as well as to women. All single parents need to recognize that no role, no matter how socially acceptable, is as important as their happiness and the best possible growth conditions for their children. Any single parent who refuses to take steps that might broaden life experiences, and who uses as an excuse a fear of appearing unmanly or unwomanly, is giving too much importance to the sexual standards our society accepts.

Who Pays for the Baby-sitter?

One of the most common financial issues faced by single parents who have physical custody of their children is the question of who will pay the cost of providing child care when the parent dates. Opinions vary widely, however, among both men and women.

Many single mothers expect, as a matter of course, that their dates will pay for the baby-sitter, or at least chip in to cover part of the cost. One young, attractive mother who dates frequently informed me that, if a man wasn't willing to pay the baby-sitter for her eight-year-old daughter, she wouldn't go out with him. She declared that she's barely able to cover the necessities of living and wouldn't dream of paying for a baby-sitter in order to have an evening out. "If he wants to date me, he pays," she stated emphatically. But many young single mothers who date less often and aren't as confident of their ability to attract men say they'd be afraid to expect, much less demand, that a date pay for a baby-sitter.

Indeed, many men feel deep resentment when women automatically expect them to pay for a sitter. One male client of mine expressed it this way: A smart woman will make sure she provides for the baby-sitter herself, at least at first; there are enough problems in becoming involved with a woman who has children without having to deal with this financial issue right away, and there are too many attractive single women to choose from, women who don't have children, for him to be taken advantage of by someone who does.

The fact is that no one wants to be taken advantage of. If a single mother doesn't discuss the issue of her baby-sitter before a date and then expects the man to pay the sitter, she is forcing him into a corner. If he pays, he might feel that he was tricked into spending more money than he can afford or that he budgeted for the evening. If he refuses to pay, he appears to be selfish and inconsiderate.

Some men resent the notion that a woman might expect them to pay for a baby-sitter but feel compelled, out of politeness, to at least offer to pay and appreciate it when a woman declines. One man with whom I spoke took the position that a woman who's "on the ball" will already have paid the sitter, but added that a fair compromise might be to split the cost.

The truth is that there are as many approaches to this issue as there are men and women who deal with it. I've encountered men who have come to accept the payment for a baby-sitter as part of the normal cost of a date, so they automatically offer to pay. They generally feel that it helps when a woman acknowledges the payment and expresses appreciation rather than just taking it for granted. Other men feel they might be insulting a woman if they offer to pay for the sitter—as if they were assuming she couldn't afford to care for her own children. But the issue is not one-sided. I worked with a widower with three children who could not afford both the date and the baby-sitter. He was embarrassed and angry when a woman he asked for a date wasn't more sensitive to his situation.

Many women, and especially those who are financially successful and secure, do interpret the offer to pay a sitter as an insult to their competence in being self-supporting. They take pride in their ability to cope with all facets of their lives without help, including the paying of costs for social activities and child-care expenses.

But even some of those who are having a difficult time financially feel that depending on a man for such monetary support is an affront to their sense of integrity. They handle the problem by developing a network of friends with whom they trade off baby-sitting chores. Such an arrangement makes them feel more independent, as well as satisfied that they're taking care of the responsibilities they have to their children.

Many single mothers agree that insufficient money influences their decisions. A mother who became single when her daughters were six and nine, and who lacked both money and a support system, dated only one man for some time because he accepted her children and arranged for the child care when they went out. But she believes that, if she could have afforded baby-sitters herself and had gone out with other men, she might have found someone she felt more strongly about.

There can be cultural overtones to this issue, too. A woman who raised her young daughter in Puerto Rico recalled dating a wealthy doctor who offered to pay for child care. She refused, stating she'd feel there was an implication that she was being kept.

Many women don't want to be obligated to the men they date. If a date pays for the sitter, they feel they owe him. While they realize this is an irrational point of view, they can't help the feeling. They believe some women become involved sexually with a man out of a sense of obligation and as a trade-off for the money spent on them, and that there's an implicit, but never openly acknowledged, understanding of such a trade-off on the part of both participants.

Others who view their options more clearly believe that, even if a man pays for the social activities or the baby-sitter, they have no obligation to repay in any form, since there's been no agreement between them regarding any such arrangement. If a man invites them out, he's making a free choice without any strings attached. However, some acknowledge that if a man pays for the expenses of a date, including the cost of a baby-sitter, they'll later reciprocate by preparing a dinner at home, or inviting him to some event, much as they would repay a friend for a kindness.

It should be noted, however, that men don't always agree with this view. Jacqueline Simenauer and David Carroll, in *Singles: The New Americans*, report that "more than three-quarters of men feel that women should pay or occasionally help pay for a date."* Many men might not consider a dinner at home adequate reciprocation for a number of expensive dates where they also covered baby-sitting costs.

Timing with regard to the stage of a relationship between two people is important in determining attitude in these matters. Even men who resent the expectation that they cover the cost of a sitter tend to think that, once a relationship is well established, the subject of who pays for what should be openly discussed and negotiated on a fair basis.

*Jacqueline Simenauer and David Carroll, *Singles: The New Americans* (New York: New American Library, 1982), p. 100.

Financial arrangement with respect to dating—especially the payment to a baby-sitter—is a highly individual matter. No assumptions should be made beforehand. In this touchy area, as in all other aspects of a relationship, frank and open communication is the best way to avoid misunderstandings.

I advise my clients to cover their own baby-sitting costs, at least for the initial dates, or, preferably, to establish friendships with other single mothers and two-parent families so they can arrange child care on an exchange basis. This matter is dealt with in more detail in chapter 8 under Networking: The Buddy System.

Who Pays When the Kids Come Along?

The same factors that pertain to the question of who pays the baby-sitter apply when children accompany their parent on an outing or other family entertainment. Ideally, the parent is still responsible for their expenses. However, practically and fairly speaking, this may not be feasible.

There are many exceptions, of course. Not all women are facing financial difficulties, and many take pride in handling all aspects of their children's care. Nevertheless, it is common for women to appreciate it when a man offers to pay for the costs of the children's social activities while they're together. As one woman expressed it, the offer tells her something symbolically about her date's willingness to give, how accepting he is of her children, and how prepared he might be to assume some responsibility for them if this were to become a committed relationship. She generally responds to such an offer by saying, "No, but thank you," even if she feels close to the man. But when a date fails to make the offer, she thinks less of him.

Be that as it may, there are many men who believe women use them financially. They resent women who expect them to pay for everything as a matter of course. Furthermore, many men, even if they want to, can't afford to pick up the tab. Women dating single fathers whose funds may be limited should consider ways in which they can share the costs of social activities. If they think an offer to pay some of the expenses might offend their lover, they can plan economical outings, of which there are many, or reciprocate in some other way that doesn't involve the actual exchange of money.

This is a sensitive subject under all circumstances, but it must be faced. I suggest that, in considering the financial aspects of dates, with and without the children, you follow these simple guidelines:

1. Don't make assumptions or take things for granted.
2. Talk about the issues openly.
3. Be fair.

Don't manipulate or use your date to lighten your financial load without first getting an agreement.

Money Is Power

As we've seen, money has many levels of meaning. It can be thought of as a symbol of status, or security, or a source of power. And with money goes control. People who can provide can also withhold. A person who's dependent upon another financially is indeed in a vulnerable position.

In *Mirror, Mirror,* Elissa Melamed states that "the dependency of the married state is a mixed blessing. . . . We will never know how many stay in destructive or dead-end marriages out of fear that they will not be able to survive economically on their own. Or even the effect on a good marriage when a wife has to think of her husband not only as a partner but also as a meal ticket."*

A single person—most often a woman—who allows herself to

*Elissa Melamed, *Mirror, Mirror: The Terror of Not Being Young* (New York: Simon and Schuster, 1983), p. 21.

become financially dependent upon her lover places herself in a similarly vulnerable position. This can occur in both subtle and blatant ways, as Judy's story shows.

Judy described how, shortly after her divorce, when she was frightened of how she was going to manage financially, she drifted into a relationship with a man who was generous with his money. She soon discovered, however, that the trade-off was in the demands he made of her and her children. He tended to be perfectionistic, domineering, and controlling.

Nevertheless, Judy accepted these demands without question, since she was convinced she could not survive alone. At first, she let herself become accustomed to his taking her and the two children out to dinner and to movies and other social activities. These were things she enjoyed, and wanted her children to have, but couldn't afford on her own. Gradually, with no discussion, he assumed other financial responsibilities, such as helping with her daughter's orthodontic expenses, defraying summer camp costs, and handling other special expenses her budget didn't cover.

It soon became painfully clear to Judy that she was duplicating a pattern of living she'd experienced with her former husband—one in which she'd remained for years, subjugating her own personality and desires to his because of her financial dependence upon him. Once she recognized this pattern, she began to free herself from this second controlling and dependent relationship. It was a difficult task, but she knew its importance to herself and her children. She became more self-supporting and, because of her new awareness, avoided entering into such a relationship again.

Economic realities and feminist politics notwithstanding, it's remarkable in this time of supposed greater enlightenment that teenaged girls continue to believe they'll someday be taken care of by a man.

Judy Edmondson, a coauthor of *Choices: A Teen Woman's Journal for Self-Awareness and Personal Planning*, stated in a telephone interview that, in her numerous contacts with teenaged girls, she has found that most of them continue to believe they will marry, have children, and be supported by their husbands. Yet reality is far from this dream. Statistics reveal that 90 percent of today's teenaged girls will work outside the home for at least twenty-five years, with an almost 50 percent chance they'll be divorced and very possibly become single parents.

Of particular concern is the fact that the greatest rise in pregnancy of any age group is among ten- to fourteen-year-old girls, many of whom are keeping their babies. It's a sobering picture. It's difficult to imagine how these young single parents, still children themselves, will handle the issues discussed in this book.

Economic realities affect every aspect of a person's life. The wish to be Cinderella often leads one not to the palace but back to the hearth and ashes. There's wisdom in directing one's energies into being as economically self-sufficient as possible. This will minimize the financial problems you, as a single parent, face when you date. It will also help you to avoid choosing a lover primarily because of an ability to provide what you can't get for yourself or your children. Best of all, such independence will help you, with the partner of your choice, to develop a bond based more on sharing than on dependency.

13 Love Me, Love My Kids

Helping Your Lover Understand Your Children

A single parent establishing a new relationship with another adult faces a special problem not encountered by single adults who don't have children. The time will come when all the plans that have been made while they were alone will come up against a very crucial test. Does my lover understand and love my children? Many promising relationships between single parents and would-be partners have ended when this question is finally faced and answered.

Why is this such a critical point in a relationship between a single parent and his or her lover? Why is it so difficult for a new lover to enter an established family? There are a number of basic reasons. The most obvious are:

1. There's a natural resistance to change. If you're aware of this resistance, you can work on it with your children and your lover.

2. Some people welcome the idea of being involved with children. But there are probably many more who'd prefer if you didn't come as a package.

3. The addition of any new element to a relationship is threatening. You, your children, and your lover will all feel additionally insecure during this period of change, and insecurity often results in disruptive behavior.

If a single parent and lover marry without first reaching a satisfactory solution to these problems, lack of understanding and lack of love between children and the new adult in the house can contribute to the breakup of that marriage. If the two adults try to maintain their love relationship in spite of the discord, unresolved daily conflict is quickly reflected in bed. It's difficult to feel romantic, loving, and tender if you're angry.

Caught in the Middle

Single parents, in this situation, face a dilemma. Both legally and emotionally, they're loyal to the children in their custody. They love them. Their lives are intertwined. But they now have another loyalty—a new love. They see in this lover a chance for a fresh start and a better adult relationship than has existed before. In the back of their thoughts is an awareness that the children will eventually grow up and leave. But the lover, who seems so right, may very well stay on until, in the words of the marriage ceremony, "death do you part."

The choice is not a simple one. Compounding the usual problems single parents face is the awareness that a lack of affection and love between their children and the new adult in the family may seriously harm the children's emotional growth.

There's another complexity to add to this confusion. In our imperfect world, few adults are mature in all areas of their personalities. Single parents carry loads of unresolved problems that originated in their own childhoods. So do their lovers. These immaturities frequently remain hidden until some special condition stirs them up. Then, when they surface, reason often flies out the window.

If, under these circumstances, the insecure adult is expected to deal rationally with children who have their *own* fears and insecurities, the result can be total disaster. When single parents are caught in the middle of a conflict between their lover and their children, the problems that exist can grow to unmanageable proportions. The only solution seems to be to side with one and reject the other.

This was the conclusion reached by Elaine when she came to me. She had been optimistic when Alvin, her lover, came to live with her, since he had made it clear he loved children, and was prepared to accept her thirteen-year-old boy as if he were his own. She believed that Henry, too, had been properly prepared, since she'd told him of the plan at least a week before Alvin actually moved in. She'd conveniently forgotten the problems that had developed between the two on those few occasions when they'd met earlier in her relationship with Alvin. Back then, if she'd noticed any upsets at all, she'd merely reprimanded Henry for being foolish, or teased Alvin for acting childish. Now, she was so eager to have her lover move in with her, she couldn't admit that any difficulties had occurred in the past or might arise in the future.

But, as soon as Alvin moved in, the arguments began. He seemed critical of everything Henry did. True, the boy wasn't doing too well in school, but he wasn't as bad as Alvin seemed to feel he was. Alvin even complained to neighbors, as well as to Elaine, about Henry's faults. And Elaine was aware that her lover resented any time she spent with her son. Henry, meanwhile, became more and more difficult. His problems in school increased.

Finally, Elaine considered asking Alvin to leave. She hated to do it. She loved him, and was convinced he loved her. But she was close to the end of her rope. She couldn't endure the conflict between her son and her lover any more.

This is typical of the dilemma faced by many single parents. Fortunately, before Elaine made that critical decision, she sought help. In therapy, she was able to recognize how she'd failed to take the precautions that might have avoided the problem now confronting her, and she saw a way to resolve the situation, too.

She should have started discussions with her son regarding how he felt about Alvin living with them far earlier than she did. This would have allowed him to express his fears and concerns so that she could deal with them. It would also have given the boy more time to adjust to the change.

She should have talked more with her lover, too. Alvin would have been better able to deal with Henry had he first been helped to identify his own inner child. He should have been prepared for some rejection by Henry, so that he didn't try to push for intimacy too fast. Moreover, the two of them should have clarified their expectations regarding the child. They should have decided who would take responsibility for discipline, as well as the manner in which it would be meted out. Most of all, it would have helped if she'd realized that Alvin might feel threatened and insecure as a newcomer to the family.

Until this time, Elaine had been afraid to get involved in the feuding. But now, with guidance, she began to try the steps that have proven effective for others. She came to recognize that both her lover and her son felt insecure in this new relationship and needed reassurance. Both depended upon her continued loyalty for their happiness. She learned how to mediate when Alvin and Henry disagreed, without seeming to side with either one or destroying whatever respect each had for the other.

Most of all, she came to recognize the need for patience. She'd dated her lover for over a year before they decided to live together, yet she'd been expecting him to take to her child after very few encounters. And she'd expected the same quick adjustment from her boy.

She also learned to anticipate periods when there would be a conflict of life-styles. She and Henry had established their own family routine while they were alone. Alvin had been accustomed to thinking only of himself. Now all three of them had to change. But because of their increased understanding of the problems involved, these adjustments were made with a minimum of distress.

Showing Your Love

Adult newcomers to single-parent families inevitably feel a bit on the outside. They're certain to approach their new, ready-made families with some trepidation and stress. Will the children like them? How can they help out in discipline as well as in other matters that arise?

They're aware that, one way or another, their lovers have managed the children alone. It's difficult for them not to wonder if they might arouse resentment if they try too soon to help solve problems that have, until this time, been kept within the family. And, most of all, they wonder when—if ever—they'll become as much a family member as the others. Will there ever be enough blending of attitudes toward life so the new family feels, and is, united?

Because they're under this stress, lovers who have recently moved in with a single parent need reassurance. They need to know that their every action isn't being scrutinized and condemned. They should be complimented when they deal effectively with the children, and given a thoughtful, understanding analysis of what happened when they fail.

This was one of the steps Elaine took when she decided to try straightening out the trouble that had been compounding ever since Alvin moved in. Quietly, she noted the times when Alvin, who was a computer programmer, helped Henry with his schoolwork. She recognized that during these periods things seemed to go smoothly. So she began by complimenting Alvin on his capabilities in this area.

Along with this greater display of appreciation for Alvin's talents, Elaine also began to reassure him of her love in many small ways. The compliments and the reminders of her love served to make him feel more secure. He'd begun to fear that he'd soon be thrown out because of his competitiveness with Henry, which, at the beginning, seemed to be all Elaine noticed.

Fostering Mutual Understanding

When a lover and child are fighting, single parents may feel they're dealing not with one adult and one child, but with two children. And, in truth, they are. Most adults have tender spots caused by the burdens of problems that were never solved when they were young. When those tender areas are touched, otherwise reasonable adults suddenly turn into unreasonable, overly emotional children. Until someone recognizes the cause of this irrational behavior, there's no chance for it to be controlled.

The first thing Elaine had to do was recognize Alvin's insecurity. Before he moved in, he'd had very little contact with her boy, which was one of their first mistakes. He hadn't realized how close her relationship to the child actually was. Nor was he aware of the family routine to which Henry was accustomed. When Elaine saw that Alvin's repeated criticism of her son was motivated by his inner child reacting to insecurity, she was able to handle the situation. She understood that children often belittle competitors in hopes of pushing them out of favor.

As Elaine improved in her ability to show her love for Alvin, he gained control of his inner child. She was able to talk more with him about his personal insecurity and help him keep it under control. Once this was settled, she was able to help Alvin understand her son's reactions and fears. Once more, Alvin was able to approach the adjustment not as a frightened child, but as the mature adult he usually was.

At the same time, she had quiet talks with Henry. She knew that he, too, was feeling insecure, and she reassured him of her continued love. Then she helped him see Alvin's point of view. It surprised Henry to realize that both Alvin and his mother were sometimes frightened by new situations and sometimes insecure as well. This new understanding gave him more confidence. He was better able to compromise with Alvin when he no longer saw the man as an unyielding, rigid enemy, but rather as a human being with foibles and sensitivities just like his own.

Giving It Time

One of Elaine's main problems vanished when she stopped expecting the immediate creation of a firm, loving family relationship between her child and Alvin. She was so eager to establish her new family and, perhaps, to alleviate some of the burden of parenting she'd carried alone that she'd been unwilling to put the needed energy into helping her son and her lover adjust.

What surprised her was the realization that Alvin had shared her eagerness. He had pushed to assume the role of father before his new son was willing to accept him, before, in fact, Henry knew him well enough even to *like* him. With her new insight, Elaine helped Alvin relax and accept the necessity for establishing a good personal relationship with her child. She encouraged him to help Henry with his math and to teach him some of the intricacies of computer programming. She also encouraged them to spend some time alone together.

As Henry's respect for Alvin's mathematical skills grew, and as he began to see Alvin as a confidant and friend, his willingness to accept this new man in the family increased. Time achieved what pressure had failed to do.

It's important to note that the straight talks Elaine had with Alvin were very important to the final adjustments. Elaine was able to tell him of her pain and the pressure she felt because of his quarrels with her son. She was able to urge him to snap out of his childish behavior and share adult responsibilities with her. She told him she was beginning to feel desperate and might reach a point where she could no longer bear the entire burden.

If he hadn't responded to that direct plea, Elaine might have found her love waning and her sexual response to him negatively affected. In time, this shift in her feelings toward him could have ended their relationship. As mentioned before, daytime arguments are certain to affect what happens in bed.

Avoiding Reactive Behavior

Until Elaine sought help, she was what is known as a "reactor." If her son or her lover did something that displeased her, she reacted to that specific behavior with no consideration of how this might affect their long-term relationship. Often, she reacted differently at different times to the same bickering, confusing Henry and Alvin alike. Unknowingly, she'd contributed to the very chaos and conflict that upset her so much.

After she sought help, Elaine learned to recognize her own behavior patterns and how they added to the difficulties she was facing. She began to be more consistent in her treatment of the problems she encountered. As she improved, so did the relationship between her son and her lover.

I helped Elaine recognize that no one expected her to be perfect. As therapy progressed, she came to understand that there would be times when she'd forget and *react* instead of *act* with a direction and a goal in mind. But she realized that if she remained aware of what she was doing these periods would decrease and she'd grow more skilled at being a parent.

Elaine was, in turn, able to convey this same attitude of tolerance to her son and her lover. Just knowing they'd still be loved even when they weren't perfect took pressure off them both. Their behavior improved. Many of the problems that had brought Elaine to my door were beginning to fade.

Sharing Dreams

As the stress under which they'd been living began to abate, Elaine and Alvin approached the next step in improving family relationships. They were ready to explore their expectations for themselves, for each other, and for the new family they were creating. This is something I advise single parents and their lovers to do *before* they move in together, but it's better to do it later than not at all.

This exploration often starts with the single parent stating his or her hopes for the children and the new relationship. But that opening has its hazards. Parents may easily become very touchy where their children are concerned. They grow angry and defensive if any criticism is made or even implied. To avoid having this important discussion degenerate into a fight, I advise that a single parent and lover *begin by discussing general issues*.

Reach an agreement about what you want for yourselves. When you feel united in that goal, look at how and where the children will fit in. Consider their ages. How long will they be dependent upon you? Do you want to send them to college? Your aims here may differ, depending on the personality, personal goals, skills, and aptitudes of each child. Discuss the goals you had before you divorced, or lost your mate through death, and how they've changed over the years. These past objectives may still have meaning to you and your children and should be considered.

Tell your lover all you know about your children's loyalties to their missing parent. To the degree that your lover recognizes those loyalties and respects them, some clashes may be avoided. Also, your lover will be prepared to encounter them and won't be hurt when that happens.

As the discussion progresses, it will soon become obvious that you'll have to talk about your respective childhood years. If you had a very happy childhood but your lover was mistreated, you need to know this. Did you have a firm conviction that your parents loved you? Did your lover have to fight for every sign of parental affection? What kind of expectations did each of your parents have for you? Were they accepting or critical? How were you disciplined? Were you treated harshly, ignored, or showered with affection? Your past experiences have a strong effect on your present attitudes.

I've found in my clinical practice that, as we explore these questions, parents begin to understand their own expectations for their children. They begin to sort out their own dreams and to differentiate between them and those *their* parents had in the past. When both single parent and lover go through this session of remembering, they're better able to recognize those areas where they see eye-to-eye and those where they oppose each other. With the parameters clearly established, they can reach agreement, or at least empathy and understanding, even in those areas where they began in complete opposition.

Your problems will be minimized if you and your lover both had parents who were understanding, accepting, and affectionate. You'll both instinctively want to behave in a like manner to your children.

But if one or both of you had parents who provided poor guidance, who were reluctant to show affection, and who never seemed to understand your needs, you may try to compensate by being too rigid, or you may simply accept this poor method of handling children as the only way to behave. If this is the "unfinished business" you have to contend with, you'll first need to recognize where *your* parents failed so that you can behave differently. This type of situation is difficult to cope with. Often, understanding can't be reached without the help of a third party, such as a therapist, to keep the discussion on track.

Many times, just the opportunity to talk together about these experiences brings an awareness of how you or your lover may be repeating bad patterns from your past as you deal with your children. This insight may be enough to cause a change in behavior. At the very least, it generally serves to diminish anger and to provide a better atmosphere for solving differences that seemed insurmountable before.

At this point, because of increased understanding, you may be able to explore the expectations both you and your lover have for your children without battling when you encounter differences of opinion. You can emphasize the similarities and compromise in areas where disagreements are extreme.

Special concepts to discuss are:

1. Does your lover want to be involved with the care and control of the children?

2. Who will discipline them, and how?

3. What is an equitable way to deal with expenditures so that you and your lover aren't being denied while the children are overindulged, or vice versa?

4. What household chores are appropriate for each child?

5. Who will deal with school problems, and what are your expectations for your children's education?

6. How will you spend your leisure time? Your vacations? Will the children always accompany you?

7. What about the visitation or joint-custody rights for your ex-spouse? Does your lover feel excluded when your ex-partner is around?

8. Do you both agree on how emotions may be expressed? Do you let your son have the freedom to cry although your lover feels that it's shameful for men to shed tears? Can you both tolerate a show of emotion?

9. How do your family routines differ? Are you both prepared to adjust in your search for a new family identity?

10. Are you prepared to recognize and honor those routines that are important to your children?

There may be other questions that apply only to your relationship. Discuss them, whatever they are, when you're both calm and feeling unthreatened. If you're angry with each other, or if one of you feels insecure, these discussions will be difficult, if not totally useless.

This last point is very important. In counseling sessions, when I ask my clients if they've discussed something, they'll often answer yes but that "talking doesn't help." If I explore further, I usually find that the talk took place when they were angry.

Private Talking Helps

Sometimes a single parent faced with disagreements between the lover and the children feels that the only way to tackle each difficulty is through a family conference. I've found, however, that more is accomplished if the discussions begin with one person at a time. This avoids humiliating anyone, or wounding fragile egos.

When Elaine realized that her lover had a problem brought on by his own insecurity, she didn't try to get him to admit this to her son. Neither did she ask her son to stand by as she explained to Alvin Henry's loyalty to his alcoholic father. By dealing with each issue separately, and with only the person who needed to understand what appeared to be an irrational behavior on another's part, she kept the discussions from reverting to hurt feelings and an exchange of invectives. When she was sure Alvin and Henry each had a better understanding of the other, she was ready to suggest a full family discussion. Both were now prepeared to compromise and be less judgmental.

Direct contact between lover and child can be of value, too. Sometimes, your presence puts both of them under stress. They're too aware of your hopes for their relationship, and they react to that pressure. One of the factors contributing to the improvement of relationships in Elaine's new family was the friendship that developed between Alvin and Henry when they explored the world of computers together. In time, this accord spread to other areas of their relationship, and the tension that had almost driven Elaine to give up on her attempt to incorporate Alvin into her life dissipated.

Most problems have solutions. However, until people are able to face them squarely and without destructive emotion, the answers may be hard to find. You may need guidance, as Elaine did. But, if you study the list of questions above, you may be able to settle your own new family disputes and, at last, begin the construction of a parent-lover-child relationship that is satisfying to everyone involved.

One further note: The combining of special time and family

time is the best way to handle interpersonal problems if you choose not to seek outside help. But it isn't always easy to recognize all the aspects of a troubled relationship. Fortunately, many helpful courses are being offered today in the skills of parenthood and communication. They're to be found at local colleges, at the Y, and at adult-education centers.

I advise any single parent who's struggling to combine good child care with a balanced personal life to take at least some such course. None of us can be good parents by instinct alone. We need instruction and help. If no classes are available, and your problems are just too overwhelming, your best recourse may be to consult a family therapist. They're trained to deal with this sort of problem, and can be of inestimable value to you.

14 Unconventional Life-styles

Special Concerns of Parents with Alternative Life-styles

Our society has become increasingly liberal in the last three or four decades and, because of the sexual freedom we now experience, many single parents are choosing to live in unconventional ways. Some are homosexuals who decide to have children or are awarded custody in a divorce case because they offer their children the more stable life, despite their sexual preferences. Others are women opting for motherhood even though they have no particular interest in marriage. And one more form of single parenthood has developed where single adults are able to adopt children who, in the past, would have been placed only in two-adult, nuclear families.

These unconventional single parents face most, if not all, of the problems encountered by parents who are alone because of divorce or death, but they also face special predicaments, some of which relate directly to their life-styles and some of which are caused by societal attitudes toward them. The issues that are similar to problems faced by more conventional single parents have been dealt with in previous chapters. Those that are unique to parents with unconventional life-styles are treated below.

Conservative statistics estimate the lesbian mother population in the United States to be approximately 270,000 persons—3 percent of the nation's nine million households headed by women. But other estimates place the number at closer to three million, which is almost 30 percent of the estimated number of lesbians in the United States. It's difficult to obtain accurate figures. The societal stigma still placed on homosexuality in some areas forces many lesbians and gays to stay "in the closet."

There are no reliable statistical data available as to the number of gay men who are also fathers. Some references indicate that up to a quarter of self-identified gay men have fathered children. Since this number was acquired by studying men who identified themselves as homosexual, the assumption is that a still larger number of homosexually oriented men are fathers.

All the above statistics may be inaccurate. Only since the liberation movements of the past decade have homosexuals dared to identify themselves as such, and many still prefer anonymity. It's possible that in the future the numbers will be seen to be much greater.

Divorces are usually caused by disagreements over money, drugs, or cultural standards—or simply incompatibility. But if one partner in the dispute admits to being homosexual, all other issues, including those related to the best welfare of the children involved, may be ignored. Stereotypical notions regarding both male and female homosexuals persist despite much publicity to the contrary.

Being a good parent depends on the ability of a person to provide a warm, firm, consistent, safe environment in which each child's unique and individual needs are understood and met. Such an environment can be provided by any adults, regardless of sexual orientation, who are secure, happy, and confident of their self-worth.

The Lesbian Mother

Traditional attitudes regarding homosexuals often affect custody decisions. This is illustrated by the cases involving Ms. Driber and Ms. Koop, lesbian mothers sharing a home. Each had three children living with her, and each had an ex-husband who sued for change of custody because of the mother's lesbianism. Two separate social workers, one working with each woman, recommended that custody remain where it was. The household environment and all relevant evidence were the same. But the cases were heard by two different judges.

In the case of *Driber v. Driber* (No. 220748, Washington Superior Court, Pierce City, September 17, 1973), custody was awarded to Ms. Driber without qualification. Note was made that the mother's sexual orientation was irrelevant to her parental capabilities.

The case of *Koop v. Koop* (No. 221097, Washington Superior Courts, Pierce City, September 17, 1973) was decided quite differently. This judge granted custody of the two youngest Koop children to their father, calling Ms. Koop's living arrangement "abnormal," "not stable," and "highly detrimental" to the children. Five years later, Ms. Koop did finally receive permanent custody of her children.

The Gay Father

Little research exists dealing with the specific situation of homosexual fathers. Brian Miller, a psychologist in Los Angeles, sees this neglect as part of the general avoidance of the tender aspects of the male role by our society, which equates masculinity with insensitivity and the "macho" image. But he's found gay fathers who show great responsiveness to their children's psychological welfare. He states that some homosexual fathers value their children more highly than their need for public acceptance, and continue to hide their sexual preference in order to assure their right to custody of their children.

In 1979, Dr. Miller conducted in-depth interviews with forty gay fathers and fourteen of their children. He focused on four questions directly related to the stereotypical view of gays that are most often raised in child-custody cases where homosexuality is an issue:

1. Do gay fathers have abnormal needs for compensatory behavior, such as fathering children?
2. Are gay fathers in risk of molesting their children, especially their sons?
3. Does the sexual preference of a gay father have a negative effect on his children's development?
4. Is the child of a gay father more apt to be sexually molested (possibly by the father's friends) than are children of heterosexual single male parents?

Dr. Miller concluded that there was no foundation for affirmative responses to any of those questions. He stated that "there are as many styles of gay fathering as there are of heterosexual fathering."[1]

Special Legal Concerns of Homosexual Parents

Many homosexual parents live in fear that they may lose custody of their children or have their visitation rights restricted because of their sexual preference. Such decisions often depend on the attitude of the judge toward unconventional life-styles or on the state and the area in which the children live.

However, there has been a noticeable change in such decisions over the years. In 1959, for example, courts explained their reluctance to grant custody to a homosexual parent by claiming that the moral character of homosexuals was in question. This still happens, as in the case of *Koop v. Koop*, but the homosexual parent does have recourse now that wasn't available in the past.

*Brian Miller, "Gay Fathers and Their Children," *The Family Coordinator* (October, 1979), pp. 544–52.

Courts sometimes deny a homosexual parent custody on the grounds that the children may grow up to be homosexual, even though no evidence exists to support that belief. Other unfounded assumptions also affect custodial decisions. Some judges have awarded custody of children to the heterosexual father because they believe that a homosexual woman can't be a good mother—this in spite of studies to the contrary.

The greatest change has occurred within the homosexual community. Since the middle of the 1970s, homosexual parents have begun to show a willingness to challenge the negative assumptions about their abilities to be good parents. As a result, both mental health and legal professionals have been forced to examine society's stereotypes and to recognize that, if decisions are made on antiquated concepts of what homosexuals can and can't do, the children are often the ones who suffer.

These positive changes in legal attitude make it important that homosexuals who are good parents have the right to demand custody of their children. If you're a homosexual involved in divorce, you can expect that you'll face some angry accusations, especially if you ask for child custody. If you can, try to keep any fights between you and your spouse isolated from the children. A good solution is for both of you to visit a counselor who can supervise the verbalizing of these negative feelings. The heterosexual partner may feel victimized and deceived, and may be determined to hurt back. That shouldn't be surprising. Any rejection hurts. Counseling can be of great help in easing the pain of this kind of separation.

Sometimes, in order to avoid unnecessary fighting, the homosexual partner may be willing to give up anything just to be free. Yet this may be harmful to the children, especially if the departing parent is actually the one who is best able to manage the children. The best idea is to seek legal advice from an attorney in family law. If you both can agree that the children's welfare is more important than getting even, a solution that's most beneficial to the children can be reached.

A homosexual trying to obtain or retain custody of the children should be aware that some ex-spouses interrogate their children about every aspect of the other parent's life. This practice, a superior court judge noted, is very damaging to children, yet parents whose feelings are hurt often forget about their children's welfare in their eagerness to find some basis for revenge. If you know that your ex-spouse is inclined to litigation, you need to behave in a manner that will protect you and your children.

It appears that the problems encountered by lesbian mothers in contested child-custody cases are more readily predictable and often can be overcome. There is a slight but growing trend in the courts to require some concrete proof of a relationship between the mother's sexual preference and a negative effect on the child before taking steps to deny the mother custody or limit her rights of visitation. It appears that to a somewhat lesser degree this is also true for homosexual fathers.

All this is to the good, of course, so that the relationship between children and their parents is not arbitrarily disrupted. To add to the help now available to lesbian mothers are articles and publications that offer advice on how to help children deal with the issues of lesbianism at home and at school. Many of these, too, can be useful to the homosexual father seeking guidance.

Helping Children to Understand

When a single parent is without a partner of the opposite sex because of sexual preference, certain unique problems may arise. A single lesbian mother with a son, or a gay father with a daughter, may encounter the following concerns:

1. Children with opposite-sex gay or lesbian parents need a same-sex role model. Such an individual may be found in a neighbor, a friend, or, if there's been a divorce, by regular contact with the other parent.

2. These children need love and special reassurance of their value from the gay or lesbian parent. The possibility exists

that such a child might feel the homosexual parent's choice of a same-sex partner is an unspoken rejection of all people of the opposite sex. Betty Berzon, a contributing author in *Our Right to Love: A Lesbian Resource Book*, corroborates this. She indicates that this situation is common enough to deserve the attention of any gay or lesbian parent with a child.[2]

3. It's especially important that a child of a gay or lesbian single parent be free to disapprove of the parent's life-style. There's a danger that homosexual parents who aren't secure in their identity may unconsciously demand that their children support their choice. No adult should expect a child to provide such reinforcement. A homosexual parent needs to be as self-accepting and confident as a heterosexual parent, or perhaps more so, since the social pressures against the homosexual life-style are greater.

A colleague of mine described a family with whom she worked where the issue was the lesbian mother's unrecognized discomfort with her sexual choice. She sought approval from those around her, including her fifteen-year-old son. The boy was involved in normal adolescent activities and seemed to have no difficulty with his own sexual identity, but he didn't respond as she wanted him to regarding her life-style. He was angry with her choice, displaying obvious disapproval, which the mother couldn't tolerate.

The boy appeared to have two major difficulties. First, it was possible some of his anger resulted from a fear that his mother's choice of a same-sex lover indicated a rejection of him. If that was so, he needed to understand that his mother could prefer a female lover yet be very happy with his strong male identity.

Second, he needed to be helped to accept and love his

*Betty Berzon, Ph.D., "Sharing Your Lesbian Identity with Your Children—A Case for Openness," *Our Right to Love: A Lesbian Resource Book*, ed. Ginny Vida (Englewood Cliffs, NJ: Prentice-Hall, 1978), pp. 69–77.

mother even though he might never approve of her life-style. Neither of these goals could be reached quickly. Both required preparation and planning before they could be achieved. What's more, he probably would never learn them unless his mother provided him with a good example.

But the mother also needed assistance. It was necessary for her to recognize that her boy could still love her even though he disapproved of her life-style, if she showed him how. She also had to accept her own sexual choice so that she wouldn't demand validation from society, and particularly from her son. And last, she needed to acknowledge her son's right to his own feelings, even if they differed from hers.

The mother had to be taught how she could positively influence her son's reaction to her life-style. She learned to demonstrate by her own behavior and tolerance of his attitude toward her that it is possible to love another person and still not agree with everything he or she does. She came to recognize that any attempt she made to force her son to accept her only resulted in additional resistance on his part.

Dealing with these problems took time and effort, but their solutions were well within reach of this woman and her son. With proper guidance they did overcome their difficulties and establish a mutually satisfying relationship in which both of them felt loved and appreciated.

4. A child of a gay or lesbian single parent needs time to develop a gradual understanding and acceptance of his or her parent's right to choose a life-style. Many homosexual parents fear that their children will hate them when their unconventional choice becomes known.

This might happen, it's true, if the disclosure comes as a shock. No one, child or adult, likes such surprises. Dr. Berzon recommends planning for disclosure, rather than letting children find out by default. She also suggests that the children's ages should influence how they're told. Simple explanations are called for if the children are very young; adolescents may need more details.

If children are close in age and the parent is accustomed to having a family time, it might be best to make the disclosure then. But before the subject is brought up, a parent needs to think through the questions that might be asked so that answers can be prepared. It's also important that a parent anticipating such an open discussion remember the value of remaining calm. If questions are met with anger or resentment, the children may be afraid to speak up. This would be harmful to them. Children of all ages need to be reassured that their rights as individuals to make their own separate choices are recognized.

5. Children of lesbian or gay single parents need to develop the strength to resist outside pressures, including those from their significant others, that might cause them to reject their parents because of life-style.

Dr. Berzon suggests that lesbian parents disclose their sexual preference to significant others, especially to ex-spouses. This gives the mother a chance to try to gain understanding, which will provide support for the children involved. What Berzon applies to lesbian mothers can also be applied to gay fathers. Such a disclosure has an additional benefit: It relieves the children of the burden of having to maintain a secret. It also makes it more difficult for any significant other to use the single homosexual parent's sexual preference as an opening for manipulation. *

Special Concerns of Elective Single Parents

In past generations, the child of an unmarried woman would have either been given up for adoption or, if the mother was a young, dependent girl, been raised as her sibling. Old novels are full of unfortunate heroines who spend six months visiting relatives with their mothers and return with a new brother or sister. The

*Betty Berzon, "Sharing Your Lesbian Identity with Your Children."

entire remainder of some of these books is devoted to the agony the young mother feels because of her inability to acknowledge her baby.

Fortunately for the mental health of single women who become pregnant, that is no longer the scenario. Today, many single women who have no intentions of marrying, but who find they're pregnant, still decide to have and keep their children. Others, concerned about time running out on their biological clocks, deliberately become pregnant without deciding to marry.

Marilyn Nelson, of The Single Parent Connection, an association for single parents in Los Angeles, has encountered many elective single parents. She's found that 40 percent of them are working women in their thirties. In spite of having little available money, because there are no men from whom they receive support payments, many of them seem to function better than single mothers who have gone through divorce or lost a partner through death.

These intentionally single parents don't have to contend with conflict over visitation rights, or deal with intrusions by an ex-spouse or in-laws. However, some do seem troubled by their single status, especially when their children begin to ask questions. When a child asks, "Do I have a daddy?" they are sometimes unsure of what to say.

If the child is young, Marilyn Nelson advises the mother to respond by saying, "Yes, of course you do. Everyone has both a mother and a father. But your daddy doesn't live with us." If the child asks where the father is, an honest reply is best, even if it's "I don't know."

If the child is older, a more detailed answer is called for. The mother might explain, "I was dating your father and became pregnant. I wanted to keep my baby—you. But your dad wasn't ready to be a father. So we didn't stay together." If that isn't the case, she should describe the true situation as best she can. For example, "I didn't marry your father because I didn't feel we'd be happy together. We just didn't get along very well in day-to-day living." Or, "I really didn't want to marry. I wanted my independence." Be as honest as possible. Nothing is gained by providing a child with a fantasy, especially if it's contrary to the truth.

The Single Adoptive Parent

Today, since the elimination of regulations governing the makeup of acceptable homes into which children may be placed (two-adult households with a male and female parent), it's possible for single adults to adopt children. These new-style single parents, like elective single mothers, have an advantage over those who are alone as the result of divorce or death.

Single adoptive parents have chosen to have a child with an awareness of the special problems that lie ahead. Often, they have higher-than-average incomes and so aren't troubled by the various economic difficulties that affect many single parents with less money. They're more apt to be well established in their careers, too, so they can adjust their lives to the new responsibilities of parenthood.

Nevertheless, they still encounter problems, unique to their situations, which they may not have anticipated. If the adopted children are older, which is not uncommon, they have in all probability spent some years moving from one foster home to another. These children have a special need for reassurance and a display of love. And they may react more intensely to any alteration in routine once it's been established.

Single adoptive parents who begin to date after gaining custody of their children may be faced with a considerable display of insecurity and anger, especially when they decide to bring a lover home. This problem is actually not very different from that faced by any single parent in a like situation, except that the child's need for reassurance may be greater, especially if the child wasn't an infant when the adoption took place.

An adoptive single parent may encounter some special problems because of a child's fantasies about the relationship that exists between them. When children are waiting to be adopted, they dream about how life will be after the great event takes place. Most picture an "ideal" situation in which they're the center of their new parents' attention. They also fantasize regarding their natural families and what might have been, idealizing them while, at the same time, feeling anger at having been rejected.

An adopted child may assume that the relationship formed with his or her new parent is very special to them both, eliminating the need for additional companionship. For this reason, it's important that a single parent immediately establish a special time when he or she can have good communication with this new member of the family. During these times, there should be considerable discussion of the expectations both parent and child have for the new relationship.

The single parent needs to help his or her child recognize which expectations are attainable—and which are unrealistic fantasy. The more possibilities explored, the better. The child should be helped to understand that the single parent will want to date and may have a lover. But it should be made clear that no association developing with another adult will in any way threaten the security of this new family.

A child's fantasies may have a strong effect on his or her behavior, especially when a lover moves into the home. *Any* newcomer is apt to be considered an intruder by an adopted child, who may still feel insecure and defensive in this new position. But if both parent and lover recognize the existence of the child's particular fantasies, they'll be prepared for problems that arise and might even be able to avoid some of them.

One other consideration should be mentioned. Adopted children will be more threatened by a series of lovers than will natural children, because most adopted children have been shuttled around for some time and have lived through many rejections themselves. Adopted children who are aware of one lover after another appearing and then vanishing may fear for their own security. They may decide that each lover who disappears has done something very wrong. Since such children are already apt to worry that if *they* do too many things wrong they'll be rejected again, this fear may inhibit them when they're asked to communicate with their new parent.

If you are a single adoptive parent who has more than one lover, you can help your child get rid of such fears. Explain that your affection for one particular lover might fade, since you are still looking for just the right adult partner—one you will be willing to make a commitment to. Emphasize that you've already made a firm commitment to your child. Whatever problems the two of you have you'll work out together.

A child may not be the only one with unrealistic fantasies. A lover, too, may not understand why an adoption took place. Possibly he or she may assume that the bonding between adoptive parent and child is not overly strong. Then, if the lover is still controlled by his or her inner child, a real problem will develop. The lover may be jealous of the adopted son or daughter, who appears to be a rival, and may deliberately attempt to cause the single parent to give up on the adoption. This would create great insecurity for the child, and certainly might destroy the adult love relationship. Such fantasies must be faced and removed so the lover's feeling of competition with the child is reduced.

The lover may also have fantasies regarding why the parent adopted a child. Whatever they are, if they don't fit with facts, they should be examined and any distortions corrected so the lover does nothing to threaten the child's sense of security. As in so many interpersonal issues, open communication is essential. An adopted child whose feeling of being accepted and loved is challenged can be severely shaken.

I worked with a woman who almost let her fantasies regarding her lover's adopted daughter destroy her relationship with him. When she came to me, Elena, a single career woman, was dating Thomas, a successful businessman with an adopted daughter, Gloria, age sixteen. From the start, Elena had a false picture of the situation. She considered the possibility that Gloria was Thomas's daughter, whose mother he hadn't married. But there was no resemblance between Gloria and Thomas, so she dropped that idea.

Other explanations for the adoption seemed far more troublesome. It was clear that Gloria and Thomas were very fond of each other, and that served to direct Elena's fantasies into dark, unsavory areas. Because she was worried about the situation, Elena began to withdraw from Thomas.

When he became aware of a cooling of his relationship with Elena, he refused to accept it without discussion. He insisted on coming with her to a therapy session. Highly emotional, Elena admitted her wild, unpleasant fantasies. She also exposed, for the first time, her own inner child, insecure and filled with self-doubt.

Thomas explained that he met Gloria through a lawyer friend who knew the child. Both her parents had been killed in a boating accident, and he had adopted her because he missed his own daughter, who was living across the continent with her mother. Now he loved Gloria for herself and no longer thought of her as a substitute for another child. When Elena understood the true circumstances of Gloria's adoption, her unpleasant fantasies faded. She was able to relate to Thomas again. For them both, Gloria remained a very special person.

Choose Your Neighborhood

Where you live may be important both to you and to your children, especially if your life-style is in any way unconventional. When you look about for housing, you need to consider many issues. Some major ones are:

1. Cost of housing and living
2. Quality and safety of the neighborhood
3. Availability and quality of schools
4. Availability of work
5. Prevailing attitude toward your life-style

The first four considerations might cause a single parent to look for a place in a small town. Certainly, cost of living and housing, quality and availability of schools, and quality and safety of the neighborhood can be excellent in such areas. Work may even be available in the community, making it appear to be an ideal location for your home.

However, if your life-style is unconventional, a small town can be stifling. Neighbors often feel they have the right to criticize each other's choices. Children in the neighborhood, accustomed to conventional, nuclear families, can make life miserable for a classmate who has only one parent whose social and sexual standards differ from those to which they're accustomed.

It may be possible for an adult to ignore such pressures, but children often find them difficult to handle. Otherwise happy children may become fearful and disturbed if the pressure of their peers causes them to feel ashamed of the life their parent prefers.

For this reason, many single parents whose lives aren't conventional choose to live and work in larger cities. They can find decent neighborhoods there, though possibly not quite as good as those available in small towns. Cost of living may be a bit higher, but the extra expense seems small compared to the increased privacy and independence gained.

There are other balances, too. Salaries tend to be higher in big cities. More jobs are available. But, most important of all, there are many other single-parent families. Here, children from one-parent families can find many friends who come from similar households, friends with whom they feel comradeship and understanding.

Anticipating and Avoiding Conflicts

With each form of unconventional life-style comes unique possibilities for conflict. If one partner decides to come out of the closet, the issue of homosexuality cannot be avoided. If a single mother has never married, she may face prejudice because she's dared to flout society's requirement that children be born, if not conceived, in wedlock. A single parent who has adopted a child may encounter special problems when a lover enters the picture.

These various difficulties, if not faced squarely, can disrupt the peace and happiness of single-parent families. Yet, if they're anticipated, and some preparation is made before they arise, they not only become manageable but, in some cases, lose all power to disrupt the lives of the persons involved.

During a divorce, there is often a struggle over children, property, and assets. If one partner has an unconventional life-style, it's bound to be brought up and used as an excuse for vilification. At such times, both partners are apt to be emotional and accusative, as well as defensive. Things are said that might be avoided in more peaceful situations. And the attempt to get even, to pay back for hurts and insults, can cause one of the participants to strike out at the other without considering how such behavior might affect the children. This antagonism may spill over into the necessary contacts that occur between the separated parents after the divorce is complete.

Anticipation of problems and their prevention go hand-in-hand. Common sense dictates that effort put into maintaining a reasonably amicable relationship with an ex-spouse can eliminate the danger of future bickering. Name-calling, accusations, and additional legal actions that could, ultimately, harm the children can be avoided.

Most of the problems faced by single parents whose life-styles are unconventional are, to one degree or another, common to all one-adult households. Heterosexual men or women who take a live-in lover may face condemnation by their ex-spouse or extended family. Legal actions by angry or hurt relatives can occur no matter what the sexual preference of the single parent. Children may be teased by their peers whatever life-style the single parent chooses. Any or all of these situations can be detrimental to the children.

When a single parent establishes a relationship with a lover, whether it be casual or permanent, homosexual or heterosexual, it's advisable that he or she consider the impact of that action on the children. For this reason, I recommend that any parent who might have read this chapter to the exclusion of some others reconsider and look into every part of this book. Adapt what you read to your circumstances. Even parents with more traditional lives must do this, since no example or advice can be tailored to fit every situation.

15 *Unfinished Business*

Hassles with Your Ex-spouse and Extended Family

*I*n the previous chapter we dealt briefly with some of the problems single parents with uncommon life-styles might encounter when dealing with their ex-spouses and their extended families. Single parents who have relatives, even if there's no ex-spouse involved, can be confronted with interference that may threaten to disrupt not only their families but any relationships they seek to establish.

It is not uncommon for interference to go far beyond what might be expected if it merely expressed concern for everyone's happiness. When this happens, it becomes a disruptive element—a *hassle*.

If you're divorced, it may be nearly impossible to avoid hassles with your ex-spouse completely. If communication had been good, chances are you wouldn't have separated in the first place. Most probably, many of your predivorce battles dealt with adult incompatibilities. Now, however, your disagreements may center on your social life and how it's affecting your children.

This issue may arise not only when you deal with your ex-spouse but also when you have contact with his or her parents and siblings. After all, they still have an interest in what happens to you. Despite your divorce, they're still your children's grandparents, aunts, and uncles. They may defend every attempt they make to influence your social choices by claiming that their only interest is in helping your children have what they feel is a decent upbringing.

If your husband or wife has died, this problem may still exist—with embellishments. Your in-laws may unconsciously resent the fact that their child is dead while you are still alive. They may even feel that you neglected your duties to your spouse and so were, in an indirect way, responsible for their loss. They may also fear, with their son's or daughter's influence removed, that their grandchildren will acquire attitudes under your influence that they find objectionable or even harmful.

If you now see them infrequently, they may feel sadness or even anger at losing you, especially if your relationship with them was close and gave them gratification. But if you've begun dating again, their greatest distress may be motivated by the realization that, if you remarry, their grandchildren could be further removed from them, perhaps never to be seen again.

The biggest problem with the hassles that arise from these emotional ties and disruptions between you, your ex-spouse, and your ex-spouse's relatives is that not all of them can be recognized for what they are. Hassles generally fall into two categories: covert and overt.

Covert hassles are always hidden behind other issues. For example, if you're a single mother, your child-support checks may be late in arriving whenever you date a man your ex-spouse disapproves of. Or you may find that your ex-partner gives your children money for things you've told them they shouldn't have and justifies it by explaining that money will never make up for the daily love you can give them. Covert hassles are sometimes difficult to identify, because they always seem to have some other basis than just the desire to make your life difficult.

Overt hassles are far more identifiable. A parent who constantly questions the children about the other parent's behavior—which happens often if one parent is gay or lesbian—is hassling in a very obvious manner. If an ex-spouse is openly critical of the other parent's behavior, making it difficult for the maligned parent to deal with the children, that, too, is overt hassling. However, the most obvious overt hassling is done when one parent takes the other to court in an attempt to force changes in custody or support payments—or, sometimes, even to demand a change in the life-style of the other parent. This has been done by in-laws, too, though not as frequently.

These two forms of hassling, covert and overt, are usually done by an ex-spouse and his or her family members, but they can also involve your own relatives. Sometimes, all of your extended family seems determined to keep you from enjoying any adult relationships. If this occurs, you may feel very frustrated and angry.

Your ex-spouse and your relatives and in-laws generally realize that they have no right to object to your having a normal social life after divorce or the loss of your spouse through death. Therefore, they may unconsciously redirect their anger to an area where it can have a more telling effect—how your new relationship is affecting the children. This displacement is often the only indication that a true emotional separation hasn't taken place between you, your ex-spouse, your in-laws, or your own family.

So complete may this transfer of anger from one area to another be that none of the adults involved can recognize it for what it truly is. Yet there are clues that may help you to identify the real motivation behind the interference that upsets you.

The first step to take when you're confronted with what seems to be unreasonable criticism from your ex-spouse, your ex-spouse's family, or your family is to look at your own actions. Face this question squarely. If you deceive yourself by not facing the facts, you'll be frustrated in your attempts to stop the hassles.

1. Am I giving my ex-spouse, my in-laws, or my own family mixed messages? Do I sometimes act like a child to them,

so they feel I'm not competent to care for my children and need parenting myself?

If you answered yes to this question, you need to deal with your own behavior and inner confidence. You can't expect your parents, your ex-spouse, or your in-laws to treat you as a competent adult if you repeatedly approach them as a child in need of guidance.

If you have difficulty dealing with this problem, you may need to seek professional help. It's not easy for a person to address the inner child without some guidance. But it's essential if you want to get control of your life. And only when you're beginning to take charge of your decisions and behavior can you deal effectively with the hassles from your ex-spouse and extended families.

If you feel you're managing your life without unnecessarily calling for family assistance and advice, then the next step is to analyze any new love relationship you may have. How is it affecting your children? To determine your response, ask yourself the following questions:

2. Do my children appear to feel rejected because of my new lover?

3. Do they communicate with me regularly? Can my children talk to me about their worries and fears?

4. Does my new lover get along with my children and understand their needs? Do we agree on how to handle my children?

5. Do my children's teachers and other concerned adults consider them to be happy and well adjusted?

6. Are my children doing well in school?

If you had no difficulty with the first question, and answered yes to the last five, you can be reasonably sure the objections raised by your in-laws or your ex-spouse are actually motivated by resentment at your newfound relationship and not by any legitimate concern for your children.

If you answered no to some or even all of these questions, that doesn't necessarily exonerate your interfering relatives. They still might be hassling you out of malice or resentment, rather than because of real concern for your children's welfare. In that case, you would still have the right to try to stop their interference, but you would also need to work at improving your situation, so that your children and you would have a better life.

Hassles from Your Ex-spouse

If your ex-spouse is the one who's hassling you, determine how you plan to handle yourself when you confront him or her. Do you believe you'll get action only if you resort to a show of anger? If so, I suggest you try to decide why you feel this way. I've found that anger only confuses the issue and advise my clients to keep their tempers down so communication remains open.

If you get no response even when you remain calm, have you any recourse? What social services, like a family counseling center, are available to you? Can you get affordable legal counsel? Be prepared before you confront the person who is hassling you. You don't want to threaten legal action, for example, if you can't carry through.

When you begin your talks with your hassling ex-spouse, you can approach each problem as it arises, but you'll also need to deal with the overall issues. If your ex-spouse expresses hostility through your children, you need to help them separate themselves from the problem. If you feel demoralized by your ex-spouse's disapproval, you need to reaffirm your own sense of inner security. If you're constantly being put on the defensive, you need to clarify your own opinions so you aren't intimidated when others disagree with you.

You'll get further if you anticipate the arguments you'll face and are sure you're comfortable with the choices you've made that might be offending or angering your ex-spouse. If you're a woman, you need to recognize that your ex-husband may still adhere to a double standard for social-sexual behavior. He may feel that you, as a woman, have no right to sexual self-determination.

You need to be prepared to stand up to this double standard or decide to comply with his demand—but, either way, you should make a free choice. If you choose to go against his preference, and you might have divorced because of that disagreement, be prepared for some continuation of the hassles. If you comply, you must realize that your social life may be very limited. This entire subject will be dealt with in greater detail later in this chapter.

When Your Ex-spouse Uses Your Children to Express Hostility

Since your children are often the only bridge remaining between you and your ex-spouse, they sometimes become involved in the unfinished business that was left after your divorce. Some arrangement will have been made for joint custody or for your ex-spouse to visit with your children. Essential as those contacts may be, they can also open the door to endless hassles.

If antagonisms between adults haven't been settled, the children may be involved during those visits, even if only accidentally. Especially if your ex-spouse can't accept an appropriate share of responsibility for your divorce, a problem may develop: The blame shifts so that the guilty person manages to appear pure while all the bad things are being done by someone else—you.

This was done very subtly by Joseph, the well-educated, financially successful, divorced father of Aletta, sixteen. Joseph never accepted his responsibility for the breakup of his marriage, although he'd left his wife, June, to live with another woman. He didn't remain with the woman who was the initial cause of his desertion, but met another with whom he lived and later married. June, who had custody of their daughter, established a comfortable relationship with an old-time friend. They had sex occasionally. Sometimes he spent the night with her.

Reassured by his own return to conventionality, Joseph began to scold June for her "immoral" behavior. He completely ignored the reality of her life—and his own. Unable to tolerate the guilt and bad feelings he had about himself, he transferred them all to June and what he described as her "unconventional" life-style. When she came to me, June was under great stress because of his accusations.

Aletta was placed in the middle. Every time she visited her father, she heard long lectures about the damage her mother was inflicting upon her through her "sinful" behavior. Joseph's unwillingness to accept responsibility for the divorce, or to face his guilt, resulted in an inner anger that he foisted upon his daughter, who then carried it back to her mother.

Aletta was the unwitting victim of her father's unresolved guilts. Because she was used as the go-between and took on her father's anger, it was more difficult for her to identify with her mother, which she needed to do at that stage of her development. Joseph's behavior was destructive to his daughter, but it also hurt June, causing her to be demoralized and to feel less able to carry out her role as parent.

Sometimes, a child may be used to spy on one parent and report back to the other. This might be more common when one parent's life-style is unconventional, but it happens in almost any situation. Louis, who worked with another therapist, described bringing his date, a single mother, home after the evening and going up to her apartment with her for sex. Her twelve-year-old daughter, Sally, heard them come in, waited until they were together in her mother's room, and then phoned her father, who stormed over and kicked in the door. "It was embarrassing—and frightening," Louis said. "For a while I was afraid he might even harm us. But I got out with no damage, and he left soon after. I waited outside, though, until he did. I wasn't going to leave that poor woman alone with a madman who might beat her up."

How should Susan, Sally's mother, handle such a situation? She should begin by having a talk with her ex-spouse after he has calmed down, explaining that this behavior is actually damaging the child. She should ask if that is what he really wants to do.

If Susan can't carry on such a discussion without outside help, she should arrange a meeting between her ex-spouse, her pastor, a counselor, or some respected friend, and herself. In such a situation, her ex-spouse might be more willing to listen to what she has to say. She should enlist help from any friends her ex-husband respects to get his attention. If he doesn't change she should seek legal advice.

If Sally's father continues this behavior, then Susan will have to go to her child and have a long talk. Since Sally is twelve, she's old enough to understand reason. Susan can begin by explaining that she understands that Sally wishes the divorce had never taken place. Then she can continue: "I wish it hadn't been necessary, too. But your dad was doing things that I just couldn't put up with any more [no need to elaborate on his many infidelities]. I just can't trust him to be honest with me any more."

She might get a grudging nod from Sally. She will have to accept that and continue. "Would you like it if I spied on what you did when you were with your friends?"

To this she'll get a more definite response on which to build her next argument. "Well, I don't like it when your father spies on me. And I don't think it's fair of him to use you to do the spying. Do you?"

Again, Sally's response might be limited. But Susan can still continue. "If I used Ruth, your best friend, to spy on you, you'd be very angry at me, wouldn't you? And if, after Ruth called me, I came storming in and began to threaten you with a beating, you'd be frightened of me and angry at Ruth all at the same time, wouldn't you?"

You can see the direction the discussion is taking. By relating Sally's position with Ruth's in this hypothetical situation, Susan will be able to get Sally to see how unfair her father's behavior is. It also will help Sally to understand why Susan objects to being spied upon, and the danger of such spying. It is important that Susan shows understanding of her ex-spouse's frustration, but makes it clear that feeding it by spying is only going to exacerbate the situation. If the child is younger, the explanation must be simplified. But, generally speaking, relating the situation to the child's friends makes it understandable, no matter what the age of the child.

Problems with Extended Families

Grandparents can also contribute to the problems a single parent has when trying to maintain a happy social-sexual life. They can hassle the single parent in almost every area that's available to an ex-spouse, but they may be especially troublesome if their concepts of morality differ greatly from those the single parent has chosen. Grandparents who disapprove of the "loose life-style" of their grandchild's single parent can create havoc with that child's reactions to the parent's dating.

Grandma may remark on how shocked she is that you'd bring someone in the house to sleep with you. Your child, hearing this, may pick up on grandmother's anger and, the next time your lover comes over, your child may reflect that disapproval.

This became a problem for Cathy, who was brought to me by her mother. Since the death of her father three years earlier, Cathy, ten, spent most of her summers with her paternal grandparents on their farm in a small eastern community. They were God-fearing fundamentalists who communicated both verbally and nonverbally their feeling that sex was something to be ashamed of and to avoid. This was confusing to Cathy, since her parents had been rather casual about their sexual behavior.

Being on a farm, Cathy was exposed to the sexual activity of farm animals, but her grandparents never acknowledged this, even though it often occurred in front of her. She wasn't allowed to play with the children from the neighboring farm because they talked "dirty."

Cathy loved her grandparents. They offered her security and

love, particularly at a time when her mother was foundering in her own sorrow. But Cathy was confused when she tried to reconcile her grandparents' attitude toward sex with the attitude she'd learned from her parents. This was especially difficult for her when her mother developed a new relationship and had a man sleep at their house.

Such unresolved matters must be settled. Grandparents and other relatives must finally accept the right of the remaining custodial parent to find adult companionship whether in marriage or not. They must let go of the past and accept the reality of the present. If their son or daughter has died, they must recognize the right of the surviving partner to seek new relationships. If there's been a divorce, the same rights need to be acknowledged. Until this is done, every contact between child and grandparents poses the threat of more dissension in the newly established relationship between the custodial parent and a lover.

However, this kind of situation isn't always clear-cut. Extended families need to be allowed to mourn the breakup of a member's marriage, especially if everyone felt very close. The more the single parent is able to tolerate the various stages of mourning and see them for what they are, the more likely it is that, in time, a good resolution of the problems will occur. Talking openly about the conflicting loyalties in-laws or one's own parents may have can ease the hurt and relieve some of the problem.

Communication about everything that's happening is important. The closer you can get to the underlying reasons for the intrusiveness and the hassles, the better are your chances of resolving the difficulties. When disagreements are allowed to fester, out-and-out battles may result. Single parents feuding with their extended families may deny them visitation rights. But just cutting all ties doesn't work. Some grandparents have united to demand the opportunity to see their grandchildren, and, in fact, new laws have been passed to assure grandparents of this right if single parents attempt to interfere with it.

Yet, the aim of communication between extended families and a single parent should be more than just the settling of quarrels.

The goal is to get these relatives to see the parent's right to make choices, and to understand the importance of minimizing their critical communications regarding the parent's social-sexual behavior to the children who are involved. If the points of view are too far apart, however, it might be necessary to talk to your children as well, and give them help in dealing with the disparate views held by adults whom they love.

Generally, you'll be very aware of any interference by ex-spouses or relatives. If any exist in your life, list them now. If you have neighbors or friends who intrude on your affairs unnecessarily, list them, too. You have a right to live without facing daily hassles and unjust criticism. Once you have listed the people who are hassling you, deal with them one at a time. Confront them with the problem, but do it in as gentle a way as possible, at least at the beginning. After all, you probably do not want to alienate any of them. All you really want is to put an end to the interference.

Don't Look Outside for Approval

Most of us are insecure enough to need an occasional pat on the back in order to feel good about ourselves. We blossom when we're complimented and wilt when we're criticized. Yet, it's possible to build up our own self-images enough so that we can withstand periods when we don't get any special support. The stronger our self-confidence becomes, the less we feel hassled when someone criticizes our choices.

The key words are *stronger* and *less*. No one is impervious to criticism. Confidence won't eliminate hassles entirely. But it will allow an individual to avoid upset when others disagree.

Unfortunately, many adults are still very dependent upon their parents for approval. They seem to be caught in a never-ending adolescent struggle for separation from parental ties that were necessary when they were young. Still emotionally immature, they react to their dilemma either by continuing to seek the approval they need or by rebelling.

The unfortunate fact is that, no matter what the age of the person involved, this form of rebellion is still nothing more than an adolescent cry of protest. It may result in what appears to be true independence, but that appearance is false. Such adolescent adults still aren't comfortable with their choices. They can't make up their own minds. Everything they do is in reaction to a long-lasting, harmful dependency.

It's common for a therapist working with a single-parent family to find that this is a long-term issue. A parent may seek help because of an adolescent child who's having trouble. But as treatment continues, it becomes clear that this problem spans three generations. Not only is the child in need of help to establish a good self-image, but the single parent is still struggling with the issue, and even the grandparents may never have resolved it for themselves.

The hassles that result when a family tries to deal with such multigenerational identification problems can become very burdensome. Little if anything is solved in the merry-go-round that results. Usually, such a situation calls for professional help. But until that assistance can be found, the best thing to do is let many of the issues rest.

If you find yourself getting pulled into such endless hassles, I suggest you withdraw from the conflict. Diminish in importance, by ignoring them, those negative areas of disagreement you can't change. Focus attention elsewhere by concentrating on positive aspects of your life.

Cary, for instance, had a running problem with Gwen, with whom he shared custody of their son, Dylan. Every time Gwen came to pick the boy up, they got into a hassle. Gwen objected to Cary's lover, Maureen, even though it was clear that Maureen was good to Dylan and that the boy was fond of her. Gwen insisted that Cary should either marry Maureen or get her out of the house.

The first few times Gwen showed her disapproval, Cary was upset. Then he recognized his ex-wife's interference for what it was—an unresolved anger at the breakup of their marriage. He decided he didn't have to get upset by her refusal to accept their incompatibility. When next she began to hassle him about Maureen, he refused to be drawn into the argument. Instead, he told Gwen how happy she'd made Dylan by bringing him to a concert he'd wanted to hear. "I'm glad we're beginning to cooperate in giving our son an appreciation of good music," he remarked.

Gwen was put off balance by his compliment. Instead of complaining, she smiled and told Cary she'd heard he'd bought a computer for their boy. "That was nice. He needs to feel at home with those things. I sure wouldn't be able to help him work one."

By gradually changing the tone of their meetings, Cary was able to stop the bickering and make his encounters with his ex-wife periods when they reinforced each other by acknowledging contributions to their son's welfare.

Avoiding Defensiveness

It's possible that every single parent should place in a prominent position at home this simple motto: *Adults don't have to justify their position to other adults.* This isn't to say that adults shouldn't be willing to explain their motives or seek understanding from adults they love or care about. Such understanding removes barriers to communication between friends and relatives. But such explanations should never have to be made in self-defense.

This applies to your ex-spouse and your in-laws just as surely as it does to your own relatives. If they respect you as an adult, they should be able to keep hands off your private business. And if you're assailed with unwelcome questions or bits of advice, you have the right to disregard their proffered help. "That's something I don't care to talk about" is one way of telling them your personal choices aren't up for discussion.

If a relative offers unsolicited advice, you can say "thank you," and just ignore it. But if you do, you might be criticized later for not doing something they assumed you had agreed to do. Far better to express your objection immediately to such interference. Dare to voice your objection. "I know you mean well," you may say, "but this is really a private matter. Thanks, just the same."

If a relative offers you moral advice with which you disagree, state your position calmly. "We apparently have a difference of opinion about that" may stop the preaching. But if it doesn't you might add, "I prefer not to discuss this." If the lecturing continues, you'll have to be more firm in your response. "If you persist," you can say, "I'm going to leave," or if this hassle is taking place in your home, "I'll have to ask you to leave."

If you can't get away immediately (if you're visiting relatives in another town, for example), at least separate yourself from the hassling person for a while. Take a walk or go into another room. Then, when you're calm, be alert to any opening that might lead to a repeat of that kind of hassle. Stop it before it starts by bringing up a different, more pleasant subject far removed from the issues on which you disagree.

Sometimes, this solution to hassles can result in a general improvement in other relationships, as well. Whenever Hugh took his sons to see his ex-wife's family, her mother would bring up the question of his lover, Ruby, who lived with him. For a time, he considered stopping the visits altogether. Then he found a better solution. He made careful plans for the entire period of each visit, keeping everyone so busy that there was no time for long personal discussions.

The results were surprising. Both his children and their grandmother looked forward to their days together with greater enthusiasm. Even Hugh enjoyed himself more than he had in the past. After a few more visits, the suggestion was made that he bring Ruby along next time. The implication was that Ruby must have been, in some way, responsible for the change in Hugh's attitude.

Being Comfortable with Your Choices

Some of the choices you've made that upset your family, your ex-spouse, or your in-laws may seem very clear-cut to you. You aren't disturbed if they're criticized. But others may be more difficult. You're unsure about them. Did you choose correctly? Were other options better than the one you took? If those decisions are criticized by your family or relatives, you'll have more trouble responding calmly.

Many young single parents today have responded to the new freedom that exists and are aware of many options their parents didn't have. What's acceptable today may not have been considered a possible alternative ten years ago. Living together as an alternative to marriage, for example, has only been generally accepted since the early to middle seventies.

With more options comes greater responsibility. You can no longer depend upon established rules to guide your decisions. However, those rules may be behind the attitudes expressed by your parents or your in-laws. You may feel you're okay in a live-in arrangement that they find very upsetting. When that happens, you need to respect their feelings even though you aren't obligated to act upon them.

Yet, because this change in attitude is fairly recent, it's possible you may not be thoroughly comfortable when your decisions are questioned. If you recognize this and accept it, you'll be better able to deal with any objections your ex-spouse, relatives, or in-laws may have to what you're doing.

An example of the way unclarified attitudes can cause one to behave illogically can be found in Joyce's actions before her divorce was finalized. Joyce was divorcing her husband because she wanted to marry Bart. She asked him to move in with her and her children six months after the separation, but some time before the divorce was final. Custody had not yet been awarded to her, though her teenaged children were staying with her during that time.

She was very uneasy with her decision, even though she loved having Bart nearby. She was fearful that, if her husband learned of his presence, he might sue for custody of their children, so she told them to be careful never to mention Bart when they visited their father. Her uneasiness with her choice should have been a cue to her that it was a bad one. It caused her much distress, and it put the children in an awkward position of being deceptive to their father. She should have considered her reactions before Bart moved in with her. Then she might have delayed that step until there was no chance that his presence could affect her custody claims.

If You've Moved Back Home

A different problem results if, after a divorce or death, a custodial parent returns to his or her parents' home to live. One of the most difficult issues is the right of single parents in this situation to act autonomously. They seem to lose their identity as adults when they return to the nest, even though they did quite well as long as the households were separated.

Sometimes, the responsibility for this lies with the single parent who expects the preferential treatment given to a dependent child. A woman recently wrote to an advice columnist regarding her divorced daughter who brought two children, aged nine months and three years, to live with their grandma. The mother and daughter disagreed as to whom the daughter should date. The mother also felt that she had no time to herself, since she cared for the babies while her daughter worked and also on the evenings when she went out socially.

This was recognized by the columnist as being typical for adults who couldn't see that they should discuss the problems they were sure to face at such a time. She recommended that mother and daughter work out an arrangement in which the mother had time off, too, and the daughter resumed responsibility for her children on weekends and evenings. She also advised the women to stay out of each other's personal lives.

The problem is aggravated under special circumstances, and sometimes in certain religious or ethnic homes. Louise was a single mother of thirty-three. Her parents, who had disapproved of her marriage but still felt her divorce was "sinful," insisted they wouldn't stay home and baby-sit for her. Every time she had a potential date, her parents would plan to go out themselves, which would have left her eight-year-old son alone. As a result, Louise often had to take her child with her on her dates or remain at home, since an outside baby-sitter wasn't always available.

This tendency of adults to resume parent-child relationships even after the child has grown up can cause many difficulties. But before they can be settled to everyone's satisfaction, the change of status of the former child needs to be recognized. Both parents and adult child need to face the issue directly. They need to talk about how their relationship has changed. The adult child has a right to expect to be treated as an equal, but then must be willing to accept full adult responsibility in the home.

If talking over what you see as an unsatisfactory adult relationship in this new situation doesn't work for you, then I recommend that you join a singles group. There you'll get moral support and the wisdom of others who have experienced similar difficulties. You'll also be in touch with people who may be able to help you by establishing a network. Therapy with a family counselor may be helpful, too. The important thing is to choose the form of help that brings results, for this dependency relationship needs to end.

Don't Get Angry

A person who isn't quite sure a decision is the right one can easily become irate if it is questioned. If you find yourself responding with irritation to criticisms of your actions, slow down your responses. Take deep breaths and relax your body. You'll never be able to communicate until you have your anger under control. While you're regaining your equilibrium, think. Did you get angry because you aren't sure you're doing the right thing?

If your answer is yes, then take the time to analyze what you've decided to do. Consider all possible alternatives. Would another choice be better? People who are genuinely at ease with the choices they've made don't usually have to get angry and defend what they've done. Lack of conviction, a fear of being wrong, causes a person to jump into battle when another person shows disapproval.

When you have your anger under control, you can make an attempt to turn your critic into a helper. If the criticism comes from your extended family, it may be voiced in a negative manner. "Why waste your time with Larry? Your children need you now." If you hear only the first sentence you'll miss the point. The second half offers a different perspective. The worry is that your children are left alone too much or don't have your love.

This is a point on which you can give reassurance. Respond lightly to the comment about the time you spend with your lover. "I know, Dad, I worry about it sometimes, too. But if I don't keep some balance in my life I get very short with the kids. Larry's wonderful. He keeps me on track."

Then move on to the real issue—the welfare of your children. "I'd love to spend more time with the kids, and I would, if I didn't have to cover so many bases." Explain that, in addition to working, you have to come home and do the cleaning and laundry. If they truly want to help, perhaps they can supply you with someone to do the laundry and cleaning, which you can't afford.

Another suggestion you might offer is that they take your children for an evening or two during the week, or possibly for a weekend once a month so you have time away from parental duties to devote to your own needs. If you have some other special need *spell it out clearly*. If the criticism was sincere, you might get some much-needed assistance. If it wasn't, you might succeed in shutting it off.

Most grandparents enjoy a visit with their grandchildren, especially if their own child no longer has custody. They feel left out after the breakup of your family. They are sometimes fearful they'll be forgotten altogether. So if you ask them to help, you may also be reassuring them that their relationship with you and your children is going to continue no matter how your life-style changes.

If the hassles are coming from your ex-spouse, such pleas for cooperation may fall on deaf ears. However, many divorced parents still maintain reasonable communication with their ex-spouses and, when they do, hassles are minimized.

The Old Double Standard

Periodically, someone announces that we've finally eliminated the double standard. But there's too much evidence against this. A man who leaves his children is not condemned as vehemently as a woman who agrees to give custody of her children to her husband. Similarly, men are still expected to try to get as many dates as they can into bed, but when a woman has a number of men sleep over she may be accused of being promiscuous. That word, incidentally, is rarely applied to a man, even if he has a new woman every night—he's a Don Juan, a superlover. The names used to describe him are complimentary.

Ex-spouses, in-laws, and relatives are all influenced by these societal attitudes. A single mother is somehow expected to be less sexual than a single father. Often, criticism of a single mother's love relationship is based on this moral double standard.

Children, too, seem to accept this outmoded belief. Perhaps it's because the custodial parent is usually a mother, and if her life is in any way criticized or unsettled their home and security seem threatened. Also, as mentioned in chapter 3, children, especially adolescents, are forming their own moral standards and in the process accept, at least for a time, the standards in evidence around them.

Many modern women, however, choose not to be controlled by this antiquated morality. They may decide to face up to their own sexual needs in spite of the attitudes of their relatives and in-laws. That's fine. But it may require a special confidence on their part.

If you've made the decision to live a normal, full, sexual adult life even though you're a single mother, you need to be prepared for possible criticism that's inspired by this old belief in the double standard. Examine your own attitude carefully. Recognize your own insecurities. Get help if you need it to reinforce your conviction that you have a right to live your life as you wish. Don't be your own worst enemy and accept a moral standard that's imposed by another generation or an attitude you don't feel is your own.

One more note. In custody cases men often seem to be more able than women to articulate the importance of having time for themselves. *Clearly, women need to be more self-assertive.* This is especially true when it comes to demanding their right to a personal life, even if they have children.

Creative Counseling and Mediation Services

Various jurisdictions have their own legal codes or regulations controlling the use of mediators when children are involved in divorce actions. You may already have asked about the existence of any regulations or provisions for arranging custody when you spoke directly with the court in your area or with a family law attorney. If your ex-spouse is interfering with your life on the pretext of helping your children, you may be able to return to the mediation services for help.

If you're presently working out the conditions of your divorce, these services may be available to help you establish a custody agreement that will diminish inappropriate intrusiveness. It's usually easier to prevent problems than to solve them after they've become big issues in your life. Most of all, remember that the hassling is often expressed as concern for the children. If your children's needs remain in focus during the divorce process, there will be less basis for complaining later.

Robin Drapkin, of the Family Mediation and Conciliation Service of Los Angeles Superior Court, author of "Child-focused Mediation: What the Family Law Attorney Needs to Know," remarked in an interview on the need for attorneys to keep the child's welfare in mind during all divorce and custody disputes. She emphasized that this is particularly essential when the parents are tangled up in their own past hurts and disappointments. She also noted that many parents who are obviously enmeshed in bitter conflict may claim that the children are "just fine," when actually the ongoing fighting is causing the children great distress. She advised lawyers and others dealing with divorcing couples to insist on meeting personally with the children.

If your problem is legal, go to a qualified attorney. But if mediation of disagreements is required, you can get help from other mental health professionals who specialize in these matters. Their experience in the intricacies of family relationships may enable them to help their clients reach decisions a lawyer might not consider.

When You Need Legal Help to Stop Excessive Intrusions

Sometimes the most tactful handling of overly intrusive ex-spouses, relatives, or in-laws fails to eliminate the problem. You've tried discussing things calmly and redirecting the concern to more positive channels. But you still find your private life being invaded and upset. Under such circumstances, you may have to take legal steps to end the harassment.

This is difficult for most to do. It may be hard to use the law to defend yourself against intrusion. You may hesitate to fight for your right to live without interference if you're uncertain about a decision you've made. Maybe you think your ex-spouse, in-laws, or relatives might be right after all. Obviously, this question needs to be resolved before you seek legal redress. Certainly reconsider, if you feel the need, any decision of which you're unsure. You don't want to get into legal hassles and then change your mind.

Domestic issues involving support payments or custody are dealt with by trial judges in local jurisdictions. Occasionally, an appeal may be made to a higher state court. However, such an appeal is usually time-consuming and expensive as well as emotionally exhausting. This is particularly true if a child's custody is being disputed. Children placed in the middle of this kind of battle are rarely unaffected by the dispute. Most suffer emotional scars that last a lifetime.

Each state has authority over domestic matters, and domestic cases can be taken into a federal court only if there's a constitutional issue involved. Local trial judges have great latitude. Their rulings usually reflect the cultures of the communities in which they live and work. What may be the local and prevailing standard in one part of the country can be very different in another.

If you believe anyone is attempting to subvert your decisions regarding your children, if you're being unduly harassed and interfered with by your ex-spouse, relatives, or in-laws, or if any one of them is trying to take custody of your children away from you, you *can* take legal action. Such assistance doesn't have to be expensive. In many communities, legal aid societies offer help to those unable to afford private lawyers.

But how do you decide that your only recourse is the law? You start by using more subtle means of getting your relatives or in-laws off your back. You try every suggestion I've made, and any other ideas you may have. You seek the aid of your pastor, your rabbi, or some other person you believe may have influence on whoever is causing you trouble.

If all those channels fail, I suggest you inform whoever is causing you distress of your intention to seek legal redress. Occasionally, that warning is enough to stop the difficulty. But if it continues, proceed with your suit. You'll be acting in the best interests of your children as well as yourself.

16 The Balancing Act

Weighing the Scales for Your Happiness

Single parents are confronted with many problems, most of which they can deal with on their own. However, they sometimes feel overwhelmed by guilt or confused as to how they should apportion their attention, time, energy, and money between their own needs and the needs of their children.

They're troubled by the necessity of cutting up a limited "pie"—themselves and their resources—in an equitable manner. They often feel discouraged and overwhelmed by the multiple demands put upon them. It's no wonder they frequently make less-than-perfect decisions. Feeling powerless when confronted with conflicting needs, a parent may simply push the entire matter aside and refuse to think about it until forced to do so by circumstances. But if decisions aren't thought out, the apportionment will be made in a random, unpredictable, almost unconscious manner, dictated by the emotional need of the moment. This far too often results in choices that are unsatisfactory to all concerned.

Many single parents struggle with a sense of overwhelming inadequacy. They feel guilty because they don't have their lives under control. They believe they've failed because they no longer have the cultural ideal—an intact nuclear family.

But guilt and self-deprecation have only negative effects. They destroy one's ability to operate at maximum efficiency. Single parents who suffer from excessive guilt are unable to deal well with the various demands that crowd each day. They may try to ignore their nagging consciences, but this requires so much effort that there's no energy left to solve real difficulties in a logical, thoughtful manner. If they feel inadequate to deal with life, they may lose their ability to utilize their own common sense, which, if it had been allowed to operate, could have pointed the way to the solution of many family problems.

The reality today is that increasing numbers of children are being raised by single parents. According to the latest Census Bureau figures, one in every five children in America lives in a one-parent household. This is a 54 percent jump since 1970. There is little indication that this upward trend is coming to an end.

Yet, to claim that single-parent families are automatically handicapped—unable to function well—is to ignore the facts. Many single parents have systematically made satisfactory decisions regarding their social-sexual lives and their responsibilities to their children. They've arrived at a comfortable balance regarding the divisions of the pie upon which the well-being of their families depend.

They begin by recognizing their own limitations and the fact that, though they may never achieve perfection, they can accept themselves and do their best. They strive to create a reasonably happy, secure environment for their families in which the needs of each person, including themselves, are met as appropriately and fairly as possible.

What do they use as their guides? Many get help from organizations formed for the specific purpose of assisting single parents in their decision making. National groups such as Parents Without Partners (PWP) and local groups to be found in every state as well as in many larger cities throughout the country serve as meeting centers for communication where single parents can pool information. The friendships formed among members of these groups contribute to the mental health of the participants. The discussions and lectures they provide cover all aspects of relationships between single parents and children as well as the problems single parents face in maintaining satisfactory social-sexual lives.

But groups are not the only source of inspiration for single parents seeking a balance in their lives. Books that offer sound advice are available in increasing numbers. A network of neighbors and friends can share the responsibilities that might overwhelm one lone parent. And if the burden of guilt and feelings of inadequacy grow overpowering, professional help is available in both large cities and small towns.

Dating Ethics

When you are dating, whether you are having one-night stands or developing a serious relationship with a lover, there are certain ethics that would be in your best interests to follow. A good survey of the areas you should consider has been developed by Garnett E. Phibbs, of Parents Without Partners.* I have adapted his ideas below with the thought that they may serve as a guide to considerate dating, and perhaps to more successful relationships.

The first step is to decide what your moral standards are and act on them. For your peace of mind, you need to feel comfortable with your behavior and not be unduly influenced by what others are doing. If, for example, you're uneasy with one-night stands, respect your feelings and don't let someone pressure you into engaging in them.

Respect your partner's integrity as well. Don't try to force into bed a date who has made it clear that he or she considers

*For more information, contact the Parents Without Partners organization in your area.

nonmarital sex bad, or who has simply indicated a desire to know you better before becoming intimate.

Regarding one-night stands, try to keep your children sheltered from such temporary arrangements.

Be willing to consider the impact of your relationship on your lover's children. Remember that, if you establish a close relationship, the responsibility for the children's mental welfare rests on both of you.

Consider the reputation of yourself and your partner. Don't insist on "your place" if you know your lover has neighbors who will spread gossip that might be harmful to either your lover or the children.

Consider carefully the methods we have discussed for telling the children. Don't expect their automatic approval, and don't spring surprises on them.

Be aware that children should not be permitted the same sexual liberties that you have a right to allow yourself. Understand and work to avoid the imposing of a double standard on adult relationships: if liberal sexuality is all right for men, it is also acceptable for women.

Everyone should have the right to refuse a date or the suggestion for sex. Try to reach a point where you can accept refusal without feeling put down and refuse others without making them feel denigrated.

If you are more experienced than your date, you have a responsibility not to push too hard, especially for sex. Remember that if you take advantage of another's ignorance or innocence you are sure eventually to stir up animosity and resentment.

As parents, you have a responsibility to protect your children, who truly are innocent and inexperienced. Protect your minor children from physical or sexual abuse by your adult companions.

Be someone who can keep confidences. Often, during an intimate time, people say things they wouldn't want repeated outside the bedroom. And just because a person has sex with you doesn't mean they're promiscuous. Don't be a person who kisses and tells.

Remember the importance of friendship. Be friends with your lovers. Sometimes minor disagreements that could break up a love affair can be weathered by lovers who are also friends.

The possibility of contracting venereal disease is greater if you have one-night stands. Have regular medical checkups and, if you do become infected, remember that the only ethical thing to do is to warn any other partners you've had so they, too, can get medical help.

Try to reach some understanding with your lover regarding your expectations about your relationship. If your lover wants to play the field and you want a monogamous relationship, one of you will have to change. It is a rare union that can survive with disagreement in this critical area.

Remember that the best relationships are those where both partners want to be together. Loving someone does not mean you own that person. These are simple rules that seem basic to any good relationship.

Accepting Your Right to Happiness

In my clinical experience, I've found that those single parents who feel good about themselves and have a healthy respect for their own needs are best equipped to be good parents. They've learned to accept their own inner child. They show empathy and tolerance of their own lack of perfection. And this tolerance expands to include their children and their lovers as well.

Because they like themselves, they usually like and respect their children. This helps them to carry on their interfamily relationships from a perspective of mutual respect rather than from guilt. Their children may not always approve of every choice that's made, but they're generally able to recognize and accept their parents' warm, consistent, firm, nonambivalent messages. This self-understanding and acceptance greatly influence single parents as they decide how the pie should be sliced.

None of us has ever met a truly perfect person. We all have our faults. It's how we deal with these faults that matters in our lives. If you're overly judgmental of yourself and put down your inner child, you can't escape guilt and feelings of inadequacy. But if you recognize the inner child and see your tendency to criticize yourself for what it is, you can exercise good judgment in your life and avoid overly harsh dealings with yourself and with your children.

When you recognize that you deserve happiness and the right to some time of your own, you'll be able to make decisions about your social-sexual life that you're comfortable with. You won't be compelled to accept the choices of your ex-spouse, your extended family, or your children.

This isn't to say the children's individual and developmental needs and feelings shouldn't be considered. Communication should be open and your children should know you respect their opinions. However, you don't *have* to accept every idea they present, nor are you obligated to do what they suggest. Accept your own right to self-determination, knowing that understanding your children's ideas and opinions puts you under no obligation to concede to their wishes.

When you are developing an adequate social life for yourself and at the same time are continuing to be a good parent, approach the problems you encounter slowly. Before you act, mentally rehearse the steps you'll take. Visualize your new "family" in happy communication. Get the feel of the satisfaction you'll experience. Then keep that sense of peace and happiness as you seek to balance your needs with those of your children and your lover.

A sensitive verse, dated 1692 and found in Old Saint Paul's Church in Baltimore, states in part: "Beyond a wholesome discipline, be gentle with yourself. You are a child of the universe, no less than the trees and the stars; you have a right to be here." You, as a single parent, would do well to keep this in mind. As you struggle with the choices and the needs that dictate your slicing of the pie that is your energy, time, and resources, remember that you, too, are entitled to an equitable share.

Resources

Audiocassette Series on Parenting

Preschool and Infant Parenting Service (PIPS). "Puzzling Behavior of Infants and Toddlers." 8730 Alden Drive, Room E101, Thalians Mental Health Center, Cedars-Sinai Medical Center, Los Angeles, CA 90048.

Books on Parenting

Atlas, Stephen L. *Single Parenting: A Practical Resource Guide*. Englewood Cliffs, NJ: Prentice-Hall, 1981.

Boston Women's Health Book Collective. *Ourselves and Our Children: A Book by and for Parents*. New York: Random House, 1978.

Elkind, David. *All Grown Up and No Place to Go: Teenagers in Crisis*. New York: Addison-Wesley, 1984.

Elkind, David. *The Hurried Child: Growing Up Too Fast Too Soon*. New York: Addison-Wesley, 1981.

Erikson, Erik H. *Childhood and Society*. New York: W. W. Norton, 1950, 1964.

Fraiberg, Selma H. *Magic Years: Understanding and Handling the Problems of Early Childhood*. New York: Charles Scribner's Sons, 1984.

Gordon, Thomas. *P.E.T., Parent Effectiveness Training: The Tested New Way to Raise Responsible Children*. New York: New American Library, 1975.

Miller, Alice. *For Your Own Good: Hidden Cruelty in Child-Rearing and the Roots of Violence*. New York: Farrar, Straus and Giroux, 1983.

Miller, Alice. *The Drama of the Gifted Child*. New York: Basic Books, 1983.

Parents Without Partners. *The Single Parent Magazine*. Suite 1000, 7910 Woodmont Avenue, Bethesda, MD 20814.

Patterson, Gerald R. *Families: Applications of Social Learning to Family Life*. Rev. ed. Champaign, IL: Research Press, 1975.

Sanderson, Jim. *How to Raise Your Kids to Stand on Their Own Two Feet*. New York: Congdon and Weed, 1983.

Wallerstein, Judith, and Joan B. Kelly. *Surviving the Breakup: How Children and Parents Cope with Divorce*. New York: Basic Books, 1980.

Sex Education Books for Younger Children

Andry, Andrew C., and Steven Schepp. *How Babies Are Made*. Alexandria, VA: Time-Life Books, 1968.

Calderone, Mary S., and James W. Ramsy. *Talking with Your Child About Sex: Questions and Answers for Children from Birth to Puberty*. New York: Ballantine Books, 1984.

Cole, Joanna. *How You Were Born.* New York: William Morrow, 1984.

Mayle, Peter. *Where Did I Come From?* Secaucus, NJ: Lyle Stuart, 1973.

Sheffield, Margaret. *Before You Were Born.* New York: Alfred A. Knopf, 1984.

Sheffield, Margaret, and Sheila Bewley. *Where Do Babies Come From?* New York: Alfred A. Knopf, 1973.

Stein, Sara Bonnett. *Making Babies.* New York: Walker and Co., 1974.

Sex Education for Adolescents

Bell, Ruth. *Changing Bodies, Changing Lives: A Book for Teens on Sex and Relationships.* New York: Random House, 1981.

Gale, Jay. *A Young Man's Guide to Sex.* New York: Holt, Rinehart and Winston, 1984.

Madaras, Lynda, with Dane Saavedra. *The "What's Happening to My Body?" Book for Boys: A Growing-up Guide for Parents and Sons.* New York: Newmarket Press, 1984.

Madaras, Lynda, with Area Madaras. *What's Happening to My Body? A Growing-up Guide for Mothers and Daughters.* New York: Newmarket Press, 1983.

McCoy, Kathy. *The Teenage Body Book Guide to Dating.* New York: Simon and Schuster, 1983.

For Protection Against Molestation

Adams, Caren, and Jennifer Fay. *No More Secrets: Protecting Your Child from Sexual Assault.* San Luis Obispo, CA: Impact Publishers, 1981.

The National Center on Child Abuse. *Child Abuse Prevention: Tips to Parents*. P.O. Box 1182, Washington, D.C. 20013.

Helping Children Deal with Divorce

Gardner, Richard. *The Boys and Girls Book About Divorce*. New York: Bantam Books, 1971 (third to ninth grades).

Hyde, M. O. *My Friend Has Four Parents*. New York: McGraw-Hill, 1981 (ages ten to fourteen).

Sinberg, Janet. *Divorce Is a Grown-up Problem*. New York: Avon Books, 1978 (preschool to kindergarten).

Stetson, J. S. *Now I Have a Stepparent and It's Kind of Confusing*. New York: Avon Books, 1979 (ages three to ten).

Sex Education for Adults

The Boston Women's Health Book Collective. *The New Our Bodies, Ourselves*. New York: A Touchstone Book, Simon and Schuster, 1984.

Comfort, Alex. *The Joy of Sex: A Gourmet Guide to Love Making*. New York: Crown Publishers, 1972.

Masters, William H., and Virginia E. Johnson, with Robert J. Levin. *The Pleasure Bond*. New York: Bantam Books, 1976.

Montagu, Ashley. *Touching: The Human Significance of Skin*. 2nd ed. New York: Harper and Row, 1978.

Uncommon Life-styles

Berzon, Betty. "Sharing Your Lesbian Identity with Your Children: A Case for Openness." *Our Right to Love: A Lesbian Re-*

source Book. Edited by Ginny Vida. Englewood Cliffs, NJ: Prentice-Hall, 1978.

Cutrow, Michelle, Peggy Hoppman, and Jessica Lehman. "Children of Lesbian Mothers: Their Perceptions of Their Relationships with Family and Peers." Master's Thesis, University of Southern California, Los Angeles, 1980.

Hitchens, Donna J. *The Lesbian Mother's Litigation Manual*. San Francisco: Lesbian Rights Project, 1982.

Hitchens, Donna J., and Anne G. Thomas. *Lesbian Mothers and Their Children: An Annotated Bibliography of Legal and Psychological Materials*. San Francisco: Lesbian Rights Project, 1983.

Kirkpatrick, Martha, Ron Roy, and Katharine Smith. "Studies of a New Population: The Lesbian Mother." *Modern Perspectives in Psychiatry: Middle Age*. Edited by John Howells. New York: Bruner/Mazel, 1981.

Lewin, Ellen. "Lesbianism and Motherhood: Implications for Child Custody." *Human Organization* 40(1):6–14. Washington, DC: Society for Applied Anthropology, 1981.

Miller, Brian. "Gay Fathers and Their Children." *The Family Coordinator* (October 1979), pp. 544–52.

Guide for Parental Negotiations

Fisher, Roger, and William Ury. *Getting to Yes: Negotiating Agreement Without Giving In*. Boston: Houghton Mifflin, 1981.

Support Groups

Children of Gays/Lesbians, 691 South Irolo St. #2003, Los Angeles, CA 90005; phone: (213) 650-0060.

Committee for Single Adoptive Parents, P.O. Box 15084, Chevy Chase, MD 20815.

Displaced Homemakers Network, 1010 Vermont Ave. N.W., Washington, D.C., 20005; phone: (202) 628-6767.

Fathers' Rights of America, Inc., P.O. Box 7596, Van Nuys, CA 91309; phone: (818) 789-4435.

Fathers United for Equal Rights, P.O. Box 9751, Baltimore, MD 21204; phone: (301) 539-3237.

Joint Custody Association, 10606 Wilkins Ave., Los Angeles, CA 90024; phone: (213) 475-5352.

Lesbian Rights Project, 1370 Mission St. (4th floor), San Francisco, CA 94103; phone: (415) 621-0674.

Mothers Without Custody, P.O. Box 56762, Houston, TX 77256-6762; phone: (713) 840-1622.

National Federation of Parents and Friends of Gays, 5715 16th St. N.W., Washington, D.C., 20011; phone: (202) 726-3223.

National Gay Task Force, 80 Fifth Ave., New York, NY 10011; phone: (212) 741-5800.

National Self-Help Clearing House, Graduate School in University Center, 33 W. 42nd St., City University of New York, New York, NY 10036; phone: (212) 840-1259.

National Single Parent Coalition, 225 Park Ave. South, New York, NY 10003; phone: (212) 475-4401.

North American Conference of Separated and Divorced Catholics, 1100 S. Goodman St., Rochester, NY 14620; phone: (716) 271-1320.

Organization for the Enforcement of Child Support, 119 Nicodemus Rd., Reisterstown, MD 21136; phone: (301) 833-2458.

Parents Anonymous, 22330 Hawthorne Blvd. #208, Torrance, CA 90505; phone: (213) 371-3501.

Parents Without Partners (PWP), Suite 1000, 9718 Woodmont Ave., Bethesda, MD 28814; phone: (301) 654-8850.

Self-Help Center, 1600 Dodge Ave. #S-122, Evanston, IL 60201; phone: (312) 328-0470.

Single Mothers by Choice, Box 207, Van Brunt Station, Brooklyn, NY 11215; phone: (212) 965-2148.

Single Parent Project, 5715 Lindo Paseo, San Diego, CA 92115; phone: (714) 286-9472.

Sisterhood of Black Single Mothers, P.O. Box 155, Brooklyn, NY 11203; phone: (718) 638-0413.

Stepfamily Association of America, 28 Allegheny Ave. #1307, Baltimore, MD 21204; phone: (301) 823-7570.

Stepfamily Association of America, 900 Welch Ave., Palo Alto, CA 94304; phone: (415) 493-8813.

Toughlove, P.O. Box 1069, Doylestown, PA 18901; phone: (215) 348-7090.

The support groups listed above are national in scope. Some have more to offer in a specific locality, but all have indicated a willingness to provide information nationally wherever possible. There are also numerous local groups available to single parents. To locate them, contact the Family Service Agency, Child Psychiatric Clinic, or State Social Service Department in your city: inquire at a church or synagogue; or check listings in local newspapers and the telephone book.

Index